Greece & Rome

NEW SURVEYS IN THE CLASSICS No. 47

PLUTARCH

BY
GEERT ROSKAM

Published for the Classical Association
CAMBRIDGE UNIVERSITY PRESS
2021

CAMBRIDGE UNIVERSITY PRESS
Shaftesbury Road, Cambridge CB2 8BS, United Kingdom
One Liberty Plaza, Floor 20, New York, NY 10006, USA
477 Williamstown Road, Port Melbourne, VIC 3207, Australia
Ruiz de Alarcón 13, 28014 Madrid, Spain
Dock house, The Waterfront, Cape Town 8001, South Africa

www.cambridge.org
Information on this title: www.cambridge.org/9781009108225

Printed in the United Kingdom by Bell and Bain, Glasgow, UK

A catalogue record for this publication is available from the British Library

ISBN 9781009108225

CONTENTS

Contents

ACKNOWLEDGEMENTS

Plutarch of Chaeronea in 166 pages: that sounds like trying to pour the ocean into an aquarium! A project like that seems a priori undoable, for Plutarch is an extremely rich and versatile author and he wrote so many works on so many different themes. His *Parallel Lives* alone contain far too much information for a small volume like this one, and the same holds true for his *Moralia*. Therefore, the invitation of the New Surveys editors on behalf of the Classical Association to write this book was a real challenge and I'm grateful to them for their trust in me and for their support during the publication process. Inevitably, the focus of this volume will often be on bare essentials. Yet I also hope to give the reader an idea of the dynamics of Plutarch's thinking and indeed arouse a passion for this interesting author. Briefly put, my goal will be reached when my reader enthusiastically throws this book away (or, perhaps better, carefully places it on a shelf), runs to the library, and begins reading Plutarch for themselves.

In writing and finalizing this book I have greatly benefited from the advice and remarks of many colleagues, who blended their accurate and helpful criticisms with the kind frankness of genuine friendship. I am most grateful to Jeffrey Beneker, Mauro Bonazzi, Frederick Brenk, Bram Demulder, Tim Duff, Franco Ferrari, Rainer Hirsch-Luipold, Phillip Horky, Heinz Gerd Ingenkamp, Katarzyna Jazdzewska, Delfim Leão, Michiel Meeusen, Judith Mossman, Israel Muñoz Gallarte, Anastasios Nikolaidis, Jan Opsomer, Christopher Pelling, Dámaris Romero Gonzales, Philip Stadter, John Taylor, Frances Titchener, Luc Van der Stockt, Laurens Van der Wiel, Lieve Van Hoof, and Alexei Zadorozhny, all of whom read (parts of) the first draft of this book. Their valuable feedback, comments, and suggestions significantly improved the final result, saved me from many mistakes, and helped me a lot in clarifying and nuancing my arguments.

I'd also like to thank my colleagues at the University of Leuven, especially Johan Leemans, Peter Van Deun, Gerd Van Riel, and Joseph Verheyden, with whom I have been collaborating for ten years now on several big projects.

Warm thanks finally go to my wife, Kristin – who easily surpasses blameless Timoxena – and to my children – who easily surpass Plutarch's sons in intellectually challenging their father. Not only do they know how much effort it has taken to write this book but they were also kind enough to welcome the old Plutarch so often as a fellow banqueter and a member of our family, and this intellectual hospitality, no doubt, has contributed immensely to this book.

I. PLUTARCH'S LIFE

The fifth and fourth century BC were truly the pinnacle of Greek history and culture. In those golden days, one could deliberate on political matters with Themistocles and Pericles; discuss our human condition with Socrates and Plato and the past with Herodotus and Thucydides; watch the superb plays of Aeschylus, Sophocles, and Euripides; visit the brand-new Acropolis at Athens or consult Apollo at Delphi; drop in at Polyclitus' workshop or marvel at a skilfully decorated black-figure Panathenaic amphora. It was, however, also a period in which Greeks were still Greeks, whereas the rest were conveniently despised as barbarians. Greeks confidently bashed barbarian brains in (at Marathon, for instance, or Plataea) and were even proud of it. After all, they did it in a culturally justified way. With fellow Greeks, matters were somewhat different. Their brains were likewise crushed, to be sure, and even in such cases, the slaughter was usually not devoid of a certain feeling of ideological superiority, yet to refined Greek ears, the cracking of Greek skulls must have sounded differently from the smashing of the skull of an ordinary effeminate barbarian. Athenians, Spartans, and Thebans could often drink each other's blood (in a skilfully decorated cup), no doubt, but in the end, they all remained fellow Greeks.

This moving scene radically changed with Alexander the Great. His military campaigns entailed an enormous increase of scale. More and more, Greek culture did not merely flourish in Greece itself (and, of course, in Asia Minor and southern Italy), but it also exerted its influence as far as Egypt and India. As a result, the traditional dichotomy between Greeks and barbarians had to be reinterpreted. Even former barbarians could now exercise the privilege of slaughtering one another in a culturally justified way. The world would never be the same.

In the days of Plutarch of Chaeronea, the situation was even more complex. At that time, Greece had long been subjected to Roman rule – or, according to the official Roman point of view, had been delivered from Macedonian dominion. Yet this liberation did not constitute a straightforward blessing for Greece. In 146 BC, Corinth was competently sacked by the troops of L. Mummius, the survivors were sold as slaves, and the works of art were destroyed or transported to Rome. Sixty years later, it was Athens' turn. After Sulla had quelled the Greeks' renewed hope of freedom by defeating the army of

Mithridates VI Eupator at Chaeronea, Athens was plundered. In 48 BC, Greece again provided a battlefield for Roman armies, when the legions of Caesar and Pompey clashed with one another at Pharsalus in Thessaly. These continual confrontations took their toll and entailed a general population decline and an economic crisis in Greece. Applying Calgacus' pointed maxim (Tacitus, *Agr.* 30.5), including its rhetorical hyperbole, one could say that the Romans turned Greece 'into a desolation and then called it peace'.

Even if Greece had not completely been changed into a desolate wilderness, the situation was far from rosy. In Plutarch's *On the obsolescence of oracles*, the character Ammonius describes the contemporary circumstances as follows (413F–414A):

> Greece has far more than its share in the general depopulation which the earlier discords and the wars have wrought throughout practically the whole inhabited earth, and...today the whole of Greece would hardly muster three thousand men-at-arms, which is the number that the one city of the Megarians sent forth to Plataea.[1]

This statement, again, is not without some rhetorical exaggeration for the sake of the argument,[2] yet it is not totally unfounded. The Greek mainland suffered hard times indeed.

In 27 BC, Greece became a Roman province, governed by a proconsul with praetorian rank who had his seat at Corinth (which had been refounded as the Roman *Colonia Laus Iulia Corinthiensis*). This inaugurated a period of relative stability (although the Greeks, true to their reputation, were always prone to sedition) and even a gradual economic revival. Due to the definitive loss of all their political and military powers, the Greeks had no choice but to retreat to the safe ground of their cultural supremacy. They knew well enough that they were politically toothless but invincible on the battlefield of education. Thus, they emphasized the brilliant achievements of their famous predecessors in literary works. The heroic victories over the Persians at Marathon, Salamis, and Plataea, for instance, or the lasting achievements of great figures like Pericles and Lycurgus were praised to the skies – although there was no prospect of imitating them in real life. The Greeks, in short, were relegated to their schools and there fed upon their great past, which was for them not merely a source of pride but

---

[1] The translations, unless otherwise indicated, are borrowed from the Loeb Classical Library, often with slight modifications.
[2] See esp. Alcock 1993: 25–92 and *passim*.

part and parcel of their identity. Being Greek meant being the intellectual heir of this unrivalled Greek tradition; being Greek, in short, became tantamount to being *pepaideumenos* (an educated man) – at least for those who felt they fitted that description. And the Romans, strikingly enough, soon took over this ambition and tried to be as cultivated as the Greeks. Horace's apt saying that 'conquered Greece conquered its rough victor' (*Epistles* 2.1.156) was pertinent indeed, and the attitude of the Roman members of Plutarch's circle actually provides one of its most illustrative examples (see below).

The order and relative rest brought about through the Roman rule also yielded new opportunities at the local level. Little by little, the Greek *poleis* began to recover from the previous rough times. In all likelihood, this also happened in Chaeronea, Plutarch's hometown. Chaeronea was only a little town, though with a great history. There the Greeks lost their freedom in the decisive battle against Philip of Macedon in 338 BC. There, as mentioned above, they also lost their dream of liberation when Sulla defeated Mithridates' army. Chaeronea occupied a strategic position, on the road that connected southern and northern Greece, and with a good connection to the Corinthian Gulf, which made it attractive for trade. Its vast plain did not merely qualify as a perfect battlefield but could also be exploited for agricultural purposes. The local aristocracy could benefit from this favourable location in order to increase their wealth and consolidate their power. It is likely indeed that Chaeronea, like most Greek cities in that period, was controlled and administrated by a few aristocratic families – families like that of Plutarch.

1. Plutarch's family

There can be no doubt that Plutarch was the scion of a rich and noble family that probably owned substantial pieces of fruitful land. A passage from *On the slowness of divine punishments* suggests that the family claimed descent from King Opheltas of Thessaly and from Daiphantus, a famous commander from Phocis (558A–B). About Plutarch's great-grandfather Nicarchus, we only know that he was forced by Antony's troops to carry wheat on his shoulders, down to Anticyra (on the Gulf of Corinth), with whips (*Ant.* 68.7–8). Plutarch's grandfather Lamprias is much better known. He often appears in the *Table Talk* as an agreeable, cultivated, and intelligent table companion, showing a basic knowledge of poetry and philosophy and being capable of independent thinking.[3] Plutarch's father is characterized along the same lines. Several scholars argue that he appears as less cultivated and more superficial than Lamprias,[4] but on closer inspection, he turns out to be no less familiar with poets and philosophers (615E–616B) and he even criticizes Aristotle (656C–D). Moreover, he often raises interesting questions that provide the starting point for philosophical discussions (642A; 655E–F; 656C–D). This, in Plutarch's eyes, is a typical feature of the ideal teacher,[5] so that, in this respect at least, Plutarch's father is not inferior to his grandfather Lamprias. He generally appears as a broad-minded intellectual, the kind of man, indeed, who takes care that his children receive an excellent education and are introduced into cultivated aristocratic circles.

As far as we know, Plutarch had two brothers. The elder one, Lamprias (called after his grandfather), is the main speaker in two dialogues (*On the face that appears in the orb of the moon* and *On the obsolescence of oracles*) and frequently intervenes in the *Table Talk* too.[6] He is portrayed as a particularly gifted (626A) and clever man, thoroughly familiar with the different aspects of the rich intellectual tradition, intelligent and funny, never afraid of provoking his interlocutors with controversial points of view. Like Plutarch, he had been a student of Ammonius (*De E* 385D–386A) and indeed usually thinks along Platonic lines.[7] Finally, Lamprias was apparently active at the oracle of Lebadeia (*De def. or.* 431C). In short, he had an intellectual profile that was very similar to that of Plutarch himself.

Plutarch's other brother, Timon, participates in the discussion of the dialogue *On the slowness of divine punishments* and may have been the principal speaker of the lost dialogue *On the soul*. His interventions in

---

[3] *Quaest. conv.* 622E; 669C–D; 678D–679E; 680A–B; 684A–B; 684C–D; 738A–C; see also *Ant.* 28.3–12.

[4] E.g. Ziegler 1951: 642; C. Jones 1971: 9; Sirinelli 2000: 29; cf. Volkmann 1869: i.21. In *Quaest. conv.* 641F–642A, he is characterized as an expert in horse-breeding.

[5] Roskam 2004a: 103 and 108–13 on Ammonius.

[6] *Quaest. conv.* 617E–619A; 626A–C; 643E–644D; 669C–E; 670E–671C; 705B–706E; 715A–716C; 726D–727A; 740B–D.

[7] In *Quaest. conv.* 635A–B, the character 'Plutarch' points out that his brother prefers The Walk (τὸν περίπατον) and The Lyceum (τὸ Λύκειον) to the Epicurean Garden. This statement, however, should be understood in its sympotic context, as an apt saying, meant to defend Lamprias against the attacks of the Epicurean Xenocles and to introduce an interesting topic for discussion. Moreover, the characterization is not at odds with Lamprias' Platonic outlook. As a matter of fact, every Platonist would prefer Aristotle to Epicurus.

the *Table Talk* illustrate a similar *paideia* ('education'; 616C–F and 639B–D): yet another fruit from the same tree! Plutarch underlines his warm feelings for his brother Timon in a well-known passage from *On brotherly love* (487D–E):

And for myself, though I have received from Fortune many favours which call for gratitude, that my brother Timon's affection for me has always balanced and still balances all the rest, no one is unaware who has ever had any dealings whatever with me.

Such statements are often taken at face value in scholarly literature and one easily understands why. After all, short *obiter dicta* like this one constitute by far the most important source about Plutarch's life and personality, so that it is difficult to completely ignore them. Yet we should bear in mind that Plutarch's self-disclosure is always closely connected with its argumentative context. This also appears in the above quotation, where the emphasis on Plutarch's great brotherly love in a treatise which precisely deals with this subject directly contributes to Plutarch's own image-building as a consistent and thus trustworthy philosopher who practises what he preaches. Some methodological caution is justified, then, although this does not imply that all of Plutarch's statements about himself and his experiences should a priori be regarded with great suspicion. They often provide a glimpse into his personality or an interesting snapshot from his life and can as such be used, with due caution, as an interesting source for Plutarch's daily activities and interests (see also fr. 184).

2. Childhood and youth

Plutarch was probably born around AD 45. This can be inferred from his dialogue *On the E at Delphi*, where he relates that he was present in Delphi when Nero visited the sanctuary (385B), that is, in AD 67. At that point, Plutarch was still a young man (391E). The term *neos* is, of course, rather vague, but if we may presume that Plutarch was then in his early twenties, he was indeed born around AD 45.[8]

---

[8] He may in fact have been a little bit younger. In 387F, he says that he was at that time still fond of mathematics but would soon embrace the maxim 'avoid extremes' when he had become a member of the Academy (ἐν Ἀκαδημείᾳ γενόμενος). This suggests that either he had only recently become a student of Ammonius or even that he was not yet a member of his school. In that case, the date of his birth may have been closer to AD 50.

The wealth and culture of his family guaranteed an excellent education. Thus the little Plutarch soon wrote his first letters on his tablets, was later introduced to the poets, and gradually acquired an encyclopaedic knowledge. His body was not neglected either: the young child trained his muscles and ran the *stade* and the double course. Higher studies followed, presumably in nearby Athens, where Plutarch first developed his rhetorical skills. The impact of this study of rhetoric can be felt throughout his life. Scholars have sometimes postulated an early phase in Plutarch's literary career in which rhetorical interests seem to be predominant;[9] in line with this hypothesis, a few 'rhetorical' speeches (see Chapter III, §5) are regarded as youthful works. This is not impossible, but no compelling arguments can be found for such a view, as a similar rhetorical approach is not absent from his later works either. It is prominent in Plutarch's philosophical polemics, in several discourses, in many sections from the *Parallel Lives*, and even in several late works, where we can easily find many passages that combine philosophical depth with the virtuoso panache of the brilliant orator. We do not know the name of Plutarch's teacher of rhetoric, but it is certain that he exerted a strong and lifelong influence on his talented pupil.

Plutarch's studies in rhetoric were followed by philosophical studies at the school of the Platonist Ammonius.[10] There he learned the basics of Platonic philosophy, with its radical dichotomy between the realm of intelligible being and the sensible world of becoming. There he also learned what it meant to look for the truth, to pursue virtue and insight – in short, to be a philosopher. Indeed, in Ammonius' school, Plutarch joined the guild of philosophers, at a fairly early age. He would never leave it.

During the following years, he would have further opportunities to develop his talents in the best possible way. He was still relatively young when he travelled to Alexandria.[11] There he could discover a flourishing intellectual centre with a well-established Platonic tradition and a superb library.[12] And in his hometown, Chaeronea, he entered

---

[9] See, e.g., Krauss 1912: 4; Ziegler 1951: 716–17; Flacelière 1964: 16; C. Jones 1971: 14–16 and 76; Lamberton 2001: 44; see also Hirzel 1895: ii.124–7.

[10] On the person of Ammonius, see C. Jones 1967; on his philosophical profile, see Opsomer 2009a.

[11] His grandfather Lamprias was still alive at that point: *Quaest. conv.* 678C–E. According to Stadter 2015b: 73 and 194–5, Plutarch went to Alexandria on an embassy to Vespasian's court in AD 69 or 70. See also Stadter 2015b: 188–98 on Plutarch's Alexandrias.

upon a political career. Plutarch recalls how he was sent in his youth on an embassy to the proconsul in Corinth (*Praec. ger. reip.* 816D):

> I recollect that when I was still a young man, I was sent with another as envoy to the proconsul; the other man was somehow left behind; I alone met the proconsul and accomplished the business. Now when I had returned and was to make the report of our mission, my father left his seat and told me in private not to say 'I went' but 'we went,' not 'I said,' but 'we said,' and in all other ways thus to associate my colleague in a joint report.

This charming anecdote shows us Plutarch's father as an intelligent politician but also throws light on the situation of the young Plutarch himself. The Chaeronean community apparently put its trust in the young man in order to negotiate its affairs with the proconsul. This illustrates again the influence of Plutarch's family – an ordinary farmer's son would not have been sent to the proconsul – but also shows that, at that time, the Chaeroneans already recognized the intellectual capacities of Plutarch and were willing to put their confidence in him. Even if the issue was in all likelihood not a matter of life or death, it nevertheless entailed some responsibility to represent the whole community before the proconsul. And thus, Plutarch quite early in his life came into contact with the powers that be.

He was still young when a voyage to Rome brought him to the beating heart of the empire. This first trip to Rome has more than once been understood in the context of Plutarch's supposed ambitions as an itinerant sophist.[13] In Rome, he would have tried to gain a reputation with the Roman audience and he may even have made a tour through Italy for the sake of such self-promotion. This hypothesis, however, ignores the fact that the young intellectual who went to Rome had already been studying for several years in Ammonius' school. In other words, Plutarch, in spite of his rhetorical talents, arrived in the city as a young intellectual and philosopher. In the proem to the *Life of Demosthenes*, he relates himself how he passed his days in Rome (*Dem.* 2.2):

[12] Eudorus of Alexandria helped to lay the foundations of Middle Platonist philosophy in the first century BC; see Dillon 1977: 115–35; Bonazzi 2007. Closer in time to Plutarch, Philo of Alexandria developed a sophisticated exegesis of the Old Testament on the basis of Platonist philosophy. Nothing suggests, though, that Plutarch was familiar with Philo's works.

[13] See, e.g., C. Jones 1971: 14–15. Cf. also Russell 1972: 7, who argues that Plutarch first aimed at a brilliant career as a sophist but failed and then turned to philosophy.

During the time when I was in Rome and various parts of Italy I had no leisure to practise in the Roman language, owing to my public duties (χρειῶν πολιτικῶν) and the number of my pupils in philosophy (τῶν διὰ φιλοσοφίαν πλησιαζόντων).

This suggests clearly enough that his interests and activities in Rome
had always been philosophical. His lectures probably dealt with the
same kind of topics which he so often discussed later, viz. general
moral issues or historical themes approached from a philosophical perspective. The clear distinction that is often made between a rhetorical
and a philosophical period in Plutarch's life, each with its own ambitions, is not based on tangible evidence. Plutarch never felt any difficulty in combining both, with rhetoric acting as the servant of
philosophy (*ancilla philosophiae*).

3. Adulthood

As Plutarch reached manhood, he began to manage his own *oikos*
(household), administering his property, controlling his finances,
directing his slaves, and organizing his personal affairs. This aspect of
his life is not directly discussed in his works and has received little
attention in scholarly literature, although a well-functioning *oikos* is
the material *sine qua non* of all his writing and thinking. It is likely
that Plutarch entrusted the daily management of his property to a stew-
ard, but his voluminous oeuvre is, at least indirectly, also the fruit of
hard-working slaves and a good major-domo.

Whereas we do not know the latter's name, we have more information about Plutarch's wife and children. An important source in this
respect is the *Consolation to his wife*, a letter in which Plutarch comforts
his wife, Timoxena, for the premature death of their little daughter.
Timoxena is there characterized as a virtuous and cultivated woman,
a paragon of moderation and maternal love.[14] Once again, however,
we should bear in mind that Plutarch's self-disclosure in this work
should not be taken at face value but also reflects, at least to a certain
extent, his attempt to present himself, his wife, and his children as a
model family.[15] The consolation also reveals that several of Plutarch's
children died young: apart from the little Timoxena (named after her

---

[14] In *Con. praec.* 145A, Plutarch refers to a work *On love of ornament* (Περὶ φιλοκοσμίας) written
by Timoxena.
[15] Russell 1993b; Claassen 2004. See also, however, Baltussen 2009: 85–7, for arguments in
support of the sincerity of Plutarch's personal engagement in the *Consolation to his wife*.

mother), two sons did not reach adulthood. Three other sons survived their father. Autobulus and Plutarch received the treatise *On the generation of the soul in the Timaeus* (1012A), and Soclarus is mentioned near the beginning of *How the young man should listen to poetry* (15A). Later inscriptions show that at least two of them were Roman citizens.[16]

At home, Plutarch directed his own Platonic school. This did not have a strongly institutionalized and official character, but was rather a kind of private school where a group of young students and more mature adults met one another for philosophical discussions and instruction.[17] They read and commented upon important texts from the philosophical canon, such as Plato's *Timaeus*, a dialogue that was much discussed in Platonic circles and about which Plutarch had his own idiosyncratic views (see Chapter II, §3.1). Alongside Plato, other authors from other philosophical schools likewise received attention. For instance, the polemical treatise of the Epicurean Colotes entitled *That conformity to the doctrines of the other philosophers makes it even impossible to live* was first read in a group and then systematically refuted by Plutarch (*Adv. Col.* 1107E–1108C). After Plutarch's lengthy reply, the company continued the discussion and elaborated further arguments against the Epicurean view (*Non posse* 1086D; see Chapter II, §3.2). This introduction to the philosophical tradition was further completed by a series of discourses (διαλέξεις) on different topics (ethics as well as physics, history, and literature, and so on).[18] The curriculum at Plutarch's school, then, combined a fairly broad *paideia* with philosophical depth, stimulating independent thinking and a sincere search for the truth.

Plutarch's *oikos* and his school were not separated by high walls but often merged with one another. This especially appears from the *Table Talk*, in which Plutarch recalls the philosophical conversations that were held over wine, both at his home and elsewhere. Setting aside the difficult problem of the historicity of the talks,[19] we can learn much about the kind of topics that he and his friends were

---

[16] See *SIG* 844A on Autobulus and *IG* 9.1.61.41–2 on Soclarus.
[17] See esp. Glucker 1978.
[18] See esp. La Matina 2000; also Roskam 2009b: 26–8.
[19] Most scholars now adopt a sensible middle position, arguing that the talks are rooted in conversations that really took place but that Plutarch himself significantly elaborated and polished the original arguments. See, e.g., Ziegler 1951: 886–7; Teodorsson 1989: 12–15; Pordomingo Pardo 1999; Sirinelli 2000: 379–82; Titchener 2009; Roskam 2010: 46–8; Klotz and Oikonomopoulou 2011: 3–12; Meeusen 2016: 162–5; Nikolaidis 2017: 260–3.

interested in, and about their behaviour during symposia. Several
times, young students were present at these drinking parties and even
intervened in the discussion. At such moments, the framework of the
school and the informal perspective of friendly talks blend into each
other. This results in a community of congenial *pepaideumenoi* who
pass their time in learned philosophical conversations, in short, in philosophizing together (συμφιλοσοφεῖν).[20]

At this point we may take a closer look at the circle of Plutarch's
friends and acquaintances. More than a hundred names can be
found in his works, and all of them belong to the cultivated upper
class.[21] Plutarch characterizes them as politicians and men of letters
(ἄνδρες πολιτικοὶ καὶ φιλόλογοι)[22] and they are his main target readers.[23] Not surprisingly, several of them are philosophers, not only
Platonists (like Plutarch's good friend Theon) but also Pythagoreans
(Philinus), Stoics (Sarapion), and Epicureans (Boethus). Plutarch
also mentions many doctors and several priests (including Nicandrus,
his colleague Euthydemus, and Clea, priestess at Delphi). In short,
we meet the *fine fleur* of the contemporary local aristocracy. Many of
them were politically active (like Philopappus, Herculanus, or
Euphanes) and belonged to distinguished families who had been influential for several generations. Furthermore, Plutarch's circle was open
to powerful Romans who shared the same cultural background and had
a similar intellectual profile. L. Mestrius Florus, for instance, consul
under Vespasian (Suetonius, *Vesp.* 22) and later proconsul of Asia
(*SIG* 820), is often mentioned in the *Table Talk* as an erudite interlocu-
tor and a good friend. He also obtained Roman citizenship for
Plutarch.[24] Even more important was Sosius Senecio, twice consul
under Trajan (AD 99 and 107) and one of the most powerful men of
his day. In Plutarch's works, he appears as a learned man, thoroughly
familiar with literature and philosophy, and as a close friend.[25]

---

[20] Cf. the phrase διαλέγεσθαι καὶ συμφιλοσοφεῖν ('converse and philosophize together') in *Brut.*
12.3. For the term συμφιλοσοφεῖν, which expresses the activities in Plutarch's school very well, see
also *De prof. in virt.* 77C; *De tuenda* 122B; *De genio Socr.* 578F; *Dion* 20.3; *Brut.* 24.1; *Sol.* 26.1; *Cic.*
24.8.

[21] See, e.g., Ziegler 1951: 665–96; C. Jones 1971: 39–64; Puech 1992; Sirinelli 2000: 167–98.

[22] *De tuenda* 137C; see also *Quaest. conv.* 715B; Van Hoof 2010: 23. On Plutarch's conception
of philology, see Van der Stockt 2019.

[23] For Plutarch's readers, see, e.g., Wardman 1974: 37–48; Stadter 1988: 292–3 and 2015b:
45–55; Duff 2007–8: esp. 7–11; Muccioli 2012: 44–53 (on the *Parallel Lives*); and Van Hoof
2005–6 and 2010: 19–24 (on the *Moralia*).

[24] This appears from an inscription (*SIG* 829A) which mentions 'Mestrius Plutarchus the
priest'.

Several works (including the *Parallel Lives* and the *Table Talk*) were dedicated to him.

Plutarch, then, kept in touch with many members of the ruling elite. Yet an important caveat is in place here. Contrary to what is often suggested, this extensive network did not merely consist of staunch friendships. The many dedications tell us little about the actual relationship between Plutarch and his dedicatee,[26] and often rather illustrate Plutarch's networking strategies. Similarly, the shared conviviality of Plutarch's guests or hosts at different symposia need not presuppose intimate friendship but may equally well be rooted in the politics of a social player.[27] In one of his works (*On having many friends*), Plutarch unmasks πολυφιλία ('abundance of friends') as a contradiction in terms: true friends are extremely rare indeed. Elsewhere, he points out that the politician should have a powerful Roman friend in order to help him whenever necessary (*Praec. ger. reip.* 814C). This clearly reflects an insight into the importance of strategic networking, and the use of the singular (φίλον τινά) is perhaps not only motivated by a concern for feasibility – most young politicians would be more than glad to be on good terms with one powerful Roman – but even makes this position compatible with a philosophical perspective on friendship. In this light, Mestrius Florus, and later Sosius Senecio, qualify for being called Plutarch's Roman friends in the pregnant sense of the word; the others probably do not. Similarly, a few Greek aristocrats, such as Theon, Philinus, or Soclarus, may be considered as Plutarch's intimate friends. The others are involved in a subtle game of inclusion and exclusion, in which ties are strengthened for the sake of reciprocal benefit, and amicable contacts prove advantageous for all parties.

In order to build, expand, and maintain this large network, Plutarch often invited and hosted these men at his home in Chaeronea. No less often, he was himself invited by others and thus he frequently travelled through Greece. We find him back in Athens and in Delphi, but also in Aedepsus in Euboea (*Quaest. conv.* 667C), Corinth (675D), Elis (664B), Hyampolis (660D), Patras (629F), Sparta (*Lyc.* 18.2), and Tanagra (*Cons. ad ux.* 608B). He also returned to Rome. With Florus, he traversed Italy, visiting Bedriacum (*Oth.* 14.2), Brixellum

---

[25] He was present at the wedding of Plutarch's son; *Quaest. conv.* 666D.

[26] Thus correctly Russell 1972: 10–11.

[27] This aspect of Plutarch's persona is discussed in detail by Van Hoof 2010.

(18.2), and Ravenna (*Mar.* 2.1). This tour through Italy is often connected with Plutarch's first trip to Rome, in line with the hypothesis
of his ambitions as an itinerant sophist, but since, as we have seen,
the latter theory lacks decisive proof, it is equally possible that this journey to the north of Italy took place at a later stage, after the contacts
with Florus were already intensified. In Rome, Plutarch probably
again lectured on philosophical subjects (*De cur.* 522D–E):

> When I was once lecturing in Rome, that famous Rusticus, whom Domitian later killed
> through envy at his repute, was among my hearers, and a soldier came through the
> audience and delivered to him a letter from the emperor. There was a silence and I,
> too, made a pause, that he might read his letter; but he refused and did not break
> the seal until I had finished my lecture and the audience had dispersed. Because of
> this incident everyone admired the dignity of the man.

Like so many anecdotes, this one is difficult to date. If the incident
occurred during a later stay at Rome, as is sometimes assumed,[28] it
again illustrates the continuity of Plutarch's career, in which public lectures were part and parcel of his activities as a philosopher.

All these journeys cast a different light on Plutarch's famous statement in the proem to the *Life of Demosthenes* (2.2): 'But as for me, I
live in a small city, and I prefer to dwell there that it may not become
smaller still.' This sentence is often quoted as evidence for Plutarch's
patriotism and for his devotion to his native city.[29] This is precisely
the impression that he wants to create, yet here, too, his self-disclosure
is not devoid of subtle rhetoric.[30] Plutarch never hid himself away in the
sticks. He was a citizen of Athens (*Quaest. conv.* 628A), Delphi, and
Rome, as well as Chaeronea, and we may well recall that he was not
at home when his daughter died. Chaeronea was probably, indeed,
quite small, but it often had to get along without its most famous
citizen.

There can be no doubt, though, about Plutarch's influential position
in his hometown. Through his social standing, his broad network, and
his erudition, he became one of the leading figures of the town. No

---

[28] Barrow 1967: 38; C. Jones 1971: 23; Puech 1992: 4856; *contra* Russell 1968: 132 and
Flacelière and Irigoin 1987: xxxi.
[29] Dodds 1933: 98; C. Jones 1971: 3; Aalders 1982: 15; Titchener 2002. Plutarch's patriotism
is frequently regarded as the main motivation for his attack on Herodotus. I argue against this view
in Roskam 2017b.
[30] On this proem to *Demosthenes–Cicero*, see Mossman 1999; Zadorojnyi 2005; Beneker 2016;
Chrysanthou 2018.

wonder then that he held the eponymous archonship (*Quaest. conv.* 642F; cf. 693F). An inscription (*SIG* 829A; cf. *An seni* 785C–D) shows that he was also a member of the Amphictyonic Council.[31] Moreover, he did not avoid minor political duties. A passage from the *Political precepts* shows that he was once responsible for building activities in Chaeronea (811B–C):

Epameinondas advanced the *telearchy* to a position of great consideration and dignity, though previously it had been nothing but a sort of supervision of the alleys for the removal of dung and the draining off of water in the streets. And no doubt I myself seem ridiculous to visitors in our town when I am seen in public, as I often am, engaged in such matters...But I say to those who criticize me for standing and watching tiles being measured or concrete or stones being delivered, that I am not building this for myself, but for my native place.

This is one further sample of Plutarch's sophisticated self-fashioning. It is far from plausible that he was himself actively working with shovel or pickaxe. We may presume that the *telearchy* was basically a smaller administrative task and that Plutarch cleverly used it to enhance his reputation as a benefactor of his community,[32] following the lead of the great philosophically trained statesman Epameinondas himself.[33]

Plutarch, then, was deeply involved in municipal politics, at both its higher and lower levels. This political commitment should be understood in light of his political philosophy, which in turn cannot be understood without insight into the precise situation of the *poleis* at that time and of the dynamics of local politics in general. As in most cities of Greece in that era, Chaeronea had a certain autonomy. Internal matters were decided upon by the council and the people. Though democracies by name, most cities were in fact aristocracies ruled by the most important families. These tried to keep the populace under control by large donations (for buildings and festivals, for instance) and in turn received honour and managed to maintain the social *status quo*. This so-called euergetic system is well documented

---

[31] He may also have been Boeotarch and Agonothete at the Pythian games (thus C. Jones 1971: 25–6, on the basis of *An seni* 785C; cf. Gianakaris 1970: 32), but this is beyond proof.

[32] See Carrière and Cuvigny 1984: 181: 'It is possible that Plutarch's modesty was a bit feigned, for it was very honourable, even in a small city, to take the initiative for building or to supervise works, as the inscriptions show' ('Il se peut que la modestie de Plutarque soit un peu feinte, car il était fort honorable, même dans une petite cité, de prendre l'initiative de constructions ou d'être le curateur des travaux, comme le montrent les inscriptions').

[33] See Wardman 1974: 102–3. Epameinondas broke the military supremacy of Sparta in the Battle of Leuctra (371 BC). As a result, his city, Thebes, for a while became the leading *polis* in Greece (until the Battle of Mantinea in 362 BC).

through a great number of honorary inscriptions from the whole Greek world and through literary sources, and it is also discussed in Plutarch's political works (see Chapter IV, §7).

Finally, Plutarch maintained a strong relationship with the oracle at Delphi. At a mature age, he became one of the two priests of Apollo at the Delphic shrine (his colleague was Euthydemus; *Quaest. conv.* 700E).[34] The priesthood was for life and Plutarch would hold it for many Pythiads, as he says himself (*An seni* 792F). As well as several administrative responsibilities, the office entailed active involvement in ritual acts. Plutarch summarizes his duties very briefly as 'sacrificing, leading processions, and taking part in a chorus' (792F). While growing older, the Chaeronean philosopher continued to attend the rituals, with a crown on his head. His office did not require a permanent presence in Delphi, but it is more than likely that he often stayed at the sanctuary and was involved in the daily routine. For not every day of Plutarch's life was an intellectual banquet of high-minded philosophical discussions. Often, it was business as usual, with day-to-day worries and doubtless irritations. After all, even Plutarch was a mortal.

4. Old age and beyond

Plutarch himself was only too aware of this, even more so when he crossed the baneful threshold of old age. Several passages in his work suggest, however, that he had come to terms with his existence. He gladly welcomes the revival of Delphi (*De Pyth. or.* 409A–C), pointing to

many additions in the form of buildings not here before and many restored that were dilapidated and in ruins...It is true that I feel kindly toward myself in so far as my zeal or services may have furthered these matters with the co-operation of Polycrates and Petraeus.[35]

And he repeatedly expresses his appreciation of the blessings of the *Pax Romana* (*De Pyth. or.* 408B–C):

[34] On Plutarch's priesthood at Delphi and its importance for his life and thinking, see Jaillard 2007; Casanova 2012; Thum 2013: 118–21; Stadter 2015b: 82–97.
[35] The 'I' speaking here is Theon, not Plutarch (see Schröder 1990: 15–18), yet the latter would no doubt have been willing to appropriate Theon's words.

For my part, I am well content with the settled conditions prevailing at present, and I find them very welcome, and the questions which men now put to the god are concerned with these conditions. There is, in fact, profound peace and tranquillity; war has ceased, there are no wanderings of peoples, no civil strifes, no tyrannies, no other maladies and ills in Greece requiring many unusual remedial forces.[36]

Although it is always risky to isolate such passages from their context, it is hard to resist the conclusion that the old Plutarch was satisfied with his world and that he had reached the peace of mind he valued so highly.

His old age was a period of continuity and further consolidation. He remained active in local politics and continued his priesthood at Delphi, and, of course, he kept writing. It was also a period of great recognition. According to a late source, he received the *ornamenta consularia* from Trajan (*Suda* 4.150.27–9). These were usually awarded for personal services to the emperor, but sometimes also as a mere favour or as acknowledgement of a meritorious career.[37] If Plutarch indeed received the *ornamenta*, it is reasonable to suppose that it was through Senecio's intercession. The powerful Roman could thus pay back the big literary favours he had received from Plutarch, while the latter truly reaped the fruit of his friendship with a ruler (καρπὸν ἐκ φιλίας ἡγεμονικῆς, *Praec. ger. reip.* 814C). The *Suda* adds that governors of Illyria were told to ask Plutarch's advice before taking any decision. It is far from certain whether this information is reliable but, if it is, it was the result of a political network that had been built and maintained for decades.

Another late source (Syncellus, *Ecl. Chron.* 659 Dind. = p. 426 Mossh.) tells us that Hadrian made Plutarch procurator of Greece. This information, again based on a single and late source, is to be regarded with caution, although it cannot be ruled out that the philosopher did indeed receive this honour.[38] However that may be, he had reached the sunset of his life. We still have an honorary inscription for the new emperor Hadrian which mentions Plutarch as the *epimelete*

[36] Again Theon speaking (see previous note). See also *De fort. Rom.* 317B–C; *De tranq. an.* 469E; *An seni* 784F; *Praec. ger. reip.* 805A and 824C; Bravo García 1973: 185–9; Boulogne 1994: 37–8. According to Dillon 1997, Plutarch even regarded this universal Roman peace as the end of history.

[37] Rémy 1976. Quintilian for instance, had received them under Domitian.

[38] The testimony is accepted by Ziegler 1951: 657–8; Bowersock 1969: 57, 65, and 112; C. Jones 1971: 29–30 and 34; Carrière and Cuvigny 1984: 63–4; Flacelière and Irigoin 1987: li; Lamberton 2001: 12; and others. Swain 1996: 171–2 is more sceptical. On Plutarch's possible relations with Hadrian, see also Bowie 1997.

or administrator of the Amphictyonic Council which administered the Delphic sanctuary (*SIG* 829A). What follows is silence, the silence of death. His belief in the immortality of the soul and his initiation into the mysteries of Dionysus (*Cons. ad ux.* 611D) may have comforted Plutarch in his last moments, together with the confident idea that he, after Horace's famous saying (*Carm.* 3.30.1), had completed a monument more lasting than bronze.

Plutarch's fame only grew after his death. Following a decree of the Amphictyonic Council, Delphi and Chaeronea honoured him with a herm with an inscription (*SIG* 843A). This was the beginning of an exceptionally rich reception history. He was often quoted by ancient authors and was not even forgotten in the Middle Ages. During the Byzantine period, the learned Maximus Planudes laid the basis of our Greek texts, while the first translations, and later the Aldine editions, were made in the Italian Renaissance. The famous French translation of Jacques Amyot (the *Parallel Lives* in 1559, the *Moralia* in 1572), followed by the English translation of Thomas North (1579), inaugurated a new phase in the reception of Plutarch's oeuvre, as he became a major source of inspiration of many coryphaei of Western cultural history. Authors like Shakespeare and Montaigne, Bacon, Ben Jonson, Racine, Rousseau, and many more, were deeply influenced by the Chaeronean. A detailed study of the reception history of Plutarch's work would easily fill several volumes; it falls, however, outside the scope of the present book.[39]

Plutarch, then, never died. His fame and influence lasted through the centuries.

A man from Seriphos told Themistocles that he did not owe his great reputation to his own efforts at all, but to his city. 'Very true,' retorted Themistocles, 'I should never have become famous if I had been a Seriphian, and neither would you if you had been an Athenian!'[40]

---

[39] The classic study is still Hirzel 1912. See also Aulotte 1965 (on Plutarch and Amyot); Konstantinovic 1989 (on Plutarch and Montaigne); and Pade 2007 (on Plutarch's *Lives* in fifteenth-century Italy). Also several collections of articles, including Gallo 1998; Ferreira 2002; Guerrier 2005; Aguilar and Alfageme 2006; Volpe Cacciatore 2009; Pérez Jiménez 2010; and Beck 2014a: 531–610. The most recent contribution is Xenophontos and Oikonomopoulou 2019, which contains a panorama of thorough discussions that range from late antiquity into the twentieth century.

[40] *Them.* 18.5; trans. Scott-Kilvert 1960.

In this respect at least, Plutarch surpassed Themistocles. He did not need his native city, small as it was, in order to acquire perennial fame. Moreover, from his day on, Chaeronea was no longer only the city connected with the loss of Greek freedom and the destruction of the hope for the future. It had also become the place where Greek *paideia* celebrated one of its most impressive triumphs. Chaeronea, in short, was no longer the city of the great disaster: it had become the city of Plutarch.

II. LOOKING FOR THE TRUTH: PLUTARCH AS AN OPEN-MINDED PLATONIST

Plutarch saw himself primarily as a philosopher, standing in the long Academic tradition that could be followed back to the 'divine' Plato (*De cap. ex inim.* 90C; *Per.* 8.2). But when he took his first steps as a philosopher, Plato's works had been (re)read and interpreted for several centuries. As a result, Plutarch had to acquaint himself with a rich exegetical tradition that would shape the lens through which he read Plato and would turn his attention to specific dialogues. For some Platonic dialogues had during this time received a privileged position. In particular, the *Timaeus* was intensively studied, which led to heated discussions about the correct interpretation of specific passages.[1] A detailed exegesis of this dialogue, complemented with material carefully selected from a few other dialogues, yielded a few Platonic 'core doctrines'. Many Platonists, for instance, endorsed three fundamental principles, viz. God, matter, and the Forms (the so-called *Dreiprinzipienlehre*). These Forms were often regarded as the thoughts of God, and the final end of life (the τέλος) was nearly always defined as an assimilation to God (ὁμοίωσις θεῷ) – as far as possible (κατὰ τὸ δυνατόν) – on the basis of a celebrated passage from the *Theaetetus* (176b1). Such doctrines found their way into school handbooks (like Alcinous' *Didaskalikos* or Apuleius' *De Platone*), which provided the reader with a systematized Plato. Inconsistencies in Plato's works were explained away, obscure passages were clarified, and later insights (including Peripatetic and Stoic doctrines) were used to reconstruct a coherent Platonic philosophy.[2]

This does not imply, however, that there existed in Plutarch's day a kind of standard school doctrine that strictly defined what should be considered as orthodox Platonism. The Academy no longer existed as an official institution;[3] in its place were several private schools under the inspiring leadership of local teachers who knew the exegetic tradition and its basic ideas, and dealt with it in their own way.

---

[1] Good overviews can be found in Baltes 1976–8 and Ferrari 2001b. For the Middle Platonist commentaries on Plato's *Dialogues*, see also Petrucci 2018a.

[2] Excellent discussions of Plutarch's exegetical methods are Ferrari 2001a and 2004; Bréchet 2010–11.

[3] See the seminal study of Glucker 1978; see also Nikolaidis 1999.

1. A doxographical Plutarch

Plutarch's Platonic philosophy should be understood in this light. Its leading ideas have often been studied and if we reduce them to their very core (adopting, as it were, the approach of ancient doxographers), we may end up with the following picture:[4]

- Plutarch accepts two fundamental principles: the One (identified with the Demiurge) and the indeterminate dyad.[5] The One is the principle of sameness and is situated at the intelligible level where we also find the Forms.[6] The indeterminate dyad, on the other hand, is the principle of difference. Yet the two principles are not on the same level. Although several passages in Plutarch's works suggest that he endorsed a dualistic worldview (see esp. *De Is. et Os.* 369A–371A and *De an. procr.* 1026B–C), closer inspection reveals that he advocated a mitigated dualism in which the positive pole dominates and which makes room for several middle terms.

- Plutarch is well known for his idiosyncratic interpretation of Plato's *Timaeus* (see §3.1). In his view, amorphous and obscure matter and a confused irrational soul already existed before creation. The Demiurge then gave this precosmic soul a share in his own rationality by ordering it according to numerical ratios, thus turning it into the World Soul. This World Soul then ordered precosmic matter. However, it still contains a residue of the maleficent precosmic soul, which now and then makes its influence felt, and this (not unqualified matter) explains the existence of evil.

- Between God and human beings are demons (sometimes understood as separate souls or intellects), who can act as guardian spirits and are in charge of oracles and rites. Plutarch believes in divination and in a providential God,[7] and recommends a pious acceptance of the *patrios pistis*, steering a middle course between atheism and superstition (see Chapter VII, §§2 and 6).

---

[4] Discussions of Plutarch's Platonism include R. Jones 1916; Dörrie 1969 and 1971; Dillon 1977, 1988, and 2014; Froidefond 1987; Ferrari 1995 and 2004; Opsomer 1998, 2005, and 2007a; Bonazzi 2003: 213–40; Brouillette and Giavatto 2010; Donini 2011a; Boys-Stones 2018 (*passim*).

[5] Opsomer 2007b. On Plutarch's dualism, see, e.g., Bianchi 1987; Alt 1993; Chlup 2000; Hirsch-Luipold 2002: 203–11; Almagor 2013.

[6] The precise relation between Demiurge and Forms remains unclear. Plutarch may have discussed it in his lost work 'Where are the Forms' (Lamprias catalogue 67). On his view of the Forms, see further Schoppe 1994 and Ferrari 1995: 29–34.

[7] On Plutarch's position regarding providence, see, e.g., Opsomer 1997; Frazier and Leão 2010.

- Plutarch shows a great interest in physical phenomena and in explaining their causes. He makes room for a double causality, distinguishing between divine and material causes.[8] He rejects atomistic theory and prefers the theory of the elements, which he derives in a Platonic vein from geometrical solids.[9] While recognizing that theories about the world of sense perception can at best claim plausibility (τὸ εἰκός), he also believes that this world, and several of its constituents, can function as an image (εἰκών) of the divine.[10]

- The structure of our human soul reflects that of the World Soul,[11] which entails a close link between Plutarch's cosmological thinking and his ethics.[12] Our human soul basically consists of two parts: a rational one and an irrational one (that can be subdivided into an appetitive and a spirited part; De virt. mor. 441E–442B). Virtue, then, consists in controlling the irrational passions (often seen as sickness of the soul) by reason. In doxographical terms: virtue is metriopatheia (restraint over the passions, which was the ideal of the Peripatetic school) rather than apatheia (complete eradication of the passions, as pursued by the Stoics). Furthermore, such virtue, which rests on a fundamental choice (προαίρεσις), can be taught and usually requires a long and gradual process of moral progress. Real friendship is based on virtue, as is conjugal love. In the field of politics, Plutarch accepts the Platonic ideal of the philosopher-king, while also bearing in mind the demands of a pragmatic course adapted to concrete political circumstances. He is less critical of the poets than Plato and argues that their poetry can be used as propaedeutics to philosophy. Finally, like all Platonists, Plutarch regards assimilation to God (as far as possible) – ὁμοίωσις θεῷ (κατὰ τὸ δυνατόν) – as the final end of life.[13]

- In general, scholars usually distinguish between three main strands in Plutarch's philosophy: Plato, later views developed in the Academy, and Pythagoreanism.[14] Plutarch had a very detailed knowledge of Plato's dialogues.[15] He frequently quotes from them for different

---

[8] The locus classicus is De def. or. 435F–437E. See further Donini 2011a: 341–58; Ferrari 2015; Meeusen 2016: 258–78.

[9] Opsomer 2015.

[10] See esp. the important study of Hirsch-Luipold 2002.

[11] Opsomer 1994; Ferrari 2007–8; Castelnérac 2007; Roig Lanzillotta 2015.

[12] This can be seen in different domains; see Demulder 2018.

[13] See esp. Becchi 1996; see also below, Chapter VII.

[14] Donini 2011a: 396 and 359–73; Bonazzi 2003: 237–40; Opsomer 2005: 176; Brouillette and Giavatto 2010: 3.

[15] See Brouillette and Giavatto 2010: 9–25 for a typology of Plutarch's quotations from Plato. A list of quotations can be found in Helmbold and O'Neil 1959 (though not all items listed there are equally relevant) and in Giavatto 2010b. For Plutarch's reception of the Timaeus, see Chapter II, §3.1; for the Laws, see Demulder 2017; for the Phaedrus, see Billault 1999; for the Phaedo, see Roskam 2015b.

purposes, not only concerning their basic ideas but also regarding trivial details. Academic thinking certainly exerted significant influence on him: Xenocrates in particular was an important source of inspiration,[16] but also later philosophers such as Arcesilaus and Carneades, who preferred a sceptical approach.[17] In a lost work, Plutarch defended the unity of the Academy after the time of Plato (Lamprias catalogue 63).[18] Finally, Pythagoreanism comes to the fore in number speculations and in several works such as *On Socrates' divine sign*. Its influence should not be exaggerated, although Plutarch did adopt several 'Pythagorean' ideas which could in his view be perfectly reconciled with Plato's philosophy. This holds true for other philosophical traditions as well (e.g. Aristotle's philosophy[19] and subsequent Peripatetic thinking) and even for the whole intellectual Greek tradition as such.

The above doxographical survey sketches the broad outlines of Plutarch's thought. This is more or less how Diogenes Laertius (or any other ancient doxographer) would have presented it, and, although such a picture is limited to the bare essentials, it is not wrong in itself. Yet it unduly ignores several important aspects of Plutarch's philosophy. No attention is given to the intellectual context and to the relation between Plutarch's views and those of contemporary schools or movements.[20] Even worse, the creative process of thinking through which these ideas are gradually developed and argued, and the particular way in which they are expressed,[21] are entirely ignored: this doxographical survey rests on a methodologically problematic approach in which particular ideas are isolated from their context and

---

[16] Dillon 1999.

[17] For the importance of the so-called New Academy of Arcesilaus and Carneades in Plutarch's thinking, see esp. Opsomer 1998 and Bonazzi 2003: 213–40. See also Ferrari 2005b; Shiffman 2010; Bonazzi 2014.

[18] The Lamprias catalogue is an ancient list of Plutarch's works. It is presented as a list compiled by Plutarch's son Lamprias, but, as far as we know, none of Plutarch's children was called Lamprias. The list is not entirely reliable (it does not contain all works and also includes some *spuria*), yet it remains a precious source of information for the titles of several lost books.

[19] Plutarch's attitude towards Aristotle is a much discussed topic: see, e.g., Sandbach 1982; Babut 1996; Ferrari 1999b; Donini 2004 and 2011a: 327–39; Karamanolis 2006; Roskam 2011b; Becchi 2014.

[20] See esp. Roig Lanzillotta and Muñoz Gallarte 2012; also Roig Lanzillotta 2011 on gnosticism and Boulogne 2008 on hermetism.

[21] Cf. Hirsch-Luipold 2002: 288: 'Eine Interpretation der Schriften Plutarchs, die seine Bilder nicht berücksichtigt oder den bildhaften Charakter insgesamt übersieht, wird der Intention des Autors nicht gerecht und ist deshalb methodisch problematisch' ('An interpretation of Plutarch's writings that does not take into account his images or entirely overlooks the expressive character, fails to do justice to the author's intention and is thus methodologically problematic').

presented as apodictic convictions. As a result, philosophical wonder is largely replaced by a soulless set of doctrines.

It would therefore be better to follow another approach that does justice to the dynamics of Plutarch's thinking. What did it actually mean for Plutarch to be a philosopher? And what was his philosophical method (if indeed he had one)? When we try to answer such questions, it soon becomes clear that Plutarch was far less systematic and apodictic than the above doxographical picture suggests.

2. Beyond doxographical schemes: looking for the truth

For Plutarch, philosophizing was essentially looking for the truth: philosophy is *zetesis*, that is, a seeking or searching, and a philosophical approach is tantamount to a 'zetetic' approach.[22] A good philosopher raises an interesting question and then comes up with different answers. This is a pattern that very often occurs in Plutarch's works and to which we shall return in due course. Here, I confine myself to one first example: the *Platonic questions*. This is a series of ten questions regarding the correct interpretation of a particular passage from one of Plato's dialogues: 'Why did Plato call the supreme God father and maker of all things?' (1000E, with reference to *Tim.* 28c3–4); 'What does Timaeus mean by saying that the souls were sowed in earth and moon and all the rest of the instruments of time?' (1006B, referring to *Tim.* 42d4–5); and so on. The last question is as follows (1009B–C):

What was Plato's reason for saying that speech is a blend of nouns and verbs [see Pl. *Soph.* 262b9–c7]? For it seems that except these two Plato dismissed all the parts of speech whereas Homer in youthful exuberance went so far as to pack all together in a single line, the following:

Tentward going myself take the guerdon that well you may know it. [*Il.* 1.185]

In this there are in fact a pronoun and participle and noun and verb and preposition and article and conjunction and adverb, for the suffix 'ward' has here been put in place of the preposition 'to,' the expression 'tentward' being of the same kind as the expression 'Athensward.' What, then, is to be said on behalf of Plato?

---

[22] On the importance of zetetic thinking in Plutarch, see, e.g., Opsomer 1998: 189 and 191; Bonazzi 2008; Shiffman 2010: 260–1; Kechagia 2011a: 80 and 93–104; Roskam 2017c: 200–3.

This is a typical example of Plutarch's talent for problematizing. At first sight, Plato's saying is obscure if not patently wrong. For does not everybody know that other words apart from nouns and verbs exist? The challenge of the problem is cleverly illustrated by a well-chosen verse from Homer, which contains eight parts of speech. This, then, is grammatical erudition in the service of philosophical wonder. That Plato simply had it wrong is not an option, of course. We should rather reflect about the meaning and relevance of Plato's words and see how he can be defended. As a matter of fact, several alternative solutions are conceivable and they are elaborated one after the other in the remainder of the text.[23]

Such concatenation of different possible solutions, however, should not be regarded as a mere juxtaposition of equally relevant and plausible answers to the question. As a rule, the compositional pattern of the questions shows an ascending structure in which the most convincing answer is placed at the end.[24] Yet this does not imply that the previous solutions are useless (for then Plutarch could equally well have immediately jumped to the ultimate answer). The first solutions often provide an interesting introduction to the problem, making clear where the difficulties are and what is at stake.[25] They are what Plutarch metaphorically calls an ἐνδόσιμον (*De an. procr.* 1012D; see also *Quaest. conv.* 704E): the note that gives the key to the tune. Moreover, they also have a pedagogical relevance, providing a concise synthesis of the previous tradition and illustrating the broad-ranging erudition of the *pepaideumenos* (see Chapter III).

But that is not all. These first solutions are neither a ladder that can be thrown away once the problem has become clear, nor interesting pieces of knowledge that can be secured in the storehouse of our minds. They have a relative value on their own, and omitting them would mean a clear loss in our attempt to reach the truth. We should therefore take the consequences of the 'zetetic' aspect of Plutarch's philosophy more radically than is usually done. Far too often, indeed, scholars almost exclusively focus on the final answer as the one preferred by Plutarch. For instance, Plutarch's ultimate answer to the question of the enigmatic E that was dedicated in the Delphic shrine of Apollo is simply equated with that of Ammonius, his true view of

---

[23] See Giavatto 2010a for a recent discussion of this question.
[24] See, e.g., Opsomer 1996: 83 and 1998: 203; Meeusen 2016: 88–9.
[25] Cf. Opsomer 2010.

the myth of Isis and Osiris is found in his metaphysical interpretation, and so on. This, I contend, is an oversimplifying reduction of the zetetic process. The other answers make sense too, and likewise contain germs of the truth, even the first, problematic ones.[26] Plutarch's zetetic approach is characterized by intellectual honesty and great open-mindedness. He sees that the final solution often ignores several aspects that are part and parcel of the problem, whereas earlier, less plausible answers throw an interesting light on them. Rather than ignoring these elements or explaining them away, he prefers to mention them and try to explain them by different hypotheses. As a result, the definitive answer is usually beyond human reach: it is simply impossible to combine the different, sometimes even opposite solutions and fuse them together into one comprehensive answer. Every solution remains valuable in its own way, although this does not mean, of course, that they are all equally valuable. Looking for the truth, then, means entering a field of tension, bidding farewell to peremptory truth claims and tentatively indicating the direction in which the truth may be found, while collecting as many pieces of the puzzle as possible. In short, Plutarch's zetetic philosophy is refreshingly open-minded.

Furthermore, this zetetic approach has an important dialogical aspect.[27] No wonder, then, that Plutarch wrote many dialogues. This, indeed, is a constitutive element of his Platonism. Plutarch's dialogues, however, usually lack the lively Socratic interaction with question and answer but are rather fashioned after the *zetesis* approach. An initial question is followed by several interventions in which different characters develop their own answer. These characters also interact, of course, in a critical but respectful and friendly way, as educated men (πεπαιδευμένοι).[28] Thus, in Plutarch's dialogues *zetesis* becomes *syzetesis*: a learned joint enquiry into the truth.

The genre of the dialogue yields an additional advantage, in that the characters do not merely elaborate their own view but also embody their own philosophical approach. In *On Socrates' divine sign*, for instance, the different characters illustrate through their behaviour different ways of dealing with the Academic tradition.[29] Similarly, in *On the E at Delphi*, Ammonius personifies the metaphysical approach,

---

[26] I argue this for *De Is. et Os.* in Roskam 2017c and for *De genio Socr.* in Roskam 2013.
[27] Cf. Müller 2012.
[28] See, e.g., Van der Stockt 2000a; see also Stadter 1999.
[29] See Donini 2011a: 403–22 and 2017: 17–38 and 46–59.

whereas Theon shows how a dialectician would think about this problem (386D–E), and the character of the young 'Plutarch' reveals the perspective of persons with mathematical interests (387D–F).[30] In the *Table Talk*, doctors, grammarians, philosophers, and others all illustrate different points of view. The recurrent motif of the extreme character who leaves the scene before the discussion actually starts should be understood in this light as well:[31] it is not merely an element in the setting of the dialogue but also illustrates a particular attitude, viz. that of the man who radically sticks to his own convictions and is not willing to enter the dialogical process of *syzetesis*. Such people condemn themselves to isolation and thus utterly fail to come closer to the truth.

A better insight into the zetetic basis of Plutarch's dialogues also throws light on a notorious crux in Plutarch studies. Scholars often struggle with the question of which character in a certain dialogue can be regarded as Plutarch's mouthpiece. There is a large consensus about some characters, like Ammonius in *On the E at Delphi* or Theon in *That the Pythia now does not give her oracles in verse*, but, in many cases, it is far from clear to what extent the ideas of specific characters can simply be ascribed to Plutarch himself.[32] In my view, the fundamental answer to this difficult question should be sought in the underlying zetetic approach. Just as the final answer should not be regarded as the one and only, definitive solution to every aspect of the problem, so no single character should be considered as the one and only mouthpiece of Plutarch himself. Every character in his own way clarifies the question and therefore deserves to be taken seriously.[33] Again, this does not mean that the view of every character is equally plausible, but as soon as we decide to regard one character as Plutarch's mouthpiece, we unduly undermine the dialogical and zetetic aspect of his philosophy, which is always searching.

A process of broad-minded and erudite *zetesis*, then, is Plutarch's way of practising Platonic dialectics. But next to dialectics stands myth, in Plutarch as in Plato. Plutarch wrote three big eschatological

---

[30] Here as elsewhere, I use 'Plutarch' to refer to the character in the dialogue, as distinct from the author Plutarch.

[31] See, e.g., *Sept. sap. conv.* 149B; *De def. or.* 413D; *De sera num.* 548A–B; *Non posse* 1086E; Flacelière 1959: 210; Zacher 1982: 19.

[32] Cf. Ferrari 1995: 29–34; Brenk 2009 and 2016; Thum 2013: 27–36; Brouillette 2014: 33–5.

[33] See, e.g., Babut 1988: 393–408 on Galaxidorus; Babut 1992: 216–20 and Moreschini 1996: 41 on Cleombrotus; and Roskam 2013 on Theocritus.

myths and in this showed himself to be a true follower of Plato. I here confine myself to a short presentation.[34]

On the slowness of divine punishments concludes with the story of Aridaeus of Soli, a man notorious for his wickedness (563B–568A). Due to an accident, the intelligent part of his soul leaves his body and he sees other souls ascending like flamelike bubbles, some of them straight ahead, others in a whorled movement. A kinsman then addresses him as Thespesius and tells him he is not really dead: rather, his intelligence has been detached from the rest of his soul, which still remains in the body as an anchor. Aridaeus/Thespesius also learns how the souls are punished in different ways for their crimes. Some of them are punished by Poinē ('Punishment') while still being in the body, greater criminals are penalized after death by Dikē ('Justice'), and incurable souls undergo most cruel torments by the avenging Erinys. Next Aridaeus/Thespesius is brought to a seductive chasm, called the place of Lēthē ('Forgetfulness'), where Dionysus has ascended and where the intelligent part of the soul risks being dissolved by pleasures. He is not allowed to stay there, yet is unable to reach the oracle of Apollo, since the stern cable of his soul does not allow him to proceed to such heights. Then he witnesses the excruciating torments of the bad souls (including that of his own father) and the return of the souls to a second birth, taking the form of animals adapted to their character (567F–568A):

And he saw among the others Nero's soul, which was in a bad way, not least because it had been run through with red-hot nails. The artisans had a form already prepared for him – that of the Indian viper, in which he would live once, as a foetus, he had eaten his way out of his mother; but suddenly, he said, an intense light blazed forth, and a voice arose from the light, ordering them to transfer Nero's soul to another, more inoffensive species by fashioning the form of a musical animal which could live near marshes and ponds. For, the voice announced, he had already been punished for his crimes, and moreover the gods owed him a favour for freeing the nation which, of all those he ruled, was the best and the most favoured by the gods.[35]

---

[34] On Plutarch's myths, see esp. Vernière 1977 and Frazier 2019; cf. also R. Jones 1916: 40–67; Ingenkamp 2001; Deuse 2010; Hirsch-Luipold 2014. On his view of myth, see Hardie 1992; Hirsch-Luipold 2002: 138–44.

[35] Trans. Waterfield and Kidd 1992. The passage, which is a salient example of Plutarch's erudite reception of several aspects of the philosophical, literary, and historical tradition, is discussed by Dumortier 1969; Brenk 1987a; and Zadorojnyi 1997. See also Frazer 1971 and Alt 1993: 126.

After this spectacle, Aridaeus/Thespesius is suddenly cast back into his body. He gets the message, completely changes his life, and becomes a paragon of piety and virtue.[36]

At the end of *On the face that appears in the orb of the moon* (942D–945D), Sulla tells what he has heard from one of Cronus' servitors. The main idea of the myth is that human beings consist of three parts: body, soul, and mind. Earth, the realm of Demeter, provides the body, whereas the moon, Persephone's realm, furnishes the soul, and the sun gives the mind. In consequence, we also die two deaths. First, the soul is separated from the body on earth, in a quick and violent way. The souls then dwell in the region between earth and moon, where the bad ones are punished and the good ones are purged from corporeal pollution. When they reach the moon, they live a peaceful life as *daimones*, yet they sometimes descend in order to take part in rites, take charge of oracles, or intervene in human affairs. Whenever they go wrong, they are punished and are reborn. Finally, they die a second death on the moon, when their mind is separated through love for the image of the good that can be perceived in the sun. The nature of the soul withers away on the moon, quite quickly in the case of temperate souls, less so for passionate ones. A new cycle begins when the sun sows mind in the moon, the moon adds new souls, and the earth provides the bodies.

In *On Socrates' divine sign*, finally, Simmias relates the story of Timarchus of Chaeronea, who has descended into the crypt of Trophonius in an attempt to learn more about Socrates' divine sign (589F–592E). There he lies down and suddenly has the impression that his head is struck, his skull is opened, and his soul leaves his body. He sees innumerable islands, spherical and fiery, in a vast sea, as well as a great abyss from which all kinds of lamentations emerge. A voice informs him about the region of Persephone where he is at that moment, and characterizes the moon as the turning point (καμπή) of birth. Timarchus sees many stars moving to and from the abyss. The voice explains that these are souls. Whereas some of them have completely sunk into the body, others leave outside their purest part. This part, then, is the mind (νοῦς), or better, the *daimōn*, since it remains external to the body, as a kind of buoy floating above a man's head. Those stars that seem to be extinguished are souls that

---

[36] On the similarities and differences of Plutarch's myths with other (ancient and modern) testimonies of near-death experiences, see Muñoz Gallarte 2019.

sink completely into the body; the stars that are rekindled, as it were, are souls that have left their bodies; and those that move on high are the *daimones* of men said to 'possess understanding' (νοῦν ἔχειν). Some souls move in a disordered way, struggling with their passions, while others follow a straight and regular course, being obedient to their *daimōn*.

These far too short summaries are, in a way, parallel to the doxographical survey of Plutarch's philosophy presented above. They capture the main lines and basic ideas of the myths but omit their context (every myth is embedded in a broader discussion) and their literary embellishment and lively presentation – in short, everything that makes them so attractive. Plutarch's rich myths, which are inspired by those of Plato, still repay further study. They abound in clever and subtle allusions, all combined into one sophisticated feast of intertextuality. Here, I would only underscore their philosophical value. Indeed, the opposition between *mythos* and *logos* is far too absolute, for Plutarch's myths – like those of Plato – contain an important component of *logos* too.[37] In this respect, his myths significantly contribute to the search for the truth and can be perfectly integrated within the zetetic approach, as appears from *De genio Socratis*, where the myth provides one of the answers (not the last one). Theocritus there insists that myth also touches on the truth, albeit in a less precise manner (589F). Myth, in short, is part and parcel of Plutarch's zetetic philosophy.

3. Challenging Plutarch's intellectual honesty

We have seen so far that Plutarch's philosophy is a sincere search for the truth, characterized by zetetic open-mindedness, great respect for the tradition and for all available evidence, and intellectual honesty. Plutarch readily recognizes that different, partly opposite opinions can all contain at least germs of the truth, and thus prefers nuance and qualification to oversimplification. This picture will be corroborated with many more examples in the following chapters. At this point, we should deal with two aspects of his thinking that at first sight seem to refute it.

---

[37] Cf. Hirsch-Luipold 2014: 174.

3.1. Plutarch's interpretation of Plato's Timaeus

Plutarch's treatise *On the generation of the soul in the Timaeus* is a particularly interesting work that contains much valuable information about the metaphysical and cosmological foundations of his Platonic philosophy. He there proposes his own interpretation of a notoriously obscure and controversial passage from the *Timaeus* where Plato deals with the creation of the World Soul (*Tim.* 35a1–36b5).[38] The work consists of two parts, each of which is introduced by a verbatim quotation of Plato's text (respectively 34a1–b4 and 35b4–36b5), followed by an elaborate commentary. Unlike most Platonists, who were convinced that Plato was not thinking of a real creation but only presented it as such for the sake of examination (θεωρίας ἕνεκα, 1013A; cf. 1017B), Plutarch insists that we have to take Plato's words literally. We are dealing, then, with a real creation of the World Soul, which is composed by the Demiurge out of different components.

In order to understand Plutarch's interpretation, we should begin with Plato's view. According to current Platonic exegesis, Plato probably said that the Demiurge first made three different mixtures: a blend of divisible and indivisible being, a blend of divisible and divided sameness, and a blend of divisible and divided otherness.[39] From these three preliminary mixtures he then created the World Soul:

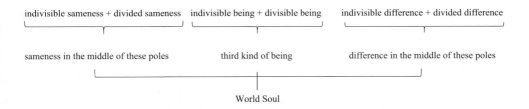

According to Plutarch's interpretation, the Demiurge first blended the indivisible and the divisible. Then, he blended this preliminary

---

[38] On this work, see esp. Thévenaz 1938; Cherniss 1976; Ferrari and Baldi 2002; Opsomer 2004. Short introductions can also be found in Hershbell 1987 and Ferrari 2001a: 267–72.

[39] The first to propose this interpretation was Grube 1932; see also Cornford 1937: 59–66.

mixture with the two extreme poles of sameness and difference. This is a considerable simplification of what Plato presumably meant:

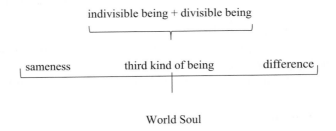

World Soul

The principle of indivisible being may be identified with the Demiurge. The radically innovative part of Plutarch's interpretation, however, has to do with the principle of divisible being (or, more correctly, the principle of being 'that becomes divisible in the realm of the bodies'; thus Plato, *Tim.* 35a2–3). This principle is equated with a precosmic soul that existed before the creation, together with eternal intelligible being and chaotic matter. This precosmic soul became the World Soul through the demiurgic process of blending illustrated by the above scheme.

Specialists in Plato now usually agree that Plutarch had it wrong. But, even worse, his general approach in *On the generation of the soul in the Timaeus* at first sight seems to be diametrically opposed to his zetetic open-mindedness, in more than one respect. First, he seems quite apodictic about his own interpretation. The views of Xenocrates, Crantor, and Posidonius are categorically rejected,[40] for they, in Plutarch's view, promote their own doctrines rather than explaining what Plato meant (1013B), and to that purpose misrepresent the latter's position (1013E). Secondly, Plutarch's usual respect for the available evidence may be seriously questioned in this case, for he even goes so far as to manipulate the texts of Plato, or so it seems. By quoting from the *Statesman* and the *Phaedrus*, he strategically omits words that may cause problems for his interpretation,[41] and he even

---

[40] Note the use of the term διαμαρτάνειν ('to be utterly mistaken'; a strengthened form of the simplex ἁμαρτάνω) in 1013B and the phrase ἐκφανῶς δὲ τούτοις ἠγνόηται ('they manifestly fail to understand') in 1013D; see also 1013E.

[41] Cherniss 1976: 139. See also Gioè 1996: 304; Ferrari 2001a: 276–8, 2002: 252–3, and 2004: 230.

changes the text of the key passage from the *Timaeus*, reading αὐτήν instead of αὐτῶν. This different reading has crucial implications for the interpretation of the passage, but, although it supports Plutarch's view, it has no manuscript authority at all. Where is Plutarch's usual respect for the tradition, or his open-minded search for the truth? Furthermore, the view which Plutarch elaborates in this treatise has important implications for his philosophical thinking as a whole, which makes the question even more urgent. What kind of *zetesis* is this?

Part of the answer may be found in the precise context in which the treatise was written. As Plutarch relates in the introduction, he wrote the work at the request of his sons Autobulus and Plutarch, who had asked their father to give a systematic presentation of the various views he had often developed on different occasions (1012B). Their question, then, is at least partly motivated by a concern for pedagogical clarity, and this pedagogical perspective indeed returns in the treatise (1012D and especially 1022C). More importantly, the question of Autobulus and Plutarch interferes with Plutarch's usual zetetic approach. After all, what they want to hear is not a nuanced survey of different perspectives that have been elaborated in the previous tradition,[42] but a straightforward presentation of Plutarch's own view. In such a perspective, the views of others can be no more than an ἐνδόσιμον (see above, §2) indeed, and it is actually characteristic of the zetetic-minded Plutarch that he nevertheless mentions them.[43] Moreover, while his criticism of other alternatives is perhaps stronger and more explicit than elsewhere, it is not unfair, and his own position is not presented as the simple and certain truth but is introduced as plausible (1014A; cf. 1013B: κανόνι τῷ πιθανῷ – 'plausibility as the criterion').[44]

Finally, Plutarch's manipulation of the evidence should not be exaggerated.[45] He may have used passages from Plato's dialogues 'creatively', but nothing suggests that he had the intention of

---

[42] Plutarch repeatedly says that they do not really need such a survey, since they are thoroughly familiar with the tradition; see 1012D and 1027A.

[43] The second part of the treatise is even organized along the basic pattern of three *zetemata* (cf. 1027C).

[44] See Ferrari and Baldi 2002: 240: 'Plutarch thus seems perfectly aware of the epistemological limits of his argumentation; its subject – the physical world – does not permit the production of assertions that are provided with absolute certainty' ('Plut. sembra cioè perfettamente consapevole dei limiti epistemologici della sua dimostrazione, il cui oggetto, il mondo fisico, non consente di produrre asserzioni dotate di certezza assoluta').

[45] See esp. Opsomer 2004.

suppressing unwelcome elements or that he was not arguing in good faith. Yet there remains the different reading αὐτήν: the fact that this reading has no manuscript authority suggests that Plutarch here deliberately changed the text. On closer inspection, however, things are not so easy and it is perfectly possible that αὐτήν was already in the text which Plutarch received from the previous tradition.[46] Nevertheless, if we assume, for the sake of the argument, that it was indeed Plutarch who changed the text, we should at least add that he was not the only Platonist to do so,[47] and that he did not regard Plato's text as sacrosanct.[48] Text changes are allowed, but only with justification, and thus it is important to see what is at stake here. In Plutarch's view, his interpretation saves Plato from an embarrassing inconsistency. For in the *Phaedrus* (245d1 and 3; 246a1), Plato called the soul unsubject to generation, whereas in the *Timaeus* he argued that it came to be. Plutarch argues that one would not even attribute such a blatant contradiction to a drunken sophist (1016A).

In Plutarch's interpretation, this problem is easily solved: the uncreated soul of the *Phaedrus* points to the precosmic soul, the created one of the *Timaeus* to the World Soul (1015F–1016D). Moreover, Plutarch succeeds in better explaining another aspect of Plato's position. Plato explicitly underlines that the soul is senior to the body (*Tim.* 34c4–35a1). In Plutarch's view, this means that the Demiurge first created the World Soul, which then in turn ordered the body of the universe. This priority of soul over body is extremely important for a Platonist: it is a matter of piety, and denying this hierarchy even amounts to atheism (1013E). All this shows how much is at stake here, and all these huge problems can easily be solved by changing one (just one!) letter in Plato's text. Again, it is far from certain whether

---

[46] See Opsomer 2004: 159–61 for a strong case that the reading αὐτήν antedates Plutarch and was already in Xenocrates' text; further evidence is presented in Opsomer 2020. If this is true, it has far-reaching implications, not only for our understanding and evaluation of Plutarch's view but also for the interpretation of Plato's *Timaeus*. For if Xenocrates' text already had αὐτήν, this reading can no longer be easily dismissed as a later distortion influenced by Plutarch's philosophical views. Xenocrates could indeed have used the copy of the *Timaeus* that was available in the library of the Academy and his text is much closer to the original than the reading αὐτῶν (which may itself result from Proclus' tampering with the text). An enquiry into the implications of all this for our understanding of Plato's *Timaeus* is far beyond the scope of this book, but it is a topic that would repay further study.

[47] See esp. Dillon 1989; Whittaker 1989; Gioè 1996; Petrucci 2018b; cf. Ferrari 2001b: 540–1. A thorough discussion of the difference between Plato's text and that of Plutarch can be found in Ferrari 1999a.

[48] In *Quaest. Plat.* 1006D, Plutarch wonders whether we should change the word χρόνου ('of time'; as in *Tim.* 42d5) into χρόνῳ ('in time').

Plutarch tampered with the text, but *if* he did so, he probably regarded the reading αὐτήν as a *conjectura palmaris* (to use a term of modern textual criticism, referring to a virtually certain text emendation that is 'worthy of a prize').[49]

On the generation of the soul in the Timaeus, then, can be perfectly reconciled with Plutarch's zetetic philosophy. He never claims to say the last word, but enthusiastically defends his own exegesis, pointing to its important advantages. He is convinced that he has thrown a new light on the truth, that his exegesis solves significant difficulties and better captures the meaning of the obscure passage from the *Timaeus*. This, indeed, is the product of genuine and painstaking philosophical *zetesis*, inspired by Plato, critical yet respectful of the tradition to which it contributes, and breathing the spirit of Plutarch's most fundamental convictions.

3.2. Plutarch's polemics against Stoicism and Epicureanism

Plutarch's Platonic outlook was in many respects fundamentally different from Stoic and Epicurean convictions. No wonder, then, that he frequently attacks these rival schools in his writings.

Many passages from his oeuvre contain polemical attacks against the Stoics.[50] More than that, several works are entirely devoted to anti-Stoic polemics.[51] In *On the contradictions of the Stoics*, Plutarch tries to show that the Stoics contradict themselves in different ways: they do not practise what they preach and they often defend doctrines that are diametrically opposed to each other.[52] In *On common conceptions, against the Stoics*, he argues that Stoic doctrine is at odds with our common convictions (the κοιναὶ ἔννοιαι).[53] Few people believe that one single drop of wine tempers the whole sea and even the whole universe (1078E), or that nothing touches anything (1080D). The whole work

---

[49] See Petrucci 2018b on the method and criteria of Taurus' ideological text emendations.

[50] The standard study of Plutarch's attitude towards the Stoics remains the monumental work of Babut 1969b. Shorter useful surveys can be found in Hershbell 1992b; Opsomer 2014; and Hirsch-Luipold 2016. See also Babut 1969a and Ingenkamp 1999 (on *De virt. mor.*); Babut 1993 (on the Delphic dialogues); Opsomer 2006 (on *De E*); Roskam 2005b: 224–47 (on *De prof. in virt.*).

[51] Apart from the extant works, see also Lamprias catalogue 59, 78, 148, 149, 152, and 154.

[52] See esp. Casevitz and Babut 2004; also Baldassarri 1976a; Boys-Stones 1997b and 1998; Weisser 2016.

[53] See Casevitz and Babut 2002; cf. Baldassarri 1976b. Plutarch's notion of κοιναὶ ἔννοιαι, however, differs from what the Stoics understood by it; see, e.g., Obbink 1992; Brittain 2005.

is one rich collection of such counter-intuitive Stoic doctrines. In Plutarch's view, Stoic philosophy 'snatches away and abducts the genuine conceptions like babes from her breast while substituting other spurious ones, brutish and uncouth, and constraining her to nurse and to cherish these in place of those' (1070C).

In *That the Stoics talk more paradoxically than the poets*, Plutarch confronts several Stoic paradoxes about the sage with stories from the poets. Caeseus, for instance, was invulnerable to iron, but the Stoic sage, sarcastically called the 'Lapith of the Stoics', forged of adamantine *apatheia*, is, though not immune to wounds, invincible, even while wounded, in pain, under torture, while his fatherland is being destroyed and he himself suffers his own disasters (1057C–E).

Epicurean philosophy is no less problematic.[54] *Against Colotes in defence of the other philosophers* results from Plutarch's teaching activities. Colotes was a friend and pupil of Epicurus and the author of a provocative work entitled *That it is not even possible to live when following the doctrines of the other philosophers*. Plutarch read this polemical work with his students and then elaborated a detailed and fairly systematic reply, in which he not only defended the distinguished philosophers from the past but also turned Colotes' attacks against Colotes himself. Not Democritus, Parmenides, or Empedocles, nor Socrates, Plato, and later philosophers are guilty of stupid mistakes, but Epicurus and Metrodorus![55] The dialogue *That it is not even possible to live pleasantly when following the doctrines of Epicurus* is the sequel to *Against Colotes*. Plutarch's students continue the discussion and now try to demonstrate the truth of this title. They argue that Epicurus' corporeal understanding of pleasure is a very shaky basis for happiness and, moreover, it deprives his followers of the much greater pleasures yielded by a contemplative and active life and by a belief in divine providence and the immortality of the soul.[56] Finally, *Is 'live unnoticed' well said?* contains a vigorous refutation of Epicurus' notorious advice to 'live unnoticed' (λάθε βιώσας). Epicurus' view is rejected with many

---

[54] See esp. the general survey of Boulogne 2003; also Flacelière 1959; Hershbell 1992a; Kechagia 2014. See also Westman 1987 (on *Quaest. conv.* 673C–674C); Roskam 2011c (on *De am. prol.*); and Horky 2017: 121–30 (on *Gryllus*). Several of Plutarch's anti-Epicurean polemics have been lost: see Lamprias catalogue 80, 129, 133, 143, 148, and 159.

[55] Good studies of *Against Colotes in defence of the other philosophers* are Westman 1955; Kechagia 2011b; and Corti 2014. See also the collection of studies in Morel 2013.

[56] On this work, see esp. Adam 1974; Zacher 1982; and Albini 1993. A detailed reading of the programmatic introduction to *That it is not even possible...* can be found in Roskam 2017a. Warren 2011 shows the Platonic bias of Plutarch's argument.

different arguments, from observations concerning daily life and the nature of man up to ethical and metaphysical reflections, culminating in an eschatological perspective. This is a short work but it illustrates Plutarch's authorial strategies and his deepest convictions as a Platonist very well.[57]

While all of these works show Plutarch's cleverness and virtuosity as a polemicist, they may also question the above conclusions regarding Plutarch's zetetic approach. As a matter of fact, these works have often been depreciated by specialists in Hellenistic philosophy: Plutarch must simply have misunderstood his opponents, as he misrepresents their position, manipulates their doctrines, and raises unconvincing and biased objections. At best, these polemics contain an oversimplifying confirmation of Plutarch's own view. We find no sincere search for the truth, let alone a genuine appreciation of germs of the truth that can also be found in Stoic or Epicurean philosophy. Where, then, has Plutarch's open-mindedness gone?

A correct answer to this question requires a great deal of nuance and fairness. To begin with, we should bear in mind the particular scope and purpose of Plutarch's polemical works. They have a completely negative purpose: that is, the refutation of erroneous views that interfere with the (Platonic) truth. In other words, in these works we enter the field of *elenchos*. This reflects only one aspect of Plutarch's zetetic philosophy. Criticism of problematic opinions does occur in the zetetic dialogues too, but there it is complemented by a more constructive pole. In such works, Sarapion the Stoic or Boethus the Epicurean can make a positive contribution to the conversation.[58] In the polemical works, however, the focus is entirely on criticism and refutation.

Secondly, this focus determines Plutarch's authorial strategies and polemical method. In these works, he is not looking for elements of the truth that can be found in Stoic or Epicurean philosophy, but only for arguments that undermine the philosophy of his opponents. To that end, he often assumes their point of view in order to refute it from the inside, revealing, for instance, the internal contradictions in their system or showing that their own goals cannot be reached by putting their doctrines into practice. Another polemical strategy is to insist on the absurdity (ἀτοπία) of the opponents' doctrines by pointing out that they endorse a view that nobody shares. In the anti-Stoic

---

[57] See esp. Berner *et al.* 2000; Roskam 2007a.
[58] Cf. Horky 2017: 125.

polemics, the Stoics prove even worse than Epicurus; in the anti-Epicurean works, Epicurus proves far less intelligent than the Stoics. Time and again, Plutarch opposes the view of his opponent to the rest of the philosophical tradition and even to widespread opinions. An appeal to sober-mindedness and common sense is one of his most frequent polemical tools. All this shows that Plutarch's *elenchos* in these polemical works is at least as much a rhetorical as a dialectical one.

Thirdly, the choice for this rhetorical approach in turn conditions Plutarch's heuristics. Plutarch is not interested in quotations that lay bare all the subtleties and technical details of the Stoic or Epicurean convictions. What he needs are the weak points in his opponents' philosophy, possible flaws or inconsistencies in their arguments, or extreme positions. Metrodorus' notorious statement that there is no need to save Greece or receive crowns for wisdom, but only to eat and drink and gratify the belly without harming it, is an easy target, of course.[59] The same holds true for Chrysippus' view that abstention from an old crone with one foot in the grave, or the courageous endurance of the bite of a fly, are also virtuous deeds, even as virtuous as abstaining from beauties like Lais or Phryne or enduring scalpel and cautery.[60] When the opponents refrain from such radical positions, Plutarch kindly lends a helping hand by himself deriving absurd conclusions from their view. For instance, according to the Stoics, friendship only exists among the sages and exists among all of them (*SVF* 1.223; 3.630–1 and 635). Plutarch translates this as 'If a single sage anywhere at all extends his finger prudently, all the sages throughout the inhabited world are benefited. This is their amity's work' (*De comm. not.* 1068F). While Epicurus emphasizes the importance of the recollection of past pleasures (e.g. fr. 138, 444, and 579 Us.), Plutarch (following Carneades) interprets this as 'gathering as from an official journal statistics about "how often I had a meeting with Hedeia or Leontion," or "where I drank Thasian wine," or "on what twentieth of the month I had the most sumptuous dinner"' (*Non posse* 1089C).

How, then, should such polemical arguments be evaluated? In these polemical works, Plutarch often fails to do justice to Stoic and

---

[59] It is quoted in *Non posse* 1098C–D and 1100D, and in *Adv. Col.* 1125D. The fragment (fr. 41 K.) is discussed in Sedley 1976: 129–32 and Roskam 2007b: 72–3.

[60] *De Stoic. rep.* 1038F–1039A; *De comm. not.* 1060E–F (= *SVF* 3.211–12). See Algra 1990; Casevitz and Babut 2004: 158–62.

Epicurean philosophy, which was usually more nuanced than he suggests. This is the direct consequence of his heuristics and his rhetorical approach. Nevertheless, his verbatim quotations are as a rule reliable and correct, and often even contain traces of nuance. In this respect, he cannot be accused of manipulation: he sticks to the material which his opponents indeed offer him.[61] But he often isolates this material from its original context, which of course makes it much easier to derive absurd or extreme conclusions from it. From Plutarch's own Platonic point of view, however, such inferences are neither unreasonable nor dishonest. Even in these polemical works, then, he is usually *bona fide*.

Moreover, Plutarch repeatedly comes up with ingenious and clever observations, and he likes to season his sharp polemical attacks with refined humour, as, for instance, in the following passage about the Stoic sage (*Stoic. absurd. poet.* 1057E–F):

The Iolaus of Euripides makes a prayer, and all of a sudden his superannuated impotence has become youthfulness and martial might; but the sage of the Stoics, though yesterday he was most ugly and at the same time most vicious, today all of a sudden has been transformed into virtue and from being a wrinkled and sallow and, as Aeschylus [*TrGF* 3.361] says,

> Lumbago-ridden, wretched, pain-distraught Elder

has become a man of comely bearing, divine aspect, and beauteous form.

Or, on the base Epicurean pleasures (*Non posse* 1093C):

Who would take greater pleasure in stilling his hunger or quenching his thirst with Phaeacian good cheer than in following Odysseus' tale of his wanderings? Who would find greater pleasure in going to bed with the most beautiful of women than in sitting up with Xenophon's story of Pantheia, Aristobulus' of Timocleia, or Theopompus' of Thebe?

Such passages characterize Plutarch's general approach in these works very well. Time and again, his polemical arguments combine sophisticated phraseology, imagery, and clever references to the rich cultural tradition with a touch of humour. His rhetorical approach, then, is coupled with a rhetorical style. More often than not, these works are entertaining reading.

---

[61] Cf. *Non posse* 1087D (χρησώμεθα τοῖς διδομένοις ὑπ' αὐτῶν; 'let us make use of what they offer us').

But what is their philosophical value? We may seriously doubt whether Plutarch's arguments were compelling or even plausible for a Stoic or Epicurean philosopher. They could, of course, explain the precise meaning of their views, point to the context of Plutarch's quotations and argue their convictions in detail. In that sense, Plutarch certainly did not speak the last word that definitively silenced his opponents.

That does not mean, however, that his polemic is worthless. There are at least three important ways in which Plutarch's anti-Stoic and anti-Epicurean polemics prove valuable from a philosophical point of view, even for specialists in Hellenistic philosophy in our own day. First, his rhetorical arguments usually appeal to non-rational reflexes, but these need not always be wrong or philosophically problematic. We often indeed *feel* that specific doctrines are problematic, even when they are supported by a series of clever arguments. The excessive claims about the Stoic sage, for instance, remain counter-intuitive. Or take the following thought experiment directed against Epicurus (*Non posse* 1099A–B):

If some person of only average weakness, on the point of death, should be granted by his sovereign, whether a god or a king, an hour's grace, to use for some honourable action or else for a good time, and then die immediately after, who in that hour would rather lie in Laïs' arms and drink Ariusian wine than slay Archias and deliver Thebes? No one, I think.

This is a clever manipulation of common-sense opinions, indeed, and there can be little doubt that Epicurus would prefer the happy hour to the heroic one. Yet Plutarch's argument at least stimulates thinking. Notwithstanding all rational arguments, we may still *feel* that there is something problematic about several extreme aspects of Stoic and Epicurean philosophy.

Secondly, Plutarch raises pertinent questions: he is not only focusing on old crones or impotent sages (*Non posse* 1094E) but also on more fundamental topics like virtue, truth, or the good life. Of course his polemical arguments often (at least partly) rest on his own philosophical presuppositions, yet this allows him to detect and lay bare blind spots in the position of his opponents.[62] Plutarch simply had it right when he regarded the precise place of the indifferents in Stoic philosophy, or

---

[62] See Algra 2014 on Plutarch's anti-Stoic attacks and Warren 2011 on the anti-Epicurean arguments. See also Boys-Stones 1997b and Ingenkamp 1999 on the anti-Stoic polemics as promotion for Plutarch's own Platonic philosophy.

the Stoic view of the final end or of divine providence, as problematic.[63] He was correct when he argued against Epicurus that a political life could be a meaningful alternative to the Epicurean unnoticed life, or that belief in an afterlife for the soul could be helpful for reaching tranquillity of mind.[64] His attacks were not always justified, no doubt, but he was not always wrong either! Finally, his polemical questions were an interesting challenge, an invitation to his opponents to render account (λόγον διδόναι) of their view. This philosophical challenge, supported itself by a thoroughly Platonic perspective, is suffused with a spirit that is perfectly reconcilable with Plutarch's zetetic approach.

[63] Cf. Babut 1998.
[64] On the latter argument, see Carter 2018.

III. LEARNING IN ABUNDANCE: THE RAMIFICATIONS OF PLUTARCH'S ERUDITION

The open-minded and penetrating search for the truth is the driving force of Plutarch's philosophy. Yet this search does not start from scratch: Plutarch knew very well that he was heir to an age-old tradition and it was never his ambition to re-invent the wheel. On the contrary, whether he was looking for the explanation of physical phenomena, discussing metaphysical questions, offering moral guidance, or dealing with history, he always tried to fall back on earlier insights. This, of course, does not imply that Plutarch was opposed to innovative answers (cf. *Quaest. conv.* 656D, where 'Plutarch' announces that he will 'stir up something of his own', ἴδιόν τι κινεῖν) but, for him, innovation should always be informed by a learned dialogue with the rich tradition. Sound philosophical *zetesis*, then, presupposes considerable erudition.

The importance of polymathy emerges from every page of Plutarch's work. It shines through in the enormous number of quotations from and allusions to other authors (not only famous but also minor ones).[1] It also comes to the fore in collections like the *Sayings of kings and commanders* or the *Spartan sayings*. These works contain a real treasury of *chreiai*, pithy sayings of famous statesmen that throw light upon their characters and thus help in developing our moral understanding. Many of them reappear in the *Parallel Lives*, which overflow with erudition as well.[2] And the treatise *On Isis and Osiris* contains an amazing quantity of references to Egyptian rites and myths (see below, Chapter VII, §6).

In this context, special mention must be made of the *Table Talk*. This is Plutarch's most extensive work after the *Parallel Lives* and it constitutes a major source for his thinking and writing.[3] It consists of

---

[1] A list of Plutarch's quotations can be found in Helmbold and O'Neil 1959 (although the list is not always reliable and notoriously incomplete on the Latin side). The abundance of quotations makes intertextuality an interesting hermeneutic tool for the interpretation of Plutarch's works; see, e.g., Gallo 2004; Sanz Morales *et al.* 2017; Schmidt *et al.* 2020.

[2] On the complicated relation between the *Apophthegmata* collections and the *Parallel Lives*, see Pelling 2002: 65–90, and Stadter 2008 and 2014; see also below, Chapter V, §5.

[3] And even, up to a certain extent, for his persona. On Plutarch's self-presentation in the *Table Talk*, see esp. Klotz 2007; J. König 2011; Vamvouri Ruffy 2012: 23–5; Egelhaaf-Gaiser 2013.

nine books in which he gives an account of the many conversations he had with his friends over wine. Few would still regard these talks as the *ipsissima verba* that were uttered during these symposia, or again as a purely literary fiction. In all likelihood, they present an idealized and artistically embellished picture that nevertheless has some historical basis.[4] The *Table Talk* should be placed in the tradition of *Symposium* literature but Plutarch also combines it with other genres (such as *problemata* and miscellany) and fully integrates it into the overarching framework of his own philosophy.[5]

In what follows, let us participate in a few drinking parties and follow the animated conversations. They will introduce us to a fascinating world in which manifold erudition is coupled with *savoir vivre* and conviviality.

1. Talking philosophy over wine

The first dinner party brings us to Athens. There, the company discusses the question if and to what extent philosophical talk should have a place in discussions over wine.[6] Ariston immediately expresses his astonishment, wondering whether there really are people who refuse to allow philosophers to participate in their parties (*Quaest. conv.* 612F). This is a motif that often returns in the *Table Talk*: even before the discussion really starts, the relevance of the topic is called into question. We are clearly among critical men who do not take anything for granted. On some occasions, this indeed entails a reorientation of the discussion (e.g. 626F–627A; 720D). In this case, 'Plutarch' confirms that such people do exist and recalls some of their arguments: philosophy is like the mistress of the house, who remains absent from drinking parties. The Persians, moreover, got drunk and danced with their concubines rather than with their wives, and even Isocrates

---

[4] See Titchener 2011: 39: the *Table Talk* presents us with 'what might have happened, could have happened, and periodically had in fact happened'. On the problem of the historicity of the *Table Talk*, see above, Chapter I, §3, with the literature mentioned in n. 19 of that chapter.

[5] On Plutarch's place in *Symposium* literature, see Teodorsson 2009; Klotz and Oikonomopoulou 2011: 13–18; see also Roskam 2010 on Plutarch's reception of Plato's and Xenophon's *Symposia*. On the importance of the προβλήματα tradition for the *Quaest. conv.*, see Klotz and Oikonomopoulou 2011: 18–21 (and, more generally, Harrison 2000; Oikonomopoulou 2013); on that of the miscellany, see Morgan 2011. Every study of Plutarch's *Table Talk* should start from the commentary of Teodorsson 1989, 1990, and 1996. Much valuable material can also be found in Montes Cala *et al.* 1999 and Ribeiro Ferreira *et al.* 2009.

[6] The talk is discussed in Schenkeveld 1996 and Klotz 2014: 210–14.

refused to speak at drinking parties because his expertise did not suit the occasion (καιρός) (612F–613A). The consistent use of the third person (εἰσίν, λέγουσι, φασι, ἀξιοῦσι) suggests that 'Plutarch' dissociates himself from this position, yet even this view is carefully argued by means of several elements borrowed from the tradition. Such convictions deserve to be mentioned and considered, and in fact challenge further reflection.

The challenge is accepted by Crato, who argues that philosophy, as the art of life (τέχνη περὶ βίον), regulates and orders all aspects of life and therefore also has its proper place at dinner parties. Thus the school doctrines about appropriate symposiastic conduct can be put into practice (613A–C). Crato's straightforward defence of philosophy may *prima facie* appear as the obvious answer for a circle of learned men like 'Plutarch' himself, yet it is not without bias: indeed, whereas Isocrates may have overemphasized the demands of the particular *kairos*, Crato risks neglecting them altogether, and it is no longer clear what the difference is between the philosopher's school and the banquet. Thus Crato, in spite of all his sympathetic enthusiasm for philosophy, cannot have the last word. Sosius Senecio intervenes and wonders about the precise limit and character of philosophical talk at such parties. This is a cleverly courteous reply, generously supporting the previous speaker (613C: 'it is not fitting to argue [with Crato] about this', οὐκ ἄξιον εἶναι... περὶ τούτων ἀντιλέγειν) while asking for further clarification.

Then, it is 'Plutarch''s turn to take up the gauntlet. He deals with the question from two angles. On the one hand, much depends on the character of the guests: if the majority of them are scholars, philosophical discussions should not be avoided, but if the company mainly consists of uncultivated men, the philosopher should adapt himself to their interests, try to philosophize without seeming to do so (φιλοσοφοῦντα μὴ δοκεῖν φιλοσοφεῖν), and accomplish the actions of the serious while jesting (614A). On the other hand, the topics of discussion should be adapted to the symposiastic atmosphere: 'The matters of enquiry (ζητήσεις) must be in themselves rather fluid (ὑγροτέρας), the topics (τὰ προβλήματα) familiar, the subjects for investigation suitably uncomplicated, so that the less intellectual guests may neither be stifled nor turned away' (614D).

'Plutarch' here mentions essential aspects that characterize many of the following table talks and it is surely no coincidence that this self-reflexive and programmatic discussion about the place of philosophy at dinner parties is placed at the very beginning of the work. First, the concern for conviviality and friendship (συμποτικὴ κοινωνία; 615A) is a leitmotif through the whole work. The scholarly but relaxed and entertaining conversations always promote socially acceptable, moderate behaviour and cultivate friendship.[7] Second, the company often consists of people with quite different kinds of expertise: philosophers, grammarians, rhetoricians, physicians, priests, local politicians, and so on. Yet they should all collaborate and examine the issue from their own point of view.[8] One answer is not necessarily better than another one. In fact, the juxtaposition of different perspectives, all put forward by specialists, adds to the erudite character of the discussion and yields the most substantial and profound investigation into the different aspects of the problem. Such a combination of complementary perspectives fits in very well with the symposiastic context[9] but no less with the dynamics of a philosophical *zetesis* and its essential openness to the value of every answer. Conviviality and philosophical search for the truth thus form a perfect match, which makes the accumulation of erudition in the *Table Talk* the result of a well-balanced συμποτικὴ συζήτησις, 'convivial co-enquiry'.

Third, this interaction between *zetesis* and conviviality also has implications for the topics to be discussed over wine, which should be 'fluid' (ὑγρός) – that is, they should easily spread over the whole company.[10] This excludes overtechnical issues and political matters that risk causing disruption and calls instead for intriguing subjects that cause wonder and thus stimulate philosophical reflection. Just a few examples of such questions that are raised at Plutarch's dinner parties:

Why do old men hold writing at a greater distance for reading? (625C–626E)
Why do men become hungrier in autumn? (635A–D)
Did the hen or the egg come first? (635E–638A)
Why does meat spoil more readily in moonlight than in sunlight? (657F–659D)
Why is hunger appeased by drinking but thirst increased by eating? (689A–690B)
What is the reason why alpha stands first in the alphabet? (737D–738C)

---

[7] These conversations also have a therapeutic dimension, as is shown by Vamvouri Ruffy 2011 and 2012.

[8] *Quaest. conv.* 614E; 643B; 644F; 660B; 664D; 679A–B; 694B; 697D; *Sept. sap. conv.* 154D and 155C. Collaboration, of course, strengthens the bonds of friendship between all those present. On friendship as the final goal of the dinner parties, see Van der Stockt 2000a: 94.

[9] Cf. J. König 2011: 195–202 and Oudot 2016: 13.

[10] Cf. Vamvouri Ruffy 2012: 67–75.

All of these questions, and many more, illustrate what Plutarch means by 'fluid' matters of enquiry. They often concern observations taken from everyday life which are not self-evident as such and thus challenge our intellect and call for explanations. Plato may long since have explained the basic outlines of the structure of the world, but what about all these striking details which everybody recognizes but about which the doctrines of the Demiurge, the Ideas, and perfect virtue largely keep silent? All this leaves ample room for clever thinking that mobilizes all available insights from the past in order to throw light on such details. By thus integrating 'fluid' questions and tremendous erudition, Plutarch admirably succeeds in both having and eating both his philosophical and his symposiastic cake.

Alongside the *Table Talk*, Plutarch contributed to the *Symposium* literature with a second work: *The Banquet of the Seven Sages*. This is an account of a dinner in which the Seven Sages took part, together with other figures, at the house of the tyrant Periander.[11] Again, the company entertains itself by a vivid and pleasant conversation about sympotic issues and food, household management, and even politics.[12] The work, which is concluded by some remarkable stories about dolphins illustrating divine providence, resembles the *Table Talk* in more than one respect, yet there are also several differences that can at least partly be explained by the difference in setting. The dinner of the Seven Sages takes place in days long gone, at the very beginning of the intellectual tradition, which precludes the incorporation of later insights. Yet even this work contains a great amount of erudition: Homer and Hesiod,[13] apophthegms of the Sages, Aesop's fables, riddles – in short, an extremely rich collection of primeval wisdom, coupled with prefigurations of later views,[14] and incorporated in a polished literary dialogue. The erudition of the sages involved less theoretical sophistication, no doubt, yet the work shows that the germs of convivial *syzetesis* were present from the very beginning.

---

[11] In Plutarch's version, the Seven Sages are Anacharsis, Bias, Chilon, Cleobulus, Pittacus, Solon, and Thales. See Defradas 1954: 16–28 or Lo Cascio 1997: 39–65 for good overviews of all the characters of the dialogue. For Plutarch's creative and innovative reception of the tradition of the 'Seven Sages', see Leão 2008: 484–8 and 2009.

[12] Other topics include love (Mossman 1997b: 126–34) and death (Jazdzewska 2013). On the motif of laughter in *The Banquet of the Seven Sages*, see Jazdzewska 2016.

[13] Stamatopoulou 2014.

[14] See, e.g., Aalders 1977 on the political philosophy of *The Banquet of the Seven Sages*.

2. Revealing the secrets of nature

Back to Plutarch's day. The next dinner party is hosted by L. Mestrius Florus, one of Plutarch's distinguished Roman friends (see above, Chapter I, §3). The point of departure for this conversation is a question of the grammarian Theon to Themistocles the Stoic (626E–F):

When we were being entertained at the house of Mestrius Florus, Theon the grammarian raised the question with Themistocles the Stoic why Chrysippus never gave an explanation for any of the strange and extraordinary things he frequently mentions: for example, 'salted fish are fresher if wetted with brine'; 'fleeces of wool yield less easily if one tears them apart violently than if one parts them gently'; and 'people who have fasted eat more deliberately than those who have taken food beforehand.'

The topics which Theon mentions have everything to arouse the curiosity of those present and thus perfectly qualify as 'fluid' issues for discussion. Yet Theon also risks violating the rules of the symposiastic game,[15] for his question clearly has anti-Stoic polemical overtones and thus forces Themistocles onto the defensive. The friendly atmosphere is jeopardized and Themistocles' unimpressed reply does little to create a better atmosphere. He briefly reminds Theon of the context and scope of Chrysippus' remarks and then abruptly reorients the discussion. Such questions, he argues, are none of his business. If Theon is indeed interested in looking for causes, he should rather stick to what he knows and wonder why Homer has made Nausicaä do her washing in the river instead of the sea (626F–627A). Themistocles thus shrewdly parries the question and avoids a technical defence of Chrysippus, which would be ill-suited to the occasion. Instead, he raises another 'fluid' question: why should we wash clothes in rivers rather than in the sea? Again we deal with one of the everyday things of life, which Themistocles subtly connects with a passage from Homer (*Od.* 6.59). Thus he seems to push Theon back into the field of his own grammatical expertise. Yet appearances are deceptive, for upon closer inspection, Themistocles' reply is less fair than it seems, since the answer to his Homeric question cannot be derived from Homer but presupposes quite some familiarity with philosophy of nature.

---

[15] This is a recurrent motif in the *Table Talk*, where grammarians frequently appear as 'problem symposiasts'; see Eshleman 2013 (esp. 154–7 for an excellent discussion of the character of Theon in this talk).

Nevertheless, Theon is able to cope with that and he claims that the problem has long been solved by Aristotle (fr. 217 Rose).[16] The latter has shown that sea water contains much earthy matter, whereas fresh water is pure and thus better soaks into clothes and dissolves stains (627A–B). For 'Plutarch', however, this explanation is 'plausible, not true' (πιθανῶς, οὐ μὴν ἀληθῶς). He prefers an alternative explanation, which he traces back to Aristotle's authority as well: sea water is oily and therefore does not clean efficiently (627B–D; cf. [Arist.] *Pr.* 932b4 and 18; 933a19; 935b18). Then, quite remarkably, 'Plutarch' adds yet another explanation (κατ' ἄλλον τρόπον): what dries quickest appears cleanest, and fresh water evaporates quicker than sea water (627D). At this moment, however, Theon interrupts: this explanation is undermined by Aristotle, who argues that people who bathe in the sea dry off more quickly than those who use fresh water (627D, with reference to *Pr.* 932b25). 'Plutarch' counters by referring to Homer, whose account of Odysseus' encounter with Nausicaä actually implies the opposite (627E–F, quoting *Od.* 6.137, 6.218–19, and 6.226).

This lively talk again illustrates the extraordinary cleverness and creativity in Plutarch's search for explanations. As usual, the different speakers avoid apodictic truth claims. Indeed, the phrase 'plausible, not true' suggests that 'Plutarch' does not come up with the definitive truth. Tellingly enough, he proposes two different explanations. Concerning such questions, plausibility is the best result we can obtain and 'Plutarch' can equally well question Theon's presuppositions and preferences as Theon does those of 'Plutarch'.

As a matter of fact, there is quite some competition in this conversation.[17] In particular, the competitiveness of the characters manifests itself in their eagerness to intrude into each other's domain of expertise. The grammarian Theon comments on the problems of Chrysippus' philosophy. The Stoic Themistocles raises a Homeric question. Theon refutes the philosopher 'Plutarch' by pointing to Aristotle. 'Plutarch' replies by referring to Homer, an authority that may especially appeal to the grammarian Theon (627E). They all wish to score points regarding problems that do not belong to their

---

[16] The question is not discussed at length in the surviving collection of *Problemata*, but for several aspects of Theon's explanation parallels can be found there; see Teodorsson 1989: 148–50.

[17] As elsewhere in the *Quaestiones convivales*: see Van der Stockt 2000a: 95; J. König 2011: 189; Stadter 2011: 245. On the many 'disruptive symposia' that appear in the *Lives*, see several contributions in Ribeiro Ferreira *et al.* 2009: 193–260.

own expertise. This obviously illustrates their great erudition, but it also lends a certain charm to their conversation. For indeed, nothing suggests that the element of competition destroys the light-hearted atmosphere of sympotic friendship. It rather reflects an aspect that is part and parcel of an age-old sympotic tradition, namely the motif of the contest (ἀγών) between those present.[18] At the same time, such a contest directly contributes to a zetetic attitude: by intellectually challenging one another, the speakers all come closer to the truth.

Plutarch's interest in questions of natural philosophy can also be seen in several other works. In the *Natural questions*, for instance, he proposes alternative answers to forty-one questions regarding different natural phenomena. The work stands in the tradition of the Pseudo-Aristotelian *Problemata*, and Plutarch frequently falls back on explanatory models that are derived from Aristotelian-Peripatetic philosophy (although other material is used as well).[19] The focus is primarily on natural causality and the divine cause is seldom alluded to.[20] As a result, Plutarch's explanations again aim at plausibility rather than certainty, since firm knowledge of the sensible phenomena of the sublunary realm is beyond human reach.[21] That does not mean, however, that all painstaking efforts to explain these phenomena are in vain and that Plutarch ends up with radical scepticism. His different explanations often clarify the general working and structure of our natural world and some of them may even be combined. Several times, indeed, alternative explanations are introduced by ἢ καί ('or is it also...'), with the copulative καί suggesting that these explanations do not exclude each other.[22] All answers have their relative value (see above, Chapter II, §2). None can lay claim to the full and definitive truth, but none is completely redundant either. Even solutions that are explicitly criticized by Plutarch still deserve mention and clarify at least a few aspects of the problem. It is clear, then, that the *Natural questions* are inspired by the spirit of Plutarch's zetetic philosophy. This is neither a dry classification of previous views nor the product

---

[18] See esp. J. Martin 1931: 127–39.
[19] Oikonomopoulou 2011; Meeusen 2016: 67–75 and *passim*; cf. Kechagia 2011a: 97–9.
[20] Meeusen 2013 and 2016: 264–74.
[21] Kechagia 2011a: 95–6 and 99–104; Meeusen 2014: 331–4 and 2016: 321–8.
[22] See *Quaest. nat.* 917C (two instances; the second one in particular is remarkable: ἢ καὶ τὸ λεγόμενον ὑπ' Ἀριστοτέλους ἀληθές ἐστιν ('or is what Aristotle says also true?'); cf. Meeusen 2016: 324); 919A; 919D. It also frequently appears in the *Roman questions*: 267E; 270B (ἢ καὶ τὸ τοῦ Θεμιστοκλέους ἔχει λόγον, 'or does Themistocles' saying make some sense too?'); 273E; 279E; 279F; 288B.

of a 'secretary of nature',[23] but scrupulous *zetesis* that combines open-mindedness and erudition with philosophical love of the truth.

A similar conclusion holds true for *On the principle of cold*. In this treatise, dedicated to Favorinus, Plutarch argues that cold is not a privation of warmth but has its own principle (945F–948A). Then he examines what this principle might be: the arguments of the Stoics, who think it to be air (948D–949F), and of Empedocles and Strato, who attribute it to water (949F–952C), are critically evaluated, whereupon Plutarch elaborates alternative arguments in support of the thesis that earth is the principle and essence of coldness (952D–955C). The work ends with an emphatic disclaimer: Favorinus has to decide himself whether he regards Plutarch's arguments as more plausible or prefers to suspend judgement (955C). Again, this need not imply that Plutarch's last word on the matter is one of radical scepticism. It is not unlikely that he regarded his own view as the more plausible one,[24] yet he was intelligent and open-minded enough to recognize possible limitations of his view, and fair enough to leave the final evaluation to his reader.

In the dialogue *On the face that appears in the orb of the moon*, Plutarch turns his attention to the moon. In the first part of the work, Lamprias argues against the Stoic Pharnaces that the moon has an earthly character and explains that the face that can be seen in the moon is nothing other than great depths and clefts containing water or misty air (935C).[25] Theon then raises the question of the moon's habitability (937D) and thus of its purpose. This is a smooth transition towards the concluding myth (see also above, Chapter II, §2) where this issue is further developed. The dialogue thus shows a perfect thematic unity: first the physical causes are dealt with, then the higher ones.[26] The first section refers to technical theories about catoptrics, eclipses, and the place and substance of the moon. Once again, an impressive amount of erudition is used to arrive at a plausible view of the moon. In the second part, the previous survey is placed in a new perspective and all material is presented in the literary framework of a polished

---

[23] This is Atticus' characterization of Aristotle (fr. 7.46–7).

[24] Boys-Stones 1997a.

[25] The first part of the work is still understudied, although much valuable work has been done by Görgemanns 1970 and Donini 2011b.

[26] Donini 2011a: 327–39 and 2011b: 71–4 and *passim*; Opsomer 2017.

dialogue that has everything necessary to arouse the admiration of Kepler himself.

We may finally point to Plutarch's works on animals.[27] In the introduction to the most extensive one, viz. *Are land or sea animals cleverer?*, Autobulus and Soclarus deal with the problem of hunting against the background of a Stoic and Peripatetic dilemma: if beasts are rational, we are either unjust to them if we kill them, or our life becomes impossible if we do not eat them (963F–964A).[28] If we are convinced that beasts have no share in reason whatsoever, the problem is solved of course, but Autobulus is willing to ascribe at least a certain degree of rationality to beasts. This calls for a more moderate and humane position (965A–B):

Living is not abolished nor life terminated when a man has no more platters of fish or pâté de foie gras or mincemeat of beef or kids' flesh for his banquets – or when he no longer, idling in the theatre or hunting for fun, compels some beasts against their will to stand their ground and fight, while he destroys others which have not the instinct to fight back even in their own defence. For I think the man who plays and enjoys himself should use cheerful partners in his game, not the sort of which Bion spoke when he remarked that boys throw stones at frogs for fun, but the frogs no longer die for fun, but truly.

Then Aristotimus and Phaedimus engage in a kind of contest, the former arguing that land animals are cleverer (965E–975C), the latter advocating the case of sea animals (975C–985C). Both present many examples of conspicuous animal behaviour that suggest at least sparks of rationality. All these descriptions presuppose careful observation of nature, notably of animals, but this observation was probably not done by Plutarch himself. He rather falls back on earlier authors. The work, in other words, is the product of his reading.[29]

The contest between Aristotimus and Phaedimus ends in a draw: Soclarus concludes that the two should join forces against the Stoics (985C). This, surely, is a clever vote: Soclarus avoids making a difficult choice and thus takes care that neither youth has to taste defeat. Instead, both are encouraged to maintain their position and henceforth

---

[27] A topic that has especially been discussed by Newmyer (e.g. 2006 and 2014); see also Boulogne 2005 and Horky 2017.

[28] See Jazdzewska 2009–10, who argues that Plutarch's view of hunting in this work should be understood in the light of his criticism of Roman *venationes*.

[29] Newmyer 2014: 225. This holds true for Plutarch's philosophy of nature in general: see Meeusen 2014: 313–14 and Longo 1992: 229 (on *On the principle of cold*).

collaborate – a nice sample of pedagogical subtlety and psychological refinement. Moreover, Soclarus lays bare the far-reaching philosophical implications of their arguments, viz. the problems which the Stoic view entails. At the same time, he keeps silent about more concrete consequences, such as vegetarianism or giving up hunting.

For such a position, we have to turn to *On the eating of flesh*, two short and mutilated speeches in which the eating of flesh is rejected with many rhetorical arguments that appeal no less to emotions than to reason. The thesis of the rationality of animals is also defended, in a particularly smart and original way, in *Gryllus*, an amusing dialogue between Odysseus and 'Grunter', a man who has been transformed by Circe into a pig.[30] Odysseus has asked Circe to turn all the Greek men whom she has changed into beasts back into their human shapes, but 'Grunter' sharply protests. He prefers to remain a pig, since he considers this condition far superior to that of a man. Indeed, he shows Odysseus how he, as a pig, easily surpasses humans in all virtues. 'Grunter' thus radicalizes the position of Aristotimus and Phaedimus regarding the rationality of the beasts.

It is clear that questions of natural philosophy occupy an important place in Plutarch's thinking. This is a field of wide learning, with ample opportunities for creative thinking, and of interest to every polyhistor. No wonder, then, that we began this section with a learned grammarian and conclude it with an erudite Boeotian pig.

3. Customs, rituals, institutions: antiquarian erudition

Our next dinner party gets us in a festive mood, for it is organized in order to celebrate the victory of Sarapion in a choral contest.[31] On this occasion, too, the topic for discussion is introduced by a grammarian. Marcus recalls the testimony of Neanthes of Cyzicus that the tribe (*phylē*) Aiantis had the honour of not having its chorus judged last. He adds, though, that Neanthes is not always reliable; however, if he is in this case, it might be an interesting opportunity for a combined investigation into the cause (628B). In any case, this is an intriguing subject that suits the occasion and perfectly qualifies

---

[30] On the dialogue, see, e.g., Indelli 1995; Herchenroeder 2008; Konstan 2010–11; Horky 2017: 121–30.

[31] See Teodorsson 1989: 155–6 for more details.

as a 'fluid' topic of conversation. Moreover, Marcus' proposal to start a collective *zetesis* fosters the general goal of συμποτικὴ κοινωνία.[32]

The first reaction comes from Milo, who insists on the caveat that Marcus himself introduced: what if Neanthes cannot be trusted (628B)? Then the problem itself would be bogus. Again the question itself is scrutinized and, in fact, Milo's critical reaction is not unjustified, even though it risks blocking Marcus' plans for an interesting symposiastic conversation. Philopappus then intervenes (628B–D):

It is not bad if the same thing will happen to us that happened to the wise Democritus because of love for learning. It seems that the juice of a cucumber he was eating appeared to have a honeylike taste, and he questioned his serving-woman about where she had bought it. When she indicated a certain garden, he got up and told her to take him and show him the place. The woman was astonished and asked what he had in mind. 'I must find,' he replied, 'the cause of the sweetness, and I shall find it if I see the place.' 'Sit down,' said the woman with a smile, 'the fact is I accidentally put the cucumber in a honey-jar.' 'That was very annoying of you,' said Democritus with pretended anger, 'and I shall apply myself not the less to the problem and seek the cause as if sweetness were proper and natural to the cucumber.'[33]

Philopappus concludes that Neanthes' unreliability should be no pretext for dismissing the question: even if the discussion were to yield no other use, it would at least serve as a good exercise (628D).

This is quite a remarkable use of a remarkable anecdote. Is Philopappus willing to cheat himself, just because he wants to keep the conversation alive? He is characterized at the beginning of the talk as a humane man and a lover of learning (διὰ φιλανθρωπίαν οὐχ ἧττον ἢ φιλομάθειαν; 628B). Now we see how far he is prepared to go in his eagerness for learning: Milo's pertinent caveat is brushed aside with the consideration that Marcus' question at least provides an opportunity for exercise. Here we come across another important aspect of the *Table Talk*: its educational dimension. During these dinner parties, existing knowledge about various topics is collected and shared. Younger students, who indeed repeatedly participate in these banquets, can assimilate all this ready-made learning and are introduced to the method of philosophical *zetesis*, whereas more mature speakers can welcome the discussions as interesting intellectual exercises.[34]

---

[32] See also Eshleman 2013: 157–8 and 163–4 on the character of Marcus in this talk.
[33] The anecdote is discussed in Meeusen 2016: 244–8.
[34] On the educational aspects of the *Table Talk*, see, e.g., Roskam 2009a and Kechagia 2011a: 81–104; cf. Titchener 2011: 45.

And thus, Milo's caveat is bracketed and the company begins to look for causes that may explain the honour granted to Aiantis. Marathon is a deme of Aiantis and Harmodius belonged to it (628D). Glaucus adds a few other pieces of historical data (628D–E) and 'Plutarch' yet more (628E–F). This is a pregnant example of *syzetesis*, in that the different speakers all collaborate in developing one basic answer. Yet 'Plutarch' also points to an evident weakness of this explanation: other *phylae* possess many honours too, so it still remains unclear why Aiantis should deserve this particular honour (628F–629A).[35] 'Plutarch' then proposes a different explanation: the custom should be understood as an attempt to placate the eponym of the *phylē*, for Ajax the son of Telamon does not endure an inferior position (629A). This is an allusion to the well-known myth of the conflict between Odysseus and Ajax about the arms of Achilles. This explanation obviously better takes into account the specificity of the *phylē* Aiantis; yet here as well, every member of the company – and every reader, too – should decide for themself whether they indeed consider it to be more plausible (σκοπεῖτε δὴ, μὴ πιθανώτερον λέγεται; 629A).

This talk illustrates another facet of Plutarch's *polymatheia*, one that has to do with the domain of history, myth, and antiquarian topics. Again, traces of this interest can be found throughout his oeuvre. In the *Parallel Lives*, but also in many works of the *Moralia*, Plutarch displays his intimate knowledge of Greek and Roman history. His antiquarian interests are especially evident in the *Roman questions* and *Greek questions*.[36]

The *Greek questions* are a collection of fifty-nine questions concerning fairly obscure local customs and institutions, often focusing on strange words.[37] To give but a few examples: who was the 'woman that rode on a donkey' at Cumae (291E–292A); what is the 'sheep-escaper' (293A); what was 'the wooden dog' among the Locrians (294E–295A)? As a rule, the answers are fairly short and clear. Different alternatives are occasionally mentioned, but most often only one answer is given, usually derived from distant local history. The work, then, is a compilation of interesting pieces of knowledge, several of which left traces in

---

[35] Cf. Ammonius' criticism of Plutarch's praise of the number five in *De E* 391E–F.

[36] Plutarch also wrote *Barbarian questions* (Lamprias catalogue 139), but these have been lost; see Schmidt 2008 for a reconstruction.

[37] Jazdzewska 2018. This work is seriously understudied. The seminal commentary remains Halliday 1928; much useful information can also be found in Payen 1998. On the importance of space and of the Delphic shrine in the work, see Oikonomopoulou 2017.

Plutarch's own day (293E; 297C; 297F; 299F; 301C). They are not just echoes of days long gone but are still relevant for contemporary readers.

In the *Roman questions*, Plutarch raises 113 questions regarding the causes of Roman customs, including: why women kiss their kinsmen on the lips (265B–E); why they adopt the month of January as the beginning of the year (267F–268D); and why they call the meat markets *macella* and *macellae* (277D–E).[38] Contrary to the *Greek questions*, the *Roman questions* as a rule contain more than one explanation, which suggests feelings of wonder if not captivation while also following Plutarch's general zetetic methodology. The overall structure of the work is not immediately clear, nor is its purpose.[39] Usually, the work is understood from the angle of Plutarch's interest in Greek and Roman identity. Boulogne interprets it as an attempt to surpass the differences between the two peoples and reach a shared identity.[40] Preston points to the differences between *Greek questions* and *Roman questions*: whereas Greek questions receive a simple answer, Roman questions are far less easy to solve. Both works thus reflect the cultural self-assurance of the *pepaideumenos* who considers and propagates his own identity.[41]

Such interpretations indeed reveal an important aspect of these works, for the question of what it meant to be Greek grew more and more important in Plutarch's day, and several passages from his works suggest that he was not indifferent to this issue.[42] Greek identity, for Plutarch, was very closely connected with *paideia*, and this can be observed in the *Greek questions* and *Roman questions* as well.[43] Yet this line of interpretation also has its limitations, for it remains true that questions of identity are hardly ever explicitly thematized in these two works. When we always have to read between the lines, we may wonder

---

[38] The *Roman questions* have received more scholarly attention; seminal studies are Rose 1924; Boulogne 1987, 1992, and 1994; see also Preston 2001; Mora 2007; Tatum 2014.

[39] According to Scheid 2012, the *Roman questions* reflect a promenade past monuments in the centre of Rome. Plutarch indeed adopted a similar approach in *That the Pythia now does not give her oracles in verse* (see below, Chapter VII, §5), but there the characters systematically follow the Sacred Way. The walker who visits ancient Rome with the *Roman questions* as his or her guide travels many unnecessary miles.

[40] Boulogne 1987: 472, 1992: 4707, and 1994.

[41] Preston 2001. Preston's view is discussed by Brenk 2019.

[42] In the *Comp. Lyc. et Num.* 1.10, Plutarch famously states that Numa was more Greek (ἑλληνικώτερον) than Lycurgus. For Plutarch's concern with Greek identity, see, e.g., Swain 1996; Goldhill 2001; Whitmarsh 2001.

[43] Pelling 1989 and 2002: 339–47; Swain 1990 and 1996: 139–45.

whether Greek identity was so important for Plutarch while writing them and whether the scholarly preoccupation with this problem of identity does not rather reflect our own postmodern obsession with it. That is not to say that it is completely irrelevant for a correct understanding of these works, yet there were other things on Plutarch's agenda that were more important to him.

Plutarch's main interest in the *Roman questions* is not in Roman (and Greek) identity but in a search for philosophical understanding. In several respects, indeed, the *Roman questions* resemble *On Isis and Osiris*. In both works, Plutarch examines the tradition of a foreign people as a source of deep philosophical truths (for *On Isis and Osiris*, see below, Chapter VII, §6). Roman customs contain many symbols of such philosophical insights, and have much to contribute to natural philosophy, ethics, and metaphysics.[44] In short, the *Roman questions* are primarily a zetetic examination of the many valuable germs of (Platonic) philosophical truths that can be found in the Roman *mos maiorum*.

4. The charms and usefulness of book learning

For our last dinner party, we are Ammonius' guests. At the festival of the Muses, Ammonius has invited several successful teachers to dinner. We are thus in the company of many scholars who put questions to one another. Let us join in the discussion at the moment when the orator Maximus asks the grammarian Zopyrio which of Aphrodite's hands Diomedes wounded (739B) – yet one more example of a 'fluid' question that arouses curiosity and stimulates thinking. Zopyrio asks a counter-question: which was Philip's lame leg (739B)? This reaction suggests that Zopyrio is baffled and considers the problem insoluble. Again, the question is itself questioned before the conversation really starts. Yet Zopyrio's attempt to escape is more than a simple *non liquet*. By alluding to Demosthenes' *On the crown* (67), he in fact most elegantly gives Maximus tit for tat. Whereas the latter confronts Zopyrio with a difficult question from his own field of expertise, Zopyrio counters by confronting the rhetorician with a problem

---

[44] Boulogne 1992: 4700; Darbo-Peschanski 1998: 25. We may add that, in the *Roman questions*, even more than in the *Greek questions*, the focus is on the present (Boulogne 1987: 471–2 and 1992: 4698–9; Payen 1998: 56–7 and 2014: 242).

concerning one of the major texts of the rhetorical tradition. This, if anything, is a courteous exchange of disciplinary *aporiai*. Again, the conversation is not without a certain competitiveness.

But Maximus is not impressed: Demosthenes' speech does not contain any evidence at all, whereas Homer's verses, so he claims, contain some clues. When Zopyrio has no answer, the others insist that Maximus should show his hand (739B). This reaction again illustrates the 'fluid' character of Maximus' question, which has succeeded in arousing the interest of the whole company. Maximus then reveals his answer, which is based on two passages from Homer. The poet says that Diomedes, before wounding the goddess, 'leaped to the side' (μετάλμενος, Homer, *Il.* 5.336). This participle (and especially its prefix) contains the vital information: standing in front of Aphrodite, Diomedes had his right hand before her left. In order to strike the goddess's right hand, he thus needed to jump to the side. This hypothesis gains support from a second passage from the same book: Athena suggests that Aphrodite has injured her hand by caressing a Greek girl (*Il.* 5.424–5) and we may safely presume that she used her right hand for this (739C–D).

In this case, Maximus' solution goes unchallenged: it is apparently accepted by the company as plausible and does not trigger alternative hypotheses. Moreover it has a positive effect on everyone's humour (739E) and thus qualifies as a beautiful example of συμποτικωτάτη πολυμάθεια. Especially noteworthy is the great erudition on which Maximus' answer rests. The rhetorician knows his Homer by heart and succeeds in beating the grammarian on his own domain. He pays attention to the smallest details, lays bare their implications, and smartly and subtly takes full advantage of them in order to explain the precise meaning of the verses.

The fundamentals of such an interpretation of the poets are explained in *How the young man should listen to poetry*. There Plutarch likewise rejects allegorical interpretations[45] and gives preference instead to a very careful and detailed reading that takes into account all the indications which the poet himself provides. Some verses contain subtle hints that the poet disapproves of a particular statement or attitude (19A–21D; 35A–C). Other indications may be derived from the context (22B–C) or phraseology (22C–25B), and the words of several

---

[45] See esp. *De aud. poet.* 19E–20B; Babut 1969b: 370–88.

poets can also be confronted with each other (21D–22A; cf. 35E–F). Such exegetical principles obviously require a meticulous reading of the poets, as is exemplified by Maximus in this talk.

In the context of Ammonius' dinner party, this careful interpretation is mainly a matter of symposiastic entertainment, a game of exegetical ingenuity, but the treatise *How the young man should listen to poetry* shows that there is much more at stake. There can be no doubt that the poets laid the foundations of the Greek intellectual tradition and that they thus received a central place in Greek education, but it is no less clear that their poems contained much material that is highly problematic from a philosophical point of view. On this point, Plutarch agrees with Plato's criticism, though he also realizes the enormous pedagogical potential of the poetic tradition. He therefore proposes using the poets as a kind of propaedeutic for philosophy. The careful exegetical method delineated in *How the young man should listen to poetry* serves this end: youths should be closely guarded (15A) and their reading should systematically be guided by philosophically justifiable criteria. This amounts to a basically utilitarian attitude towards literature that is fundamentally in line with Plutarch's Platonic outlook.[46]

Such an approach towards literature informs several other Plutarchan works. In the *Comparison of Aristophanes and Menander*, of which only a few pages survive, Plutarch explains why he prefers Menander to Aristophanes. The latter is coarse in language and subject matter, and his poetry is 'like a harlot who has passed her prime and then takes up the role of a wife' (854A). In contrast, Menander's humour and style is polished, refined, and cultivated, which obviously facilitates the philosophical appropriation of his poetry.

On the malice of Herodotus, finally, is a vitriolic polemic in which Plutarch accuses Herodotus of malice (κακοήθεια, literally a 'bad character'). The treatise opens with a list of general indications of such maliciousness,[47] and then deals with many passages from Herodotus' work where the 'father of history' gives evidence of his bad character. Plutarch shows how Herodotus time and again belittles

---

[46] The relation between Plutarch's position and that of Plato has often been discussed. Scholars have long underlined the differences between Plutarch (who was eager to benefit from what poetry had to offer) and Plato (who banishes the poets from his ideal state), but more recent discussions have shown the essential similarities between the views of both thinkers: see, e.g., Bréchet 1999; Zadorojnyi 2002; Hunter and Russell 2011: 3–9.

[47] The list is briefly discussed in Marincola 1994: 195–6.

the brilliant achievements of the ancestors, and how he trifles with historical truth and thus propagates 'absurd and false opinions about the best and greatest cities and men of Greece' (874C). This sharp attack has found little sympathy among specialists in Herodotus and Plutarch alike.[48] Scholars have shown that Plutarch can himself be called malicious on the basis of his own criteria.[49] They presume that his attack was inspired by petty patriotism,[50] and reflects a naïve spirit that rigidly repudiates every single criticism of the great past.[51] This, however, oversimplifies matters: Plutarch may have been too severe with Herodotus, but scholars should not take an eye or tooth from Plutarch for one of Herodotus. The *Parallel Lives* unambiguously demonstrate that Plutarch was no naïve and uncritical *laudator temporis acti*. His attack on Herodotus in this work is motivated by moral concerns. Plutarch has detected traces of maliciousness in Herodotus' historical account and aims at a rectification. This is his agenda in *On the malice of Herodotus* and this is what determines both his heuristics and his arguments. In short, the work should primarily be understood in light of the principles of Plutarch's ethical-utilitarian approach towards literature.[52]

5. From dining hall to writer's desk

Different drinking parties have introduced us to several domains of Plutarch's multifaceted erudition. What still remains to be done is to briefly discuss the various ways in which Plutarch organizes and presents all this material.

Often, as we have seen, Plutarch juxtaposes alternative views in a *zetema* ('object of enquiry'; pl. *zetemata*) or *problema* ('problem', 'object of criticism'; pl. *problemata*). This literary genre provides him with a convenient vehicle to collect and discuss traditional material in a fairly economical way. The *zetemata* and *problemata* usually show an

---

[48] To the literature quoted in the next notes can be added, e.g., Russell 1972: 60; Wardman 1974: 191; Bowen 1992: 2; Marincola 1994: 191.

[49] Ingenkamp 2016. See also Wardman 1974: 192; Teodorsson 1997: 443–5; Pelling 2002: 150–2 and 2007: 157–64; Dognini 2007: 501–2.

[50] Ziegler 1951: 871; Swain 1997: 171–2; Teodorsson 1997: 440; Dognini 2007: 482.

[51] Ziegler 1951: 871; Barrow 1967: 157.

[52] I develop this further in Roskam 2017b. See also Ragogna 2002: 29–30. Hershbell 1993: 154–7 points to the importance of Plutarch's educational convictions and his view of imitation.

ascending structure in which the most plausible alternatives are placed at the end of the list. But Plutarch also uses other methods of composition. He often employs the same combination of poetic quotations, imagery, references to earlier authors and ideas, concepts, and so on in different works and different contexts. In several articles, Van der Stockt has argued that such repetitive clusters of recurrent material can often be traced back to Plutarch's personal notebooks (his *hypomnemata*).[53] Plutarch informs us about the existence of these notebooks, in the celebrated introduction to *On tranquillity of mind*. There, he tells his dedicatee, Paccius, that he did not have the time to adequately meet his request for a new work on tranquillity of mind and therefore decided to collect a few ideas about such tranquillity from the notebooks he has made for himself (464F). These notebooks probably consisted of rough drafts, already written in full sentences, but without much literary embellishment.[54] The material which they contained could be recycled for the most diverse purposes and an analysis of such clusters highlights Plutarch's extraordinary versatility in creatively adapting traditional material to the demands of his argument.[55]

Moreover, Plutarch knew how to articulate his ideas. He was a particularly gifted writer who had perfectly mastered rhetorical theory and excelled in putting it into practice, as also appears from several epideictic speeches that have come down to us.[56] In *On the fortune of the Romans*, he deals with the question as to whether the Roman Empire is the product of virtue or fortune. His nuanced answer is that both are involved (316E–317C), yet in this work he especially zooms in on the role of fortune. An analogous question is raised concerning Alexander the Great in two speeches *On the fortune or virtue of Alexander*. Alexander is there praised as a dyed-in-the-wool philosopher who surpassed by his civilizing deeds distinguished

---

[53] See esp. Van der Stockt 1999a; other cases are discussed in Van der Stockt 1999b, 2002, 2004a, and 2004b. See also Van Meirvenne 1999 and 2001; Vicente Sánchez 2008; Verdegem 2010b: 141–9, 272–8, and 404–5. On Plutarch's use of his notebooks for the composition of his *Parallel Lives*, see Pelling 2002: 23–4 and 65–90; Stadter 2008 and 2014 (also Stadter 2015b: 128). The method of Van der Stockt can now be further developed by means of an algorithm-based analysis of Plutarch's corpus: see Schubert and Weiss 2015.

[54] Van der Stockt 1999a: 595.

[55] It is not always clear whether Plutarch directly reused his *hypomnemata* or drew inspiration from an earlier work (or just relied on his excellent memory); see Van der Stockt 1999a: 596–7 and esp. Xenophontos 2012; cf. Meeusen 2012.

[56] On Plutarch's general attitude towards rhetoric, see the classic study of Jeuckens 1907 and the collection of essays in Van der Stockt 2000b; see also Harrison 1987.

philosophers like Zeno (329A–B) and even Plato and Socrates themselves (328B–E). This is quite a remarkable statement for a Platonist like Plutarch, and far less nuanced than what we can read in the *Life of Alexander*.[57] But these works have completely different purposes. In the epideictic speeches, Plutarch prefers to consider Alexander's career from one provocative point of view, which is systematically developed and underlined by all kinds of rhetorical tropes, imagery, comparisons, and so on. These speeches are a beautiful sample of virtuoso and thought-provoking rhetoric that succeeds in defying the listener.

The same holds true for *Were the Athenians more famous in war or in wisdom?*, yet another epideictic speech. There, Plutarch ventures that the fame of Athens rests more on its military accomplishments than on its cultural achievements. The latter, however, were not neglected either (349A):

if we reckon up the cost of each tragedy, the Athenian people will be seen to have spent more on productions of *Bacchae*, *Phoenissae*, *Oedipuses*, and *Antigone*, and the woes of Medea and Electra, than they spent in fighting for their supremacy and for their liberty against the barbarians.

Yet the exploits of statesmen and generals outshine Athens' cultural merits. This is again a bold thesis, skilfully elaborated with rhetorical bravado. It is brilliant, entertaining, daring rhetoric, supported by considerable erudition and combining the panache of the orator with the talent of the philosopher to stimulate wonder by raising challenging questions. Even in such works, the zetetic approach is not far away.

Plutarch, then, was an outstanding philosopher, but he could also compete with every professional orator of his day. His works are written in a polished *koine* with a clear Attic stamp, but without the strictness of rigorous Atticism.[58] His smooth, flowing periods, heavily larded with images and quotations, and full of *amplificatio*, illustrate his conviction that *polylogia* is the natural consequence of *polymatheia* (*De cur.* 519C).[59] Prose rhythm is judiciously used, especially at the beginning

---

[57] On the relation between the two works, see, e.g., Wardman 1955; Hamilton 1969: xxiii–xxxiii.

[58] Studies of Plutarch's language include Giangrande 1992 and Torraca 1998. Weissenberger 1895 still remains relevant.

[59] Plutarch's periods are analysed in Yaginuma 1992. The classic study of his imagery is Fuhrmann 1964; for his philosophical view and use of images, see the ground-breaking monograph of Hirsch-Luipold 2002. On *amplificatio*, see Teodorsson 2000.

and end of his works, or in key passages, in order to underscore essential ideas or arguments.[60] Plutarch, in short, was a master of Greek literary prose.

Yet rhetoric was never an end in itself for him: it is always the content, not the form that prevails.[61] Plutarch was open to the aesthetic value and the charms of an elegant and refined style, but he always made it clear that our primary focus should be on ideas and arguments rather than stylistic *floscula* (*De prof. in virt.* 79D):

> In the case, for example, of persons who make use of Plato and Xenophon for their language, and gather therefrom nothing else but the purity of the Attic style, like the dew and the down on the flower, what can you say of them, save that they are content themselves with the sweet odour and bouquet of medicines, but have no desire for their sedative and purgative virtues, nor the power to discern them?

6. Conclusion

This chapter has only dipped at random into the wealth of relevant material. There can be no doubt that erudition is one of the most important aspects of Plutarch's thinking and writing. Every passage of his voluminous oeuvre is a feast of *polymatheia*. This erudition impregnates his zetetic philosophy and determines its peculiar character. For Plutarch, *zetesis* is not an easy-going search that is quickly satisfied with obvious answers or rashly proposes new theories,[62] but a penetrating and painstaking search for the truth, a search that always rests on an impressive acquaintance with nearly every aspect of the rich intellectual tradition. Erudition, then, fuels *zetesis*, both by providing material for explanation and hypotheses[63] and by stimulating further investigation. Philosophical enquiry and

---

[60] The study of Plutarch's use of prose rhythm is still in its infancy. An important recent contribution is Hutchinson 2018; see also Baldassarri 2000; Biraud 2014; Minon 2015. This is a domain that will still repay further study, since euphony was a crucial quality for ancient texts that were read aloud. On Plutarch's dealing with the difficult relation between orality and written texts (an issue that can be traced back to Plato's *Phaedrus*), see esp. Zadorojnyi 2007 and 2011.

[61] On the tension between this position and Plutarch's own polished literary style, see Zadorojnyi 2014: 309–10. For Plutarch's view of literary language, see Van der Stockt 1992: 62–73.

[62] See Ammonius' critical evaluation of Lamprias in *De E* 386A (with Thum 2013: 105–9), or Plutarch's comments on the ingenuity (εὑρησιλογία) of the young men in *Quaest. conv.* 656A (with Roskam 2009a: 373).

[63] See *Quaest. conv.* 734D ('great learning provides many starting points', τὴν πολυμάθειαν πολλὰς ἀρχὰς ποιεῖν), with Vesperini 2012 and Meeusen 2016: 220–1.

erudition, *zetesis* and *polymatheia,* are very closely connected for Plutarch, and it is their constant interplay that makes his works such an impressive ancient example of the human quest for wisdom and insight into the world and our place in it. The next chapters will show how the two interact in several important domains of his thinking.

IV. THE COMPLICATED PATH TO VIRTUE: PLUTARCH'S ETHICAL THINKING

Moralists are boring. Plutarch is a moralist. Thus Plutarch is boring. The following chapter will only be successful when it has shown that this syllogism, though logically valid, is wrong. Plutarch has much to say about virtue and wickedness, about moral progress and human shortcomings, but he always avoids dull moralizing and oversimplified general rules. In short, there are no wagging fingers in Plutarch's works! Moreover, in the previous chapters, we have seen that Plutarch was an open-minded thinker, carefully looking for the truth but refraining from apodictic truth claims and always open to different alternatives. We may wonder then how he was able to maintain this attitude in the domain of ethics, where norms often have an absolute character. How could he avoid replacing the vital dynamics of his zetetic thinking by a much more rigid discourse consisting of strict universal rules? How did he conceive moral virtue – the beating heart of his thinking[1] – and what did it mean for him to make moral progress?

1. The theoretical foundations

The obvious place to start is *On moral virtue*. Significantly enough, this is not a dogmatic school handbook full of prescriptions and straightforward advice but a lively polemical attack against the Stoics, more precisely against their psychological monism that regards passions as wrong judgements.[2] The implication of the Stoic view is that passions should be eradicated completely (the condition of *apatheia*), so that our conduct is entirely rational. For Plutarch, such an ideal rests on an erroneous understanding of human nature. In line with Plato, and through the method of introspection,[3] he argues in the main part of the work that we should distinguish between two parts of the soul:

---

[1] Cf. Gréard 1885: xix: 'Plutarque a touché à tous les sujets; la morale n'est pas seulement une des applications de son génie: c'est son génie même' ('Plutarch touched on all subjects; moral virtue is not simply one of the applications of his genius: it *is* his genius').

[2] All studies of *On moral virtue* should start with the seminal commentary of Babut 1969a. Much useful material is also to be found in Becchi 1990.

[3] See *De virt. mor.* 448F (συνῃσθημένος ἐν ἑαυτῷ, 'having perceived in himself'); see further Ingenkamp 1999.

the rational and the irrational (the latter can further be subdivided into the appetitive and the spirited part).[4] This implies that a complete eradication of the passions is neither possible nor better (οὔτε…δυνατὸν οὔτ᾽ ἄμεινον, 443C). Passions should rather be brought under the control of reason and thus directly contribute to virtue. They are necessary (τὴν τοῦ πάθους ἀρχήν…ἀναγκαίαν οὖσαν) but require therapy and education (451C). Plutarch argues that, if passions were completely rooted out, even reason would be more inactive too (452B) – quite a remarkable claim for a Platonist, yet fully consistent with his overall argument.

Virtue, then, consists in a due proportion and mean of the passions (συμμετρίας παθῶν καὶ μεσότητας, 443C–D).[5] At first sight, this sounds quite Aristotelian and, as a matter of fact, scholars have often pointed to Peripatetic influences on Plutarch's position in *On moral virtue*.[6] Yet this does not mean that Plutarch here argues as a representative of the Peripatetic tradition. Rather, he uses this material as a welcome polemical tool against the Stoa and fully appropriates it to his own philosophical perspective.[7] His main source of inspiration, however, remains Plato.

There is an important passage near the beginning of the work, where Plutarch points to the connection between the human soul and the World Soul. Since the former, just like the latter (see above, Chapter II, §1), consists of two parts (441F–442A), passions cannot be done away with: they should participate in reason or be mixed with it (440D).[8] Just as the Demiurge takes the disordered precosmic soul and blends it with reason, we have to blend our passions with reason in order to acquire a well-ordered virtuous disposition. This parallel shows that the core of Plutarch's ethical thinking is rooted in his metaphysics. Moreover, this metaphysical background does not merely explain his attack on the Stoics and his general conception of moral

[4] On the wide applications of the concept of reason in Plutarch's thinking, see Horky 2017: 109–12.

[5] Cf. *Quaest. Plat.* 1009A–B, with Bellanti 2007.

[6] The Peripatetic character of *On moral virtue* is especially discussed by Becchi (e.g. 1975, 1978, 1981, and 1990); see also Gréard 1885: 58; R. Jones 1916: 12–13 and 20; Russell 1972: 84; Dumortier 1975: 18–19; Dillon 1977: 195.

[7] Babut 1969a. Donini 1974: 81–8 correctly places *On moral virtue* in its Middle Platonic background. See also Roskam 2011b: 49–56.

[8] The idea is alluded to at the very outset of the work (440D) and returns at the end, in the comparison with Lycurgus' excessive destruction of the vine (451C). See on this Castelnérac 2007.

virtue but, as we will see in the remainder of this chapter, it also exerts a considerable influence on his moral methodology. We here come across a major hermeneutic key for the correct understanding of all of Plutarch's ethical writings.

2. The basics of moral progress

Controlling passions and striving for virtue is far less easy than it sounds. If even the Demiurge could not completely overcome recalcitrant matter, we should not expect that human beings will succeed in entirely subjugating their passions. Ultimate perfection may well be beyond humans,[9] yet moral progress is possible and moral virtue can even be taught, as Plutarch argues in the short rhetorical work *Is virtue teachable?*[10] And if virtue is indeed teachable – a notorious Socratic issue – we should also be able to develop a substantial pedagogical method that supports our striving for it.

The general outlines of such a method can be found in *How can one become aware of one's moral progress?*, yet another attack against the Stoics.[11] Plutarch there rejects the radical Stoic dichotomy between perfect sages and wicked fools, which in his view rules out moral progress, and goes on to provide his readers with several indications of such moral progress (προκοπή): the continuity of our course (76C–78A), mildness (πραότης)[12] and lack of jealousy (78A–E), a change in our attitude towards and use of words (78E–80E), less interest in self-display (80E–82F), untroubled dreams (82F–83E), alleviation of the passions (83E–84B), consistency (84B–85B), ability to associate with good people (85B–D), and watchfulness regarding all faults (85E–86A). The whole list of indications, which are often discussed in a lively and astute way, throws interesting light on Plutarch's understanding of moral progress.

The starting point of the whole process of our moral improvement is our insight into our own deplorable condition. Self-examination should

---

[9] See esp. *An virt. doc.* 439B; *Cim.* 2.4; Babut 1969b: 301–4.

[10] Barigazzi 1993 regards this work, together with *On fortune*, *Are the affections of the soul worse, or those of the body?*, *Is vice a sufficient cause for unhappiness?*, and *On virtue and vice*, as fragments from a lengthy work on the teachability of virtue, but his hypothesis has found little support; cf. Melandri 2003 for a critical discussion.

[11] See Roskam 2005b: 220–363 for a detailed interpretation of this work.

[12] Mildness occurs very often in Plutarch's works, as has long been observed; see esp. H. Martin 1960 and de Romilly 1979: 275–307; also Panagopoulos 1977: 216–18 and Roskam 2005b: 256–8.

reveal our disease and show that we need moral therapy. This traditional medical imagery is omnipresent in Plutarch's works: time and again, the philosopher is seen as a doctor able to cure the souls of his patients.[13] Once these patients have acquired a certain self-knowledge, they should take the fundamental decision (προαίρεσις) to enter the process of moral progress.[14] Their course will contain several intermissions and retrogressions but also show a gradual evolution towards greater stability, consistency, and authenticity. They will develop a correct value scale and begin to regard things from the right perspective, which will significantly contribute to their tranquillity of mind.

Thus, we come to another important work, *On tranquillity of mind*, where Plutarch is especially concerned with the appropriate attitude towards fortune.[15] Reason enables us to rise above fortune. We should acquire the knowledge of making the right use of the present situation (χρῆσθαι τοῖς παροῦσιν ὀρθῶς; 466C) and begin to 'live towards ourselves' (πρὸς αὐτοὺς ζῆν; 471A). Such an inner-directed attitude will give us a certain invulnerability against unavoidable adversity.[16] Indeed, we all have the treasure of our tranquillity within ourselves (473B; see also 467A). The work culminates in a beautiful comparison: life is a festival, celebrated in the holy temple of the universe (477C–D). This is a fitting conclusion of a work that generally shows an optimistic spirit without being naïve or simplistic. Plutarch does not ignore the fact that much can go wrong in life (473F–474A; 475C) but prefers to focus on the positive side, countering negative experiences with a 'yes, we can' optimism that combines philosophical ideals with sober realism.

3. Plutarch's therapy

Plutarch devoted many works to individual passions and problematic behaviour. He deals at length with anger (*On the control of anger*), talkativeness (*On talkativeness*), curiosity (*On curiosity*), excessive compliance (*On compliance*), love of wealth (*On love of wealth*), envy

---

[13] See esp. Fuhrmann 1964: 41–3 and *passim*; Hirsch-Luipold 2002: 225–81. The medical metaphor is central to *Are the affections of the soul worse, or those of the body?*.

[14] See Roskam 2005b: 350–1; see also Wardman 1974: 107–15 and Pérez Jiménez 1995 on the *Parallel Lives*.

[15] Important studies of *De tranq. an.* are Gill 1994: 4624–31; Van Hoof 2010: 83–115; Demulder 2018: 33–127. Broecker 1954 is still worth consulting.

[16] Basically the same view is developed in *On fortune, Is vice a sufficient cause for unhappiness?*, and *On virtue and vice*.

and hate (*On envy and hate*), self-praise (*On praising oneself inoffensively*), and borrowing (*That one ought not to borrow*). All of these works contain elaborate and penetrating discussions of the respective passions and together they give an excellent idea of Plutarch's psychotherapeutic methods.[17]

The key passage that reveals the overall structure of Plutarch's therapy is to be found in *On talkativeness* (510C–D):

We overcome our passions by diagnosis (κρίσει) and treatment (ἀσκήσει), but the diagnosis must come first (προτέρα δ᾽ ἡ κρίσις ἐστίν); since no one can become habituated to shun or to eradicate from his soul what does not distress him, and we only grow distressed with our passions when we have perceived, by the exercise of reason, the injuries (τὰς βλάβας) and shame (τὰς αἰσχύνας) which result from them.

The judgement or κρίσις consists in a detailed analysis of the passion, so that the patient begins to realize how harmful and shameful their condition actually is. The κρίσις is then followed by the ἄσκησις, which can itself be further subdivided into ἐπιλογισμοί and ἐθισμοί. The former are sound thoughts, which should always be reconsidered, whereas the latter consist of a series of concrete exercises: the patient should begin with small things (*De coh. ira* 464C; *De cur.* 520D; *De vit. pud.* 530E; 531F; 532B) and gradually move on to more difficult steps, while avoiding those situations that stimulate their passion (*De gar.* 513D–514C; *De se ipsum laud.* 546B–547C). The whole method thus presupposes and rests on the powerful force of habituation and requires continuous efforts and attention.[18] We should accept living under continuous treatment (ἀεὶ θεραπευομένους βιοῦν, *De coh. ira* 453D) and pay attention to every single detail (*De prof. in virt.* 85E–F). Needless to say, Plutarch's moral therapy is very demanding.

Moreover, from what we have seen so far, it also appears to be fairly traditional. It is, indeed, built around a couple of ideas that had long become common property among the different philosophical schools. Most ancient philosophers agreed on the importance of one's basic choice, considered virtue far more powerful than fortune, and underlined the importance of habituation and exercise. All this is high-minded and well-considered ethical thinking, no doubt, yet it is far from sparkling, to say the least, and the reader may be inclined to

---

[17] The classic study of Plutarch's psychotherapeutic method is Ingenkamp 1971.

[18] On habituation, see, e.g., *De coh. ira* 459B; *De gar.* 511E; *De cur.* 520D and 522E; *De soll. an.* 959F–960A. See also Ingenkamp 1971: 105–11.

think that the syllogism with which we began this chapter has so far been corroborated rather than refuted. Was Plutarch a dull moralist after all? High time to explore the true spirit and attractiveness of Plutarch's moral works.

First, these works illustrate the full wealth of Plutarch's literary mastery, his erudition and rhetorical skills (see above, Chapter III, §5). The passions are depicted with striking images that often in a few well-chosen words reveal more than theoretical definitions. The endless talking of the chatterbox is compared to the perpetual outflow of the mouth of the Black Sea (*De gar.* 503C–D) and the Seven-voiced Stoa at Olympia (502D), the busybody to a wind that pulls up our garments (*De cur.* 516F–517A), the bad judgement of the niggard to a flat intestinal worm (*De cup. div.* 524D), compliance to a low-lying and loose terrain (*De vit. pud.* 530A), envy to sore eyes (*De inv. et od.* 537A) and beetles (537F), and money-lenders to vultures (*De vit. aer.* 829A) and harpies (832A). These are a mere handful of examples out of many more.

The effect of these images is enhanced by numerous charming anecdotes. The silly behaviour of the angry man is illustrated by the story of Ctesiphon the pancratiast, who thought it right to kick back at his mule (*De coh. ira* 457A), or by that of 'the man who wished to beat the ass-driver, but when the driver cried out, "I am an Athenian," indicated the ass and said, "You at any rate are not an Athenian," and fell to beating it with many blows' (461A). The next lively story is only one of the many entertaining anecdotes by which Plutarch illustrates the incurable condition of the inveterate chatterbox (*De gar.* 509A–C):

It was a barber who first announced the great disaster of the Athenians in Sicily, having learned it in the Peiraeus from a slave, one of those who had escaped from the island. Then the barber left his shop and hurried at full speed to the city,
>   Lest another might win the glory
of imparting the news to the city,
>   and he come second. [Homer, *Il.* 22.207]
Tumult naturally arose and the people gathered in assembly and tried to come at the origin of the rumour. So the barber was brought forward and questioned; yet he did not even know the name of his informant, but referred the origin to a nameless and unknown person. The assembly was enraged and cried out, 'Torture the cursed fellow! Put him on the rack! He has fabricated and concocted this tale! Who else heard it? Who believed it?' The wheel was brought and the man was stretched upon it. Meanwhile there arrived the bearers of the disastrous news, men who had escaped from the slaughter itself. All, therefore, dispersed, each to his private mourning, leaving the wretched fellow bound on the wheel. But when he was set free late in the day when it was already

nearly evening, he asked the executioner if they had also heard 'how the general, Nicias, had died.' Such an unconquerable and incorrigible evil does habit make garrulity.

Plutarch was a born storyteller. Such enthralling stories have a clear moral relevance (here made explicit in the last sentence) but they also carry the reader along, making the message easily digestible. This is anything but dull moralizing. Plutarch's moral therapy indeed largely benefits from all the powers of his virtuoso rhetoric, although this rhetoric always serves a philosophical purpose.[19]

Second, his moral works time and again show his deep insight into human psychology and psychopathology. He lays bare the secret motivations behind our shortcomings and reveals our vulnerable spots: how we are more upset by unexpected events,[20] or how old men are prone to self-glorification while admonishing others (*De se ipsum laud.* 546F–547A). Such insights are juxtaposed to lifelike portraits of the vicious persons and their typical behaviour, like that of the curious man (*De cur.* 519E–F):

To pass by so many women who are public property open to all and then to be drawn toward a woman who is kept under lock and key and is expensive, and often, if so it happens, quite ugly too, is the very height of madness and insanity. And it is this same thing which busybodies do: they pass by much that is beautiful to see and to hear, many matters excellent for relaxation and amusement, and spend their time digging into other men's trifling correspondence, gluing their ears to their neighbours' walls, whispering with slaves and women of the streets, often incurring danger, and always infamy.

Or of the chatterbox (*De gar.* 514C):

The chatterer, if some topic comes up from which he can learn and find out something he does not know, thrusts it aside and diverts it, being unable to give even so small a fee as silence, but he works steadily around until he drives the conversation into the stale and well-worn paths of twaddle. Just so, in my native town, there was a man who chanced to have read two or three books of Ephorus, and would always bore everybody to death and put every dinner-party to rout by invariably narrating the battle of Leuctra and its sequel; so he got the nickname of 'Epameinondas'.

Such passages combine remarkable literary qualities with sound psychological insight. Plutarch's moral therapy is definitely no package of rigid generalizations and simplifications but rests on a well-considered

---

[19] See Ingenkamp 2000; Van Hoof 2010: 50 and *passim*.
[20] *De virt. mor.* 449E; *De coh. ira* 463D; *De tranq. an.* 474E–475A.

and sophisticated method rooted in a deep understanding of the human mind and careful observations of human behaviour.

Third, Plutarch always reminds his readers of their own responsibility and stimulates them to self-examination (αὐτὸν ἐπισκοπεῖν καὶ τὰ καθ' αὑτόν, *De tranq. an.* 470B; cf. 472C).[21] In that sense, his moral thinking has an important emancipatory aspect. He provides his readers with a wealth of precious ideas but leaves the rest to them. They have to decide for themselves what they will do with all this material and how they may benefit from it and apply it to their own needs. In other words, they have to look for the moral course that best fits in with their own character and needs. Thus, we again come upon one of the fundamental characteristics of Plutarch's zetetic philosophy. Plutarch indeed invites his readers to moral *zetesis*.

This moral *zetesis* has its own character. Whereas intellectual problems can be examined together, for instance at school or over wine, in an amiable context of *syzetesis*, the individual role of the reader is much greater in a moral context. It is all about the reader's own virtue, about the therapy of their personal shortcomings. Plutarch's role is adapted in light of this focus. He shares all his erudition with his readers and appeals to them with the full power of his rhetorical talents, but then retreats into the background and never takes the decision for them.

This can also be seen in his use of moral examples. These constitute an important part of his moral therapy and are useful in the most varied circumstances. We should always have good men before our eyes and consider: 'What would Plato have done in this case? What would Epameinondas have said? How would Lycurgus have conducted himself, or Agesilaus?' (*De prof. in virt.* 85A–B). To a certain extent, even such personal *zetesis* is open to a component of *syzetesis*, in that Plutarch can help the reader in looking for appropriate examples. Yet his contribution to this process is confined to a respectful and emancipatory *syzetesis* that always considers the autonomy of his reader.[22] It is this pedagogy of examples, inspired by the principles of a respectful zetetic moral therapy, that also inspires the *Parallel Lives* (see below, Chapters V and VI).

---

[21] See Van Hoof 2010: 31.

[22] Cf. *De tranq. an.* 467E–F, where Plutarch lists several concrete examples of good conduct and connects them with all kind of difficult situations, while, however, refraining from deriving clear-cut prescriptions from them. Here as well, the decision about what is relevant and how it can be used is left to the reader.

Finally, Plutarch's general approach in his moral works is characterized by a spirit of distinct pragmatism and down-to-earthness.[23] Van Hoof has shown that Plutarch carefully addresses the specific problems of his aristocratic readers, rather than trying to convert them into fully-fledged professional philosophers.[24] He certainly did not philosophize *in vacuo*, yet we may add that such a down-to-earth focus is precisely part and parcel of his zetetic philosophical project. The previous chapters have already shown that Plutarch did not keep problematic issues dark nor cheaply explain them away, even when they were at odds with his own philosophical convictions. Even then, he preferred to mention them, since they could explain at least a few aspects of a given problem. His approach towards moral problems is fundamentally the same: he does not disregard the daily problems, trivial as well as serious, that interfere with high moral ideals. It would be all too easy to overemphasize the prominent importance of virtue while keeping silent about all the potholes and bumps in the road. Matters are usually not so simple, as Plutarch knew very well. He, the learned philosopher who breathed erudition and lived by theoretical thinking, was not blind to real life but was always willing to 'look fortune in the face with open eyes' (*De tranq. an.* 476E).

This also appears from his *On exile*, written to comfort an exile from Sardis. The work contains many commonplaces, adapted to a Platonic perspective,[25] but also focuses on the concrete political consequences of banishment.[26] Similarly, the *Consolation to his wife* is a moving attempt to comfort his wife on the death of their daughter. Again, many traditional ideas are passed in review,[27] without minimizing what happened: 'I know and can set a measure to the magnitude of our loss' (608C). In such works and confronted with such circumstances, Plutarch begins by recognizing the problem and then looks for new opportunities, trying to arrive at a (more) positive outlook – not unlike the course he recommends in *On tranquillity of mind*: 'This, then, we should train and practise first of all, like the man who threw a stone at his dog, but missed her and hit his stepmother, whereupon he exclaimed: "That is not bad either!"' (467C).

---

[23] As has often been observed; see, e.g., Ingenkamp 1984; Teodorsson 2005–6: 139; Van Hoof 2010.

[24] Van Hoof 2010 and 2014.

[25] Opsomer 2002; see also Vamvouri Ruffy 2017.

[26] Van Hoof 2010: 116–50 and 2014: 141.

[27] Baltussen 2009.

This is another striking example of Plutarch's 'yes, we can' optimism, yet we may wonder whether it is not extremely banal in this kind of 'limit situation'.[28] It might be so in other authors but not in Plutarch. Even in such situations, his reflections are inspired by an authentic and sober-minded *zetesis* that modestly tries to encompass the bad with the good (τὰ χείρονα τοῖς χρηστοῖς ἐμπεριλαμβάνειν; 474B) without claiming to know the final reassuring truth.[29]

The same down-to-earth quality also appears in *Precepts of health care*. There, Plutarch advocates moderation concerning food, baths, exercises, and so on, underscoring the demands of our body. The whole work shows judicious reasonableness, underpinned by solid medical knowledge and natural philosophy and, as usual, embellished by entertaining anecdotes. Plutarch even goes so far as to state that the body suffers more from the soul than the soul from the body (135E), quite a surprising statement for a Platonist. What a difference from Plotinus, who felt ashamed to have a body (Porphyry, *Plot.* 1)! Yet Plutarch's position is perfectly in line with his general approach and even with the metaphysical basis of his ethical thinking: we should not act as if the body does not exist, nor should we be enslaved to it. The soul should rather use the body properly and, as it were, with demiurgic care, so that it can partake of a reasonable mode of living. In this light, Plutarch's general argument in *Precepts of health care* is not only sensible but also thoroughly Platonic.

We may conclude, then, that Plutarch's moral therapy is perfectly in line with the principles of his zetetic philosophy. He generally avoids dogmatic a prioris and distinct prescriptions. His moral therapy, based on a carefully elaborated method and irrigated by the streams of his multifaceted erudition, stimulates and supports a gradual process of improvement in which the individual readers take their responsibility to find and follow their own path towards moral virtue.

4. Lessons in virtue: listening to poets and philosophers

To an important extent, then, moral progress is for Plutarch a process of self-education. Every reader has to enter a process of moral *zetesis*, while benefiting from Plutarch's respectful *syzetesis*. This process can

[28] On Plutarch's dealing with such a 'limit situation', see Roskam 2012.
[29] Roskam 1999b.

be encouraged from early childhood on, through parents, pedagogues, and teachers. We thus arrive at the topic of education, which is often discussed in Plutarch's works.[30] It is a main theme in the *Parallel Lives*,[31] is no less important in the *Table Talk* (above, Chapter III, §3, with note 34) and in the polemical works, and also informs Plutarch's reflections about friendship (below, §5) and family relations (below, §6). This section briefly discusses two works that deal with two different phases of the educational process.

The starting point of *How the young man should listen to poetry*, dedicated to Marcus Sedatus, is Plutarch's observation that Sedatus' son Cleander and his own son Soclarus have got to the age where they may become interested in poetry. Yet reading the poets requires guidance (15A):

Since, then, it is neither possible, perhaps, nor profitable (οὔτ᾽ ἴσως δυνατόν ἐστιν οὔτ᾽ ὠφέλιμον) to debar from poetry a boy as old as my Soclarus and your Cleander now are, let us keep a very close watch over them (εὖ μάλα παραφυλάττωμεν αὐτούς), believing that they require oversight in their reading even more than in the streets.

In turning to the poets, Cleander and Soclarus tread on slippery ground. Plutarch frequently reminds the reader that the poets 'tell many lies' (16A; cf. 17E) and appeal to our passions: for their verses are full of disturbing factors (τὸ ταρακτικόν; 15C; cf. 25A and D) and thus constitute a potential source of immoral behaviour.

The most obvious conclusion would be a ban on all poetry, yet Plutarch realizes that such a solution would be 'neither possible, perhaps, nor profitable'. It would not be profitable because such a rigorous anathema would also wipe out the many useful insights that can be found in the poets – insights, moreover, that are expressed in a charming poetic language, which yields no slight pedagogical advantage. If Cleander and Soclarus learn to read the poets with a philosopher's eye, they will at an early age gain a foretaste of philosophical thinking. Poetry is thus turned into propaedeutic for philosophy (36D–37B). Plutarch also adds that a complete anathema would perhaps not be possible. This reflects a sober evaluation of the situation – Plutarch knew the psychology of youngsters – but is also perfectly in

---

[30] See esp. Xenophontos 2016 for a full discussion of this topic. Roskam 2004a focuses on Plutarch's views on education as a communicative process; Herchenroeder 2008 on Plutarch's subtle criticism of the extravagant claims of *paideia* in the *Gryllus*.

[31] Pelling 1989 and 2002: 339–47; Swain 1990 and 1996: 139–45; Duff 1999b: 73–8 and 2008a.

line with the view he defends in *On moral virtue* about the passions. There as well, he argues that a complete eradication would be 'neither possible nor better' (οὔτε...δυνατὸν οὔτ' ἄμεινον; 443C) and the imagery of Lycurgus' blameworthy uprooting of the vine occurs in both works (*De aud. poet.* 15E–F and *De virt. mor.* 451C). Thus, we again find the same underlying methodological approach that can ultimately be traced back to Plutarch's metaphysics.

This, however, is not the end of the story. Theoretically speaking, several options are still open. Plutarch could have chosen a selection of ready-made verses like the *Monostichae Menandri*. Such a collection has all the benefits of a perfect propaedeutic while avoiding the dangers: the material is carefully selected, easily digestible, and philosophically blameless. It is characteristic of Plutarch that he does not choose this easy way but rather defends the integral reading of Homer, tragedy, lyric poetry, and so on, including all the risky and censurable passages. Again, he refuses to ignore facts. He does not wish to create a cocoon of artificial intellectual safety, even for younger people, but prefers to face the facts and deal with them in the best possible way. In other words, he chooses to seize the verses and blend them *more demiurgico* with a rational perspective.

Such a project requires a very careful and critical reading that pays attention to every single detail (19E; 28E–F; cf. 32A).[32] Again, we see how demanding Plutarch's moral thinking actually is. At the same time, it is perfectly in line with his zetetic conception of philosophy: also, when dealing with poetry, we always have to look for what is useful (τὸ χρήσιμον ζητεῖν, 16A; cf. 14F; 30D–E). Thus, the interpretation of the poets as conceived in *How the young man should listen to poetry* also provides a *methodological propaedeutic* to philosophy.

The next step in the educative process is discussed in *On listening*. This work is not dedicated to a father who still has to guide his son but to the young Nicander, who has recently assumed the *toga virilis* and no longer stands in need of a pedagogue. We are now at the level of the philosopher's school, where Nicander will often have to listen to lectures. Again, this is both useful and dangerous (μεγάλην μὲν ὠφέλειαν οὐκ ἐλάττω δὲ κίνδυνον τοῖς νέοις τοῦ ἀκούειν ἔχοντος, 38D) – a combination that recalls the situation concerning poetry in *How the young man should*

---

[32] Plutarch's method of reading has often been discussed; apart from the commentaries of Valgiglio 1973 and Hunter and Russell 2011, see, e.g., Saïd 2005b; Konstan 2004 (Plutarch as a precursor of postmodern literary theory), and the studies mentioned above, p. 56, n. 46.

listen to poetry. And, indeed, the basic approach in both works is very similar.[33] In *On listening* Plutarch's focus is again on what is useful. Nicander has come to the school in order to amend his life and should thus assess every lecture by examining whether it has improved him (42A). Again, Plutarch thus recommends an active process of listening in which the listener should, as a fellow-worker with the speaker (συνεργὸς τοῦ λέγοντος; 45E), make a contribution himself. In general, Nicander should achieve the balance between a magnanimous and charitable attitude and a critical stance (44E–45B; 46C): 'in praising the speakers we must be generous, but in believing their words cautious' (41A).

One of the most attractive elements of this work is its many descriptions of the typical behaviour of students. We meet the know-it-all (39C–D), the envious student, regretting that the discourse is excellent and trembling with anxiety lest the remaining part prove even better (39D–40A), the over-enthusiastic student who readily agrees with everything (40F–41A), the overzealous student who time and again interrupts the speaker (42F), the student who likes to bother the speaker with problems beyond his expertise (43B–D), the student who wants to show off himself (43D), and the timid student, nodding in assent as if he understands the speaker (47D; 48A–B). All of them are characterized in a lively and attractive way, and together form a fine typology of students which, we may add, has lost little of its relevance today.

5. Friendship

The topic of friendship occurs very often in Plutarch's oeuvre. In the *Parallel Lives*, many examples of friendship can be found, like that between Theseus and Peirithous (*Thes.* 30.1–2), Epameinondas and Pelopidas (*Pel.* 3.1–4.8), and many others. It is important in family relations (e.g. between brothers, as developed in *On brotherly love*; see below, §6) and in politics (e.g. between the ruler and the philosopher; see below, §7). But Plutarch also devoted several works to questions about friendship.

In *On having many friends*, he argues that πολυφιλία ('having many friends') is a contradiction in terms. Many friends are like flies in the

---

[33] See esp. Xenophontos 2016: 79–91 on *How the young man should listen to poetry* and *On listening* as companion pieces. On *On listening*, see esp. Hillyard 1988; see also Schmitz 2012, on Plutarch's attitude towards sophistic ambition (φιλοτιμία), with particular attention to *On listening*.

kitchen, disappearing as soon as the dainties are gone (94B). Real friends are rare, for true friendship rests on three things: virtue, intimacy, and usefulness (94B), and all these entail so many duties that it is simply impossible to cultivate the bonds of lasting friendship with more than a few persons. Behind the rhetoric of Plutarch's arguments thus appears a high-minded conception of friendship.[34]

A similar and more detailed ideal is to be found in *How can one tell a flatterer from a friend?*. In this treatise, dedicated to the king C. Julius Antiochus Philopappus, Plutarch examines how we can distinguish a flatterer from a friend. This is a traditional theme that can be discussed from different perspectives: economic (flatterers being parasites filling their belly without contributing anything themselves) or political (the flatterers of influential politicians).[35] We may presume that the difficult exposure of flatterers[36] was not merely a theoretical problem for the rich and powerful Philopappus – and, indeed, Plutarch pays attention to these aspects[37] – yet the overall focus of the work is a moral one. Plutarch zooms in on the negative consequences of flattery for the victim's character and virtue. And these consequences are devastating indeed.

The philosophical foundation of the work is the moral psychology of *On moral virtue* with its division of the soul into a rational and an irrational part. The former is connected with the friend, who appears throughout the work as a benevolent and competent doctor who mitigates the passions and fosters virtue. The irrational part of the soul falls prey to the flatterer, the advocate of the passions (62B), who justifies wickedness and attacks virtue (49B; 55E–57D). He finds an easy target in our vulnerable spot, that is, our self-love, which makes us blind regarding ourselves and thus does away with our self-knowledge and sound judgement.[38] We can understand very well why Plutarch considers the flatterer so great a menace: he undermines everything that is of vital importance for authentic zetetic moral philosophy.

---

[34] Cf. Van der Stockt 2011.

[35] See esp. Cicero, *Orat.* 3.117; see further Philodemus' *On flattery* and Maximus of Tyre, *Orat.* 14. The topic of flattery is also important in Plutarch's *Life of Alcibiades*.

[36] See Whitmarsh 2006.

[37] As is often pointed out; see, e.g., Babbitt 1927: 263; Sirinelli in Klaerr *et al.* 1989: 73; Van Hoof 2010: 25; Sirinelli 2000: 146, 193, 197.

[38] *De ad. et am.* 48F, with reference to Plato, *Leg.* 731e5–753a1, also quoted in *De cap. ex inim.* 90A and 92F; *Quaest. Plat.* 1000A. See also Opsomer 1998: 150–5 and 2009b: 101–8.

Moreover, Plutarch is not dealing with the ordinary flatterer but with the true professional, the τεχνίτης κόλαξ (57F),[39] who cannot easily be unmasked, since he has many cunning techniques at his disposal. Plutarch provides us with a detailed description of the flatterer's conduct, embellished with numerous images: the flatterer is a bore-worm (49B), vermin (49C), a gadfly (55E), an ape (52B; 64E), and so on. Anecdotes and examples add a wealth of salient details: 'The flatterers of Dionysius, whose sight was failing, used to bump against one another and upset the dishes at dinner' (53F), or again: 'I personally know of one man who put away his wife after his friend had sent his own away; but he was caught visiting her in secret and sending messages to her after his friend's wife had got wind of what was going on' (54A–B). Thus Plutarch clarifies the wily behaviour of the flatterer. Such passages correspond to the κρίσις-part of his psychotherapeutic writings (see above, §3), offering an accurate diagnosis of the disease as the first step towards recovery. Such diagnosis actually constitutes the main part of the work, although more practical advice and handy hints are also scattered through it.

The final section deals with the frankness (παρρησία) of the true friend, who speaks his mind in order to reveal the truth and promote virtue. Several scholars have suggested that this section, which prima facie seems to stand on its own, was first written as a separate treatise and later added to *How can one tell a flatterer from a friend?*, but this hypothesis unduly minimizes the strong connections between the two parts.[40] In fact, the last part provides a necessary addendum to and clarification of the previous discussion. Hitherto, Plutarch has suggested that there exists a strict opposition between the salutary frankness of the friend and the deceptive words of the flatterer who only aims at pleasure (55A–E; cf. 51C on frankness as the characteristic language of friendship, ἰδία φωνὴ τῆς φιλίας). The flatterer thus only uses a counterfeit frankness, if any (51C–D; 59B; 60B). Such a clear-cut opposition implies that the friend will always frankly blame our shortcomings. That is basically true, yet Philopappus could infer that the only true friend is a rigid and severe schoolmaster with the air of a Cato. And such a conclusion would be wrong, for this is not how Plutarch conceives of frankness.

---

[39] Cf. Opsomer 2009b: 115–16.

[40] The idea was first put forward by Brokate 1913: 7 and later revived by Sirinelli in Klaerr *et al.* 1989: 68–71 and Sirinelli 2000: 146, 193, 197; see also Russell 1972: 95.

In that sense, the section on *parrhesia* is a necessary clarification and elaboration of the previous discussion. At its beginning, Plutarch again recalls the philosophical foundations of his ethical thinking: vice (notably flattery) should not be cured by another vice (that is, excessively harsh criticism) but by virtue (66C). Again we find the same ideal of achieving the right from moderation (τὸ καλὸν ἐκ τοῦ μετρίου λαβεῖν, 66D–E), the same sense of nuance, and the same sharp psychological insight.[41] Less careful doctors of the soul may be inclined to find the easy solution for flattery in its opposite – that is, a strict and straightforward *parrhesia* – but Plutarch wisely realized that such frankness can also have negative effects (66D) and that sound *parrhesia* requires a certain know-how.

This explains the addition of the second part, where Plutarch explains what such sound frankness precisely means. One of its crucial aspects is taking the right opportunity (καιρός) into account (69B–C):

For a man who is sick it is intolerable, nay, an aggravation of the sickness, to be told, 'See what comes of your intemperance, your soft living, your gluttony and wenching.' 'Heavens, man, what a time to talk of that! I am writing my will, the doctors are preparing for me a dose of castor or scammony, and you admonish me and play the philosopher!' Under such conditions, then, the very circumstances in which the unfortunate find themselves leave no room for frank speaking and sententious saws, but they do require gentle usage and help.

Furthermore, we should avoid insults, but instead mix some praise with our admonitions, not make a fuss about every single detail, and most of all proceed with mildness and benevolence. The whole section about frankness shows Plutarch to be a good and tactful judge of human character. Moreover, he as usual avoids casuistry and prefers to leave the final judgement to the reader. The last section, and the work as a whole, thus reflects the general spirit of Plutarch's diversified, nuanced, and open-minded moral thinking.

Yet there remains an obvious problem. Plutarch has argued that we need the frankness of the true friend on our way to moral perfection, but, if such true friends are rare (the lesson of *On having many friends*) and if true frankness is far from easy (as shown in *How can one tell a flatterer from a friend?*), are we then not cut off from all help in our attempts to find out the truth about ourselves? 'Since friendship's voice has nowadays become thin and weak when it comes to frank

---

[41] Cf. Opsomer 2009b: 108–14.

speaking, while its flattery is voluble and its admonition mute, we have to depend upon our enemies to hear the truth' (*De cap. ex inim.* 89B–C).

Thus Plutarch comes up with a new and quite unexpected solution: even our enemies can be very useful for our moral progress. This is the thesis of *How can one profit from one's enemies?*, which thus forms an interesting complement to *How can one tell a flatterer from a friend?*. The too rigid criticism that was rejected in the latter treatise is recovered in the former: such harsh criticism does not fit with genuine friends but it *is* fitting for enemies. Frankness is never ascribed to enemies, but their insults and attacks can be used for analogous purposes and often reveal more about ourselves than the comments of true friends. For if self-love, as we saw above, makes us blind regarding ourselves, a true friend may well, as another self, overlook our shortcomings. Enemies often have a much keener eye, as appears from the charming anecdote about Hiero (90B):

Hiero was reviled by one of his enemies for his offensive breath; so when he went home he said to his wife, 'What do you say to that? Even you never told me of this.' But she being temperate and innocent said, 'I supposed that all men smelt so.'

Enemies can thus play an interesting part in a broader project of moral (self-)therapy. The treatise in fact contains a whole method and art (μέθοδον καὶ τέχνην, 86E) of benefiting in different ways from the criticisms of our enemies. Their very existence compels us to continuous vigilance and a circumspect life (εὐλαβούμενον ζῆν, 87D). We should mildly endure their attacks and try to imitate or surpass them in their virtue. Many pages from *How can one profit from one's enemies?* illustrate the demanding character of Plutarch's ethical thinking and the high expectations he has for his readers. The work is dedicated to Cornelius Pulcher, a politician rather than a professional philosopher, but Plutarch does not lower his requirements. Pulcher is invited to surpass himself and to keep his life blameless (87D), and throughout the work, Plutarch seeks a delicate balance between demanding and edifying ideals and feasibility.

This balance even includes a dose of sober pragmatism. The starting point of the work is the observation that enmities are simply unavoidable (86C; 91E). Thus we find the same general approach as in *On tranquillity of mind* and the *Consolations*: Plutarch does not ignore this negative aspect of life, as if enmities were unimportant, but recognizes the problem and tries to transform it into something positive. The enemy ends up as an unpaid teacher (90A). Thus Plutarch again tries to organize a disordered aspect of life along rational principles. In that sense, *How can one profit from one's enemies?* is a 'demiurgic' treatise.

6. The family

Plutarch often discussed the relations in the οἶκος (household). In *On affection for offspring*, for instance, he argues against Epicurus that parental love for offspring is natural, and in *On brotherly love* he sings the praises of friendship between brothers and quite systematically shows how this can be maintained in several situations.[42] Marriage is central to two works. His *Precepts of marriage* consist of a series of short comparisons and moral reflections concerning married life, dedicated as a common present (κοινὸν δῶρον, 138C) to his students Pollianus and Eurydice. This work is a very interesting source for Plutarch's conception of marriage.[43] Husband and wife really share their lives (συμβιοῦν rather than συνοικεῖν), as in a complete blending (κρᾶσις δι' ὅλων).[44] Their marriage and household should be ruled by philosophical reason (138A).

Fishing with poison is a quick way to catch fish and an easy method of taking them, but it makes the fish inedible and bad. In the same way women who artfully employ love-potions and magic spells upon their husbands, and gain the mastery over them through pleasure, find themselves consorts of dull-witted, degenerate fools. For the men bewitched by Circe were of no service to her, nor did she make the least use of them after they had been changed into swine and asses, while for Odysseus, who had sense and showed discretion in her company, she had an exceeding great love. (139A)

It is clear, then, that the wife should be no less familiar with philosophy and general education than her husband (145C–D), and then she will be held in esteem and even reach a blessed life (145F). Yet Plutarch was also a child of his times. Throughout the work, he makes it perfectly clear that the wife is subordinate to her husband: she should have no feelings of her own (140A), should not herself make advances to her husband (140C–D), should make no friends of her own (140D),

---

[42] A detailed analysis of *On affection for offspring* can be found in Roskam 2011c; see also Postiglione 1991. For *On brotherly love*, see Postiglione 1991.

[43] Plutarch's view of love and marriage has received ample attention in scholarly research: see, e.g., Goessler 1962; Nikolaidis 1997a; Pomeroy 1999; Nieto Ibáñez and López López 2007; Boulogne 2009–10; Beneker 2012; Tsouvala 2014.

[44] *Con. praec.* 142F; *Amatorius* 769F; Boulogne 2009–10: 27–30.

and so on.[45] Eurydice should be educated by her husband and Pollianus should be her professor, philosopher, and teacher in all that is most noble and divine (145C).

If all this is 'traditional wisdom through a philosophical lens',[46] Plutarch takes it a step further in his *Dialogue on love*. In this dialogue, Plutarch's son Autobulus relates how his father long ago went to Thespiae with his young bride in order to sacrifice to Eros as a result of a conflict between their parents. While he was camped with his friends on Helicon, the group was visited by Anthemion and Pisias, who came to consult them about a remarkable question. In Thespiae lived a relatively young, beautiful, and rich widow called Ismenodora, who had fallen in love with a much younger boy, Bacchon, and wanted to marry him. The boy's mother and friends were opposed to the plan and Bacchon, still an ephebe, left the decision to his older cousin Anthemion and to Pisias, the most austere of his lovers (749E–F). Those two, however, disagreed on the question, Anthemion supporting the marriage and Pisias rejecting it, and had therefore decided to choose 'Plutarch' and his friends as arbiters.

The group of 'Plutarch' is itself divided: Protogenes praises pederastic love (750B–751B), whereas Daphnaeus replies with an attack on pederasty and a defence of conjugal love (751B–752B). The specific case of Bacchon and Ismenodora is discussed as well (752E–754E), but then follows a *coup de théâtre*: a messenger reports that Ismenodora has kidnapped Bacchon and is making preparations for the marriage (754E–F). Pisias leaves, blazing with indignation, and a bit later Anthemion also departs. This peripeteia forms the point of departure for a new discussion. 'Plutarch' makes a lengthy speech about the divine status of Eros, his domain and benefits (756A–766D). This is in several respects the culmination of the work, where, in an innovative way, Plutarch connects the ascent to the Beautiful with heterosexual, conjugal love.[47] In a final speech, now in reply to Zeuxippus' criticisms of such conjugal love, 'Plutarch' again defends the love between husband and wife, with a new attack on pederasty – a conspicuous change from Plato – and a few inspiring love stories (766E–771C). This section contains several close parallels to the *Precepts of marriage*. The same traditional perspective on marriage

---

[45] See further Auberger 1993; Roskam 2004b: 265–9.
[46] Thus Patterson 1999.
[47] See, e.g., Brenk 1988 and Rist 2001.

is thus authorized at the end of the work and we may presume that this is how Plutarch generally thinks about married life. The last paragraph of the work adds the dénouement: the marriage between Ismenodora and Bacchon is celebrated (771D–E). All's well that ends well…or is it?

Perhaps things are just a little bit more complicated. The *Dialogue on love* illustrates in a particularly expressive way how Plutarch's zetetic philosophy also examines family relations. The οἶκος should ideally be a place of stability and order, and this is indeed what Plutarch aims at in the *Precepts of marriage*. In the *Dialogue on love*, this ideal is questioned through an exceptional situation. The case of Ismenodora and Bacchon is quite singular. It may be the product of Plutarch's 'rhetoric of exaggeration', yet such a rhetoric is also philosophically relevant.[48] Plutarch here deliberately pushes the boundaries and explores how far he can go. In the *Precepts of marriage*, the man clearly dominates his wife, and, for Plutarch, that is how it should be. Yet the husband's supremacy is not based on gender but on his intellectual and moral superiority.[49] And this, of course, raises the question of what should be done in a case where such intellectual and moral superiority lies with the wife. Can she then assume the role of *erastes*? Is such an *Umwertung aller Werte* in the domain of marriage ethics really conceivable?

This is a masterly example of philosophical *zetesis*. Once again, Plutarch is not afraid of raising challenging and difficult questions and as usual carefully ponders alternative solutions. No wonder, then, that he mentions arguments both against and in support of the marriage. Pisias argues that Ismenodora will dominate Bacchon through her money (752E–753A), a point countered by 'Plutarch' (753C–754B). Protogenes points to the problem of the age difference (753A), again dismissed by 'Plutarch' (754B–E). Protogenes, however, plays his last trump (753B):

If she is really modest and orderly, let her sit decently at home awaiting the suitors and men with serious designs. For if a woman makes a declaration of love, a man could only take to his heels in utter disgust, let alone accepting and founding a marriage on such intemperance.

This is a strong argument that is fully in line with the ideal promoted in the *Precepts of marriage* and it is characteristic of Plutarch that he places

---

[48] Brenk 2000.
[49] Thus correctly Nikolaidis 1997a: 76 and 80.

it at the end of his list of counterarguments, where it receives its full effect.[50] There can be little doubt that a tension exists between the general advice of the *Precepts of marriage* and the peculiar situation discussed in the *Dialogue on love*. Ismenodora's deed is aptly called a bold act by 'Plutarch' (πρᾶγμα θαυμαστὸν τετολμημένον, 754E), and even by Anthemion (τόλμημα, 755C). If Plutarch does not argue this away, we should not do that either.[51]

This tension is also reflected in the disagreement between the characters: the opposition between Pisias and Anthemion is soon mirrored by that of Protogenes and Daphnaeus, and even by that of the gymnasiarchs of the city (756A). This, if anything, shows that the evaluation is far from easy, as the conflicting claims both have good arguments. The final decision, then, is not easy, even after the sublime reflections of 'Plutarch' and his general defence of marriage. His arguments will do for Pollianus and Eurydice, but the case of Ismenodora and Bacchon is no standard situation and the peculiarities do matter. Ignoring them would amount to oversimplifying the zetetic process.

Yet this is exactly what Plutarch seems to do at the very end of the work. Pisias has given up his resistance and has even become an enthusiastic champion of the marriage. This is another odd peripeteia, for there is nothing that can explain such a volte-face. As a matter of fact, his approval makes him a ridiculous figure (ἐπεγγελάσωμεν τἀνδρί, 771E). He had put forward strong arguments and now seems to have forgotten all of them. In that sense, the work's happy end is also a baffling one. It is no less the outcome of Ismenodora's bold act than the result of an authorial one by Plutarch himself.

Nevertheless, this unexpected end also reflects a tendency that occurs throughout the *Dialogue on love*. Philosophical arguments never influence the events. Rather, the opposite is true: the events follow their own logic and provide the starting point for philosophical reflection. And this logic of the events is the logic of the god Eros. The final sentence of the work thus contains a crucial hermeneutic clue: 'it is clear that the god takes pleasure in what happens and is benevolently present in it' (771E). At the end, everything turns out to be the work of Eros, the god whose great power has been praised earlier. Philosophy has done its work. It has provided understanding and justification, yet it cannot put life on hold: the last word should be

---

[50] Cf. Goldhill 1995: 150.
[51] Thus I side with Goldhill 1995 against Rist 2001: 575 n. 48 and Effe 2002.

for love/Love. The unexpected end is a recognition of this insight, a reverent obeisance to the god (τὸν θεὸν προσκυνήσωμεν, 771E).

7. Plutarch's political thinking

We have already seen that Plutarch was politically active, holding both minor and major offices in Chaeronea (see above, Chapter I, §3). At an advanced age, he characterized politics as an old familiar friend (*An seni* 783C). The philosophical basis of his political thinking and commitment can be found in two small works that complement one another. In *That a philosopher should especially converse with rulers*, he persuades the philosopher to associate with rulers, for, by educating these rulers to virtue, the philosopher will benefit 'many through one' and thus maximize both his usefulness and his pleasure.[52] *To an uneducated ruler* focuses on the other pole: the ruler who should listen to the philosopher's advice, control his passions by reason, and thus become the image of God in the state.[53] Just like Plato, Plutarch thus aims at an ideal combination of philosophical insight and political power. The ruler, enlightened by reason and motivated by his love of what is honourable (φιλοκαλία),[54] will guide his fellow citizens to virtue by controlling their passions and improving their character. In short, in Plutarch's eyes, honourable politics is care of the soul.

Plutarch's political project is thoroughly Platonic and we may presume that he had such ideals in view when deciding on his own political course in Chaeronea. Yet here the obvious problem of feasibility arises. Plutarch knew history well enough to know that philosophical education was no guarantee of political success. Plato's own ambitions in Sicily proved a total fiasco (*Maxime cum principibus* 779B–C; *Dion* 13.1–20.4). Alcibiades, the pupil of Socrates (*Alc.* 4.1–4; 6.1; 6.5), greatly harmed his own city. The honourable projects of Dion, Plato's close friend and student (*Dion* 1.2 and 4.4–5), and Phocion, an alumnus of the Academy (*Phoc.* 4.2 and 14.7), both ended in disaster. Time and again, history questions the feasibility of such Platonic ideals.

Plutarch was not naïve. In two other works, he examines how such theoretical ideals can be translated into political praxis. *Should an old*

---

[52] See Roskam 2009b for an interpretation of the work.

[53] On this work, see esp. the commentary of Tirelli 2005; also Harrison 1995.

[54] On Plutarch's notion of φιλοκαλία, which is central to his political thinking, see Roskam 2009b: 73–4.

man engage in politics? is a passionate plea for the political relevance of old men, who should put their rich expertise at the disposal of their fellow citizens. They should continue to participate in politics, not by assuming all kinds of offices and interfering in every single detail, but by delegating, supervising, and advising their younger colleagues to serve the public interest. Even more concrete advice is given in the *Political precepts*, by far Plutarch's most important political work, dedicated to the novice politician Menemachus of Sardis. With this work, we find ourselves in the middle of municipal politics in Plutarch's day.[55]

At that time, the Greek cities were usually a kind of political aristocracy, governed by a few rich families, the πρῶτοι or 'first citizens', as Plutarch calls them (*Praec. ger. reip.* 815A). They occupied all the important positions and their rivalry sometimes caused internal disorders that risked destroying the balance of power and undermining social order. Their power base rested on their noble birth and their financial means, which enabled them to spend large sums of money on public projects. In return for these donations, they were publicly honoured as benefactors, which of course added to their influence. The days of democracy were gone,[56] but the euergetic system at least brought about a certain stability and well-being.

This is the situation that constitutes the horizon of Plutarch's political thinking. We have already seen that Plutarch was never prone to forget the demands of real life and this is all the more true when dealing with politics. He recalls Cicero's apt evaluation of Cato the Younger, who lost the consular elections because he acted 'as if he lived in Plato's state and not in the dregs of Romulus' (*Phoc.* 3.2). Plutarch never forgot that he lived in the dregs of Chaeronea and this insight forms the down-to-earth starting point of his political thinking.[57] He was a clever, sensible politician with a full measure of common sense and a pragmatic spirit. Yet, at the same time, this sobermindedness is perfectly in line with the general philosophical approach that we have found in all his ethical thinking. Just as he preferred to control the passions rather

---

[55] On Plutarch's political thinking, see, e.g., Weber 1959; Carrière 1977; Aalders 1982; Desideri 1986; Aalders and de Blois 1992; Gallo and Scardigli 1995; Swain 1996: 135–86; Stadter and Van der Stockt 2002; de Blois *et al.* 2004 and 2005; Roskam 2009b; Pelling 2014; Liebert 2016. See also the seminal studies of the *Political precepts* by Renoirte 1951 and Carrière and Cuvigny 1984.

[56] Unless democracy is understood as the rule of the elite in the service of the people: see Plácido 1995; Teixeira 1995; Roskam 2005a: 408.

[57] Although Trapp 2004 argues that Plutarch's political ideals (esp. his thinking about euergetism) were unrealistic and at odds with mainstream civic ideas.

than to completely eradicate them, and to face misfortune rather than to explain it away, he also faced the reality of political life with all its complicated problems. He realized well enough that Lycurgus' achievement of turning his city Sparta into a *polis philosophousa* (*Lyc.* 31.3) was extremely hard to imitate in his own day. For the populace is like a suspicious and capricious beast (*Praec. ger. reip.* 800C) that should, as much as possible, be brought under the control of reason, as recalcitrant matter was controlled by the Demiurge.[58] In several respects, in fact, Plutarch's political project has a strongly demiurgical aspect. The politician himself is characterized as the best of artificers and the Demiurge of good order and justice (807C), and his task is to mix a healthy element free from passions with the diseased, faction-ridden part of the state (824A).[59]

But Menemachus is no Demiurge. Plutarch is not addressing a professional philosopher who has decided to enter politics, but a young politician, and this is something that he carefully bears in mind. Throughout the work, he starts from real life, from the dregs of the Greek *polis*, and then tries to reorient this towards a philosophical perspective. And this begins with the person of the politician himself: his political engagement should rest on the fundamental choice (προαίρεσις) to serve the public interest. A political career should not be for profit (798E–F; 819E) nor should we enter upon public life mainly for the sake of personal ambition or 'love of honour' (φιλοτιμία; 819F–822A).[60] The politician should pursue what is honourable (τὸ καλόν) and thus we can also expect of him that he has acquired a virtuous disposition (800B–801C).

How should Menemachus conceive of this honourable ideal? Plutarch provides him with much general advice, while, as usual, respectfully leaving it to his reader to decide on how to apply this to his own situation. Menemachus should always be concerned with the public interest (807B; 812B; 817D; cf. *An seni* 794D). He should cause men to be good subjects (816F) and especially avoid internal disorder and pursue concord (824D). These are traditional political ideals that

---

[58] On Plutarch's very negative view of the people, see esp. Saïd 2005a.

[59] On the politician as *aristotechnas* (a quotation from Pindar, fr. 57 Maehler), see Van der Stockt 2002 and Lather 2017: 334–44.

[60] Such an ambition is one of the main motivations of many heroes in the *Parallel Lives* and is often discussed in the *Moralia* too. See esp. Frazier 1988; Duff 1999b: 83–7; Roskam *et al.* 2012; Liebert 2016, *passim*; Aloumpi 2017 (including a comparison with Demosthenes and Thucydides). On Plutarch's view of the politician's correct motivations, see also Roskam 2004–5.

are here adopted in and adapted to a philosophical project.[61] For these ideals should indeed be reached through educating the citizens' characters and making them better. A beginning politician like Menemachus should proceed in a systematic way, by first examining the general character of the people and accommodating himself to it, and then gradually changing it for the better (799B–800A). This idea, expressed with medical imagery, remains an important motif in the whole work: the politician should act as the physician of his fellow citizens' souls. In other words, he should carry out a fundamentally philosophical project.

In order to reach this goal, he should fully master the rules of the political game. Again, Plutarch blends the often recalcitrant matter of political reality with more philosophical ideals. He recognizes the importance of virtuoso rhetoric as a means to persuade the people (801C–804C). While rhetoric is not the creator of persuasion (δημιουργὸς πειθοῦς), it certainly is its helper (συνεργός) (801C), for the people should not be led by their bellies but by their ears (802D). This does not mean, of course, that Menemachus should turn into a demagogue: his speech should be full of character, high-mindedness, and fatherly frankness (802F; cf. 815D). He should respect and use offices and office-holders, but also be prepared to overrule them whenever the public good is at stake (816A–817F).[62] He should make use of friends as his living instruments, while carefully avoiding favouritism (806F–809B). Time and again, Plutarch thus views the concrete contemporary political situation from the point of view of the philosopher, but always observes moderation and balance. An excessively strict and rigid course is consistently rejected. The politician should sometimes be indulgent on smaller details (817F–818E)[63] and can even resort to cunning tricks (813A–C),[64] without forgetting his honourable mission to educate the people to virtue.

Finally, what is the role of Rome? In politics, Rome is, of course, highly relevant: one small decree of the proconsul suffices to annul

---

[61] See, e.g., Sheppard 1984–6 (on *homonoia*) and the more general survey of the sources of Plutarch's political thinking in Aalders 1982: 61–5 and Aalders and de Blois 1992.

[62] See Roskam 2005a.

[63] The idea also occurs in *On monarchy, democracy, and oligarchy* (at 827B). The authenticity of this work, of which only a few passages survive, is controversial; see esp. Caiazza 1995; further literature in Roskam 2009b: 25 n. 52.

[64] Cf. Carrière 1977.

all the politician's efforts (824E–F). This the politician should bear in mind and abstain from silly démarches (814A):

When we see little children trying playfully to bind their fathers' shoes on their feet or fit their crowns upon their heads, we only laugh, but the officials in the cities, when they foolishly urge the people to imitate the deeds, ideals, and actions of their ancestors, however unsuitable they may be to the present times and conditions, stir up the common folk and, though what they do is laughable, what is done to them is no laughing matter any more, unless they are merely treated with utter contempt.

Menemachus must realize that he always has the Roman shoe above his head (813E), as a new sword of Damocles.[65] And even if a shoe may at first sight seem less terrifying than a sword, this shoe surely had equally devastating powers. He should therefore try to make himself and his fatherland blameless (814C) and obedient (814E) towards his rulers. At the same time, he should not exaggerate and force the Romans 'to be their master more than they wish' (814F–815A). This addendum reflects the political interest of the πρῶτοι, who had everything to win in keeping Rome at a distance and preserving their own restricted autonomy, although Plutarch cloaks this point too in philosophical terms. He argues that the politician is best placed to cure the souls of his fellow citizens in the enclosed space of his own city, administering a secret medical treatment (ἀπόρρητον ἰατρείαν, 815B), so that there is no need for external doctors and medicines (815B). To give Rome a philosophically meaningful place means to relegate it to the margin.

Thus Plutarch advocates a particularly clever and considered political course. He keeps loyal to his Platonic convictions and always translates his political aims into philosophical terms: the politician should educate his fellow citizens, promote concord, and serve the public interest. For that is honourable (καλόν). That is what Plato's political ideals can mean in the cities of Plutarch's day. At the same time, however, all these high-minded philosophical ideals serve the political ideology and interests of the ruling class. Plutarch's advice to Menemachus is a rationalization of the existing political order, a plea for a political status quo. There is no place for political revolution in Plutarch: the aristocrats should be pulling the strings, whereas the people should listen, obey, and be content. Nevertheless, we should not consider Plutarch's political philosophy as a mere façade, shrewdly developed in order to secure the privileges of his own class. Such an interpretation would be too

---

[65] See C. Jones 1971: 133; Carrière and Cuvigny 1984: 186.

cynical: Plutarch was not the man to use philosophy as a pretext. The sincerity of his philosophical ideals cannot be doubted, yet he knew how to reconcile them very cleverly with the concrete political situation of his day and with the interests of his own class, and how he could combine the happiness of the people (as he understood it) and the well-being of the city with his own self-realization as philosopher and aristocrat. For all these reasons, Plutarch stands out as a particularly intelligent political thinker.

8. Conclusion

Plutarch is a moralist. His ethical thinking is very attractive. Thus the ethical thinking of some moralists is very attractive. That, at last, is a syllogism that is both logically valid and true. One looks in vain for casuistry or black and white thinking in Plutarch's ethics. His ethical reflections are nuanced, based on sound psychological insights, and ultimately rooted in metaphysics. This theoretical basis is seldom made explicit, but it significantly informs his general method and approach in his ethical works. Moreover, the genuine zetetic spirit is not absent from these works. Plutarch raises challenging moral questions and fully acknowledges the moral complexity of real life. And he deeply respects the autonomy of his readers. He tries to help those readers on their way towards moral improvement, trying to stimulate and mould their thinking through traditional moral insights but also through a wealth of particularly attractive images and anecdotes. He makes heavy demands on his readers but always leaves the decision to them, reminding them of their responsibility. Thus the response to Plutarch's moral works always reflects the reader's own character, and reveals it. This holds true both for ancient readers and for those of our own day.

V. HISTORY AS MATTER FOR PHILOSOPHY: THE *PARALLEL LIVES*

Reading Plutarch's *Parallel Lives* is a fascinating encounter with the history of the ancient world. It includes witnessing the foundation of Athens (*Thes.* 24.1–3) and Rome (*Rom.* 11.1–12.1); participating in the battles of Salamis (*Arist.* 9.1–4; *Them.* 13.1–15.4), Pharsalus (*Pomp.* 69.1–72.6; *Caes.* 42.1–45.8), Philippi (*Brut.* 49.1–10), and Actium (*Ant.* 65.1–66.8);[1] marvelling at Alexander sitting on Darius' throne (*Alex.* 37.7); being dazzled by the wonderful buildings on the Acropolis (*Per.* 12.1–13.14); watching in dismay as Caesar is killed with twenty-three dagger blows (*Caes.* 66.1–14); sharing Pyrrhus' desperation with one more victory (*Pyrrh.* 21.14); and standing aghast at the rape of the Sabines (*Rom.* 14.1–15.7), the tragic fate of Spartacus (*Crass.* 8.1–11.10), and Hannibal's triumph at Cannae (*Fab.* 16.1–9). It is a rendezvous with so many distinguished figures of Greek and Roman history: the protagonists and antagonists of the *Lives*, of course, but also the many less-known figures behind the scene, like Mnesiphilus, the teacher of Themistocles (*Them.* 2.6–7) or Damon, the brains behind the young Pericles (*Per.* 4.1–4). The decisive moments of history, such as Caesar's famous *alea iacta est* before his crossing of the Rubicon (*Caes.* 32.8; *Pomp.* 60.4), or his *veni vidi vici* at Zela (*Caes.* 50.3), are juxtaposed with 'petite histoire' with all its juicy anecdotes: Demetrius' liaison with Lamia (*Demetr.* 27.1–14), Pericles' relationship with Aspasia (*Per.* 24.2–12), Pompey's fondness for Flora (*Pomp.* 2.5–8), and, of course, Antony's notorious affair with Cleopatra (*Ant.* 36.1–7; 53.5–12; 71.4–86.9).

The *Parallel Lives* are an inexhaustible source of information: we read how Archimedes was killed (*Marc.* 19.8–12) and how the famous sculptor Phidias met his end (*Per.* 31.5), how the opulent Crassus as a young man lived in a cave from fear of Marius (*Crass.* 4.1–6.1), how Agesilaus used a stick as a hobbyhorse when playing with his children (*Ages.* 25.11), and how Demosthenes shaved one side of his head in order to force himself to stay inside and practise his vocal

---

[1] Quite strikingly, the Battle of Chaeronea, the great disaster where the Greeks lost their freedom, is only alluded to (*Dem.* 20.2–3; *Alex.* 9.2) but never related in detail. On Plutarch's account of other celebrated battles like those of Aegospotami, Leucra, and Sellasia, see Pelling 2019.

production (*Dem.* 7.6). In many respects, the *Parallel Lives* are the *via regia* to the ancient world, and walking this road is never boring or disappointing, for Plutarch is an extremely talented storyteller. Many of his biographies contain 'great scenes'[2] that are elaborated in lively detail.[3] The *Parallel Lives* are the absolute culmination of his biographical technique.

They were not, however, his first biographical project, for he had already written the *Lives of the Caesars*, a series of connected biographies of Roman emperors from Augustus to Vitellius.[4] Only two of them (*Galba* and *Otho*) are still extant. In both, much attention is given to the Platonic idea of the precarious dependence of a commander on his army (*Galba* 1.3; cf. Plato, *Resp.* 375b4–c6). This is a guiding thought throughout these *Lives*, crystallized in the recurrent motif of severed heads.[5] Plutarch also wrote individual biographies, such as the *Life of Aratus* and the *Life of Artaxerxes*.[6] These, though not conceived as (part of) a pair, have much in common with the *Parallel Lives*.

Of these *Parallel Lives*, twenty-two pairs have come down to us. They consist of one Greek and one Roman.[7] The first pair, which does not survive, probably dealt with the lives of Epameinondas and Scipio.[8] We know that the fifth pair was *Demosthenes–Cicero* (*Dem.* 3.1), the tenth *Pericles–Fabius Maximus* (*Per.* 2.5), and the twelfth *Dion–Brutus* (*Dion* 2.7). However, the relative chronology of the whole series is particularly difficult to reconstruct, especially since the time of composition may often have been different from the time of publication. There are many cross-references between different *Lives*, but their reliability is not always clear and they sometimes even contradict one another. Nikolaidis, the most recent scholar to discuss this *quaestio vexata* in detail, proposes the following order of publication:[9]

---

[2] Frazier 1992; Duff 2015: 138–48.

[3] On the vividness (*enargeia*) of Plutarch's writing, see, e.g., Mueller 1995; see also Salcedo Parrondo 2005 (on the *Life of Alcibiades*) and Soares 2007 (on the *Life of Artaxerxes*).

[4] On these *Lives*, see C. Jones 1971: 72–80; Georgiadou 1988 and 2014; Stadter 2015b: 56–69.

[5] Ash 1997.

[6] A brief presentation of both *Lives* can be found in Almagor 2014. On *Aratus*, see further Koster 1937; Porter 1937; Stadter 2015a. On *Artaxerxes*, see Binder 2008; Mossman 2010.

[7] With one exception, viz. *Agis/Cleomenes–Gracchi*. On Plutarch's choice of the heroes, see Geiger 1981, 2002, and 2005; on his criteria for juxtaposing two heroes in one pair, see Frazier 1987 and Desideri 1992b.

[8] Unfortunately enough, this pair has been lost. There is much discussion about the identity of the lost Scipio; see on this esp. Herbert 1957 (further bibliography in Duff 2011b: 259 n. 207). The case is still *sub iudice*.

Epameinondas – Scipio
Pelopidas – Marcellus
Cimon – Lucullus
Philopoemen – Flamininus
Demosthenes – Cicero
Lycurgus – Numa
Theseus – Romulus
Solon – Publicola
Themistocles – Camillus
Pericles – Fabius Maximus
Aemilius – Timoleon
Dion – Brutus
Aristides – Cato Maior
Alexander – Caesar
Agesilaus – Pompey
Phocion – Cato Minor
Demetrius – Antony
Coriolanus – Alcibiades
Nicias – Crassus
Agis / Cleomenes – Gracchi
Lysander – Sulla
Sertorius – Eumenes
Pyrrhus – Marius

Several arguments on which this order is based remain quite hypothetical though, and the absolute chronology is no less uncertain. The most likely guess is that Plutarch began writing the *Parallel Lives* after AD 96 and continued until his death.[10]

Many of the Greek *Lives* deal with famous figures of the classical period (notably from Athens, but also from Sparta and Thebes), but Hellenistic statesmen and generals receive a fair deal of attention too (especially in later *Lives*). The Roman *Lives*, for their part, include several biographies of early kings and generals (going back to Romulus himself) but also focus on the leading figures of the Late Republic from the Gracchi to Antony.

As a rule, each book consists of four components: a proem, the first *Life*, the second *Life*, and a concluding comparison (*synkrisis*) of the two protagonists.[11] Not all books, however, have a proem or *synkrisis*. The

[9] Nikolaidis 2005; earlier attempts include C. Jones 1966 and Delvaux 1995.
[10] Thus C. Jones 1966: 70.
[11] Duff 2011b.

two *Lives* are nearly always placed in chronological order (which usually implies that the Greek comes first),[12] with the second one often providing an interesting and complicating variation of the first.[13]

1. The purpose of the *Parallel Lives*

Although many different views have been proposed concerning the goal of the *Parallel Lives*, scholars now basically agree about their moral purpose.[14] This scholarly consensus rests on the analysis of several famous proems. In the celebrated proem to the book *Alexander–Caesar*, for instance, Plutarch explains that his heuristic method is conditioned by his moral interest (1.2):

It is not *Histories* that I am writing, but *Lives*; and in the most illustrious deeds there is not always a manifestation of virtue or vice; nay, a slight thing like a phrase or a jest often makes a greater revelation of character than battles where thousands fall, or the greatest armaments, or sieges of cities.[15]

The proems to the pairs *Aemilius–Timoleon* and *Pericles–Fabius Maximus* emphasize the moral relevance of the *Parallel Lives* even more. The heroes are presented to the reader as moral examples worthy of imitation (*Aem.* 1.1–2 and *Per.* 1.3–4):

It befell me to begin the writing of my *Lives* for the sake of others, but to continue the work and delight in it now for my own sake also, using history[16] as a mirror and endeavouring in a manner to fashion and adorn my life in conformity with the virtues therein depicted (ἀφομοιοῦν πρὸς τὰς ἐκείνων ἀρετὰς τὸν βίον). For the result is like nothing else than daily living and associating together, when I receive and welcome each subject of my history in turn as my guest, so to speak, and observe carefully (ἀναθεωρῶμεν)
    'how great he was and what sort of man,' [Homer, *Il.* 24.630]
and select from his career what is most important and most beautiful to know.[17]

---

[12] On the chronological ordering, see *Dem.* 3.5 (λεκτέον δὲ περὶ τοῦ πρεσβυτέρου πρότερον, 'I must speak of the more ancient first') and *Dion* 2.7 (τὸν τοῦ πρεσβυτέρου προεισαγάγωμεν, 'let us begin with [the life of] the elder man'). There are exceptions, however: *Aemilius–Timoleon* and *Sertorius–Eumenes*. These two, together with *Coriolanus–Alcibiades*, provide the three exceptions to the Greek coming first. In one pair (*Philopoemen–Flamininus*), Plutarch juxtaposes two contemporaries.

[13] Pelling 2002: 357 and 390. See also Duff 1999b: 206 and 250; Verdegem 2010b: 88; Roskam 2011a: 212; Larmour 2014: 410; Stadter 2015b: 126–7 and 244.

[14] See Nikolaidis 1982–4 for a critical overview of the different theories.

[15] Wardman 1971 and Duff 1999b: 14–22 have correctly underlined that this programmatic statement should be understood in the context of the following pair. See also *Nic.* 1.5.

[16] On the meaning of the term ἱστορία in Plutarch, see Gómez and Mestre 1997; Hershbell 1997; Duff 1999b: 17–22 and 33–4.

Our intellectual vision must be applied to such objects as, by their very charm, invite it onward to its own proper good. Such objects are to be found in virtuous deeds; these implant in those who search them out (τοῖς ἱστορήσασι) a zealous eagerness which leads to imitation (ζῆλόν τινα καὶ προθυμίαν ἀγωγὸν εἰς μίμησιν).[18]

In the proem to *Demetrius–Antony*, Plutarch explains that he also likes to add a few bad figures as *exempla e contrario* of virtuous conduct.[19]

All of these passages clearly show that Plutarch unmistakably saw his *Parallel Lives* as an essentially moral project. Yet a problem remains: there is a certain tension between these straightforward programmatic statements, on the one hand, and the subsequent *Lives*, on the other hand, where such a moral agenda is not always equally clear. In light of this tension, Pelling has argued that the moralism of the *Parallel Lives* is descriptive rather than protreptic.[20] Plutarch is not so much interested in giving direct and unequivocal moral advice as in raising and examining different moral questions, challenging the reader and inviting him to further thinking. Pelling's view has been further developed in the seminal study of Duff.[21] This take on Plutarch's moral agenda in the *Parallel Lives* is indeed confirmed by the emphasis on careful reflection (ἀναθεωρεῖν) in the proem to *Aemilius–Timoleon*.[22] Reading Plutarch's *Parallel Lives* requires serious and painstaking thinking.

Yet even then problems remain: while some *Lives* clearly exhibit a moral interest, others are much more historical,[23] and nearly all *Lives* in fact contain lengthy sections in which historical events are told without apparent interest in the hero's character or in other moral issues. Jacobs therefore proposes regarding the *Parallel Lives* more broadly as 'pragmatic biography', that is, biography that is concerned not only with moral questions but also with teaching efficient leadership.[24] She argues that many passages deal with useful political

---

[17] The proem is analysed in Duff 1999b: 30–4. On the image of the mirror in this passage, see Stadter 2003–4; Zadorojnyi 2010; Frazier 2011.

[18] See Stadter 1989: 55–6; Duff 1999b: 34–45 and 2001.

[19] *Demetr.* 1.4–6. However, such a clear-cut distinction between good and bad heroes does not really work, for Demetrius and Antony are not presented as completely wicked characters, whereas other heroes are not entirely flawless: see Duff 1999b: 53–65; Pelling 2002: 133; Alexiou 2010.

[20] See Pelling 2002: 239.

[21] Duff 1999b; he expands the argument in Duff 2007–8 and esp. 2011a.

[22] *Aem.* 1.2; cf. *Ca. Mi.* 14.4; Roskam 2014a: 188 and 191.

[23] See Pelling 2002: 102–7 and 2011a: 19–25 (on the *Life of Caesar* and the *Life of Themistocles* as two rather 'historical' biographies).

[24] Jacobs 2018.

and military conduct that could still be imitated in Plutarch's day, and viewing them from the perspective of 'pragmatical biography' better enables us to reveal their full relevance.[25] Or does it? On closer inspection, such passages do not undermine the traditional, moralizing interpretation either, which can appreciate the lengthy accounts of great military or political achievements as extensive (and often problematizing) descriptions of examples of political and military virtue.[26] In that respect, the many implicit lessons of efficient leadership which Jacobs has collected and analysed so well can also be considered as part and parcel of Plutarch's rich ethical thinking.

Perhaps some progress can be made by turning to the concept of Plutarch's 'zetetic philosophy' as discussed in the previous chapters. The moralism of the *Parallel Lives* is *zetetic moralism*: it is moralism that raises questions and searches for the truth.[27] It takes its point of departure from historical events: the lives of the statesmen and generals of the past, their successes and failings, good and bad decisions. This historical material invites difficult questions and stimulates nuanced philosophical reflection: where in this continuous stream of events can be found traces of moral or immoral behaviour; which fundamental decisions (προαίρεσεις) were taken on the basis of rational considerations; and when did the hero yield instead to his passions? In such an approach, history becomes the matter of philosophy (ἱστορία οἷον ὕλην φιλοσοφίας),[28] not as a source for dogmatic or doxographical constructions but as an incentive to a dynamic investigation that does not smooth over the complexity of moral questions but ponders them from different perspectives in order to come closer to the truth. For, indeed, zetetic moralism is no noncommittal reflection. We have already seen that Plutarch's ethical thinking makes heavy demands on his readers (see above, Chapter IV) and the same holds true for the moral project of the *Parallel Lives*.[29] After all, their heroes are explicitly

---

[25] See also Stadter 2015b: 241, who argues that the *Parallel Lives* not only contain timeless moral examples, but have a timely relevance as well; see also Stadter 2015b: 10: 'There is every reason to think that Plutarch saw his political essays and especially his *Parallel Lives* as his attempt as philosopher to enter the cave of politics.' The timely resonance and relevance of the *Lives* is further examined in Stadter and Van der Stockt 2002.

[26] See *Comp. Per. et Fab.* 1.1 (πολιτικῆς καὶ πολεμικῆς ἀρετῆς...παραδείγματα, 'examples of political and military virtue'). Also *Comp. Arist. et Ca. Ma.* 3.1 on political virtue as the supreme virtue.

[27] As has been pointed out by Pelling and Duff (see above, nn. 20 and 21).

[28] See Cleombrotus' project as described in *De def. or.* 410B. See also Duff 2007–8: 14–15 and 2011a: 82.

[29] See Duff 2011a; also Duff 1999b, *passim*.

presented as examples worthy of imitation. We may look into the mirror they present to us and take the time to reflect on their behaviour, but we should not forget to take the consequences, 'both admiring the works of virtue and emulating those who wrought them' (*Per.* 2.2). Such imitation, however, never amounts to slavish and thoughtless copying: zetetic moralism implies careful and considerate looking for the sake of better leaping.[30]

2. The comparative approach

One of the most important characteristics of the *Parallel Lives* is undoubtedly their comparative approach.[31] Every book contains a pair of *Lives*, placing one Greek hero alongside one Roman one. Such juxtaposition yields interesting opportunities, as Plutarch realized very well. In the proem to his *Virtues of women*, a collection of brief stories about virtuous and brave women illustrating the view that man's virtue and woman's virtue are one and the same (242F–243A), he states (243B–C):

And actually it is not possible to learn better the similarity and difference between the virtues of men and of women from any other source than by putting lives beside lives and actions beside actions, like works of great art, and considering whether the magnificence of Semiramis has the same character and pattern as that of Sesostris, or the cleverness of Tanaquil the same as that of Servius the king, or the high spirit of Porcia the same as that of Brutus, or that of Pelopidas the same as Timocleia's, when compared with due regard to the most important points of identity and influence.

This is the approach that is followed in the *Parallel Lives* as well: the comparison of two heroes enables Plutarch to inquire into different aspects of their virtues. Moreover, the two protagonists of a pair are not only compared to one another but also to other figures, and the comparative reading may be applied to the *Parallel Lives* as a whole: by

---

[30] Duff 1999b: 39: 'The *Lives* arouse not simply an "eagerness" or "uplift" to imitate the subjects delineated. That could be merely an unreflective aping of the great men of the past, and as such on a much lower plane of moral usefulness and intellectual worth. Imitation is involved, and is indeed central. But there is more. The *Lives*, Plutarch claims, not only instil a desire for imitation but actually change or "mould" character (ἠθοποιοῦν). This is achieved by the observer not simply looking, but also investigating, considering, testing; applying, as Plutarch might have put it, philosophy and reason.'

[31] Much has been written about the importance of the parallelism of the *Parallel Lives*. See Duff 1999b: 250 n. 25 for a convenient list of relevant studies. A recent volume on this topic is Humble 2010.

reading several pairs of *Lives* together, we come across different perspectives on the same events and persons, and thus acquire an even more nuanced understanding of the moral qualities or shortcomings of the characters.[32]

But why did Plutarch bring together one Greek and one Roman? This has given rise to much speculation. An often-repeated view is that of Ziegler, who sees the rationale behind the comparative approach as an attempt

to bring the Greeks and the Romans as the bearers of the empire always closer to each other, to make them always better known to each other and to increase their mutual esteem; to show the Romans that the Greeks are not only despicable Graeculi but that they, especially in the past, had produced men of action who were not inferior to the best Romans; to show the Greeks that the Romans are no barbarians.[33]

Yet it is not evident that a need for such a reconciliation project remained in Plutarch's time, as there was no longer a gap between aristocratic Greeks and Romans.[34] Accordingly, his intentions could equally well be understood as a project of resistance, consisting of a Greek appropriation of the Roman tradition.[35] The problem is that Plutarch nowhere explains the motive behind this juxtaposition of Greek and Roman heroes. As a result, all theories about it cannot but remain hypothetical, and yet, frustratingly enough, we cannot simply brush aside the problem. After all, Plutarch deliberately chose and persisted in this peculiar comparative approach. That can only mean that he did not regard it as a by-product.[36]

In my view, the most likely hypothesis is that Plutarch's comparison between Greek and Roman statesmen and generals does not aim at defining and moulding Greek and Roman identity but should primarily be seen in the context of the zetetic moralism of the *Parallel Lives*. Plutarch usually selects two historically unconnected men who

---

[32] On the comparative reading of different pairs together and even of the collection as a whole, see Mossman 1992; Pelling 2002: 26, 79, and 188, 2005: 339, and 2010; Beneker 2005; Buszard 2008; Duff 2011a: 73–4; Stadter 2015b: 286–302.

[33] Ziegler 1951: 897, my translation ('Griechen und Römer als die Träger des Imperiums einander immer näher zu bringen, sie einander immer besser kennen zu lehren und die gegenseitige Achtung zu erhöhen; den Römern zu zeigen, daß die Griechen nicht nur verächtliche Graeculi seien, sondern, allerdings vor allem in der Vergangenheit, Männer der Tat hervorgebracht hätten, die den besten Römern nicht nachstanden; den Griechen zu zeigen, daß die Römer keine Barbaren seien'). Ziegler's view is accepted, for instance, by Russell 1966: 141; Bucher-Isler 1972: 89; Valgiglio 1992a: 4047–50; and Binder 2008: 14–15.

[34] Thus C. Jones 1971: 103–9; see also Barrow 1967: 57–9; Russell 1972: 109.

[35] Thus Desideri 1992b: 4478–86 and Duff 1999b: 301–9.

[36] *Contra* Geiger 2014: 298: 'the pairing of Greeks and Romans, however innovative, may well have been a by-product conditioned by his times and surroundings without a necessarily well-thought-out purpose'.

are products of different past histories and cultures. By connecting them in one overarching framework and looking at their careers with the same philosophical questions at the back of his mind, he can explore interesting similarities and differences in their behaviour and fundamental decisions.[37] His parallels are sometimes criticized as quite artificial and unconvincing: what did the historical Lysander and Sulla really have in common, or Agesilaus and Pompey? Yet such objections fail to see the scope and meaning of such parallels. The great differences in historical context precisely fuel the examination of conduct, character, and decisions. Of course Plutarch did not want to suggest that Pompey was a new Agesilaus, or Crassus a Nicias *redivivus*. His real interest was in the similarities and differences between their respective characters, virtues, and shortcomings, in how these influenced their decisions, and in the lessons we can still derive from the comparison.

In several pairs, the main philosophical themes are briefly introduced in the programmatic proem. *Aemilius–Timoleon*, for instance, deals with the relation between the heroes' prudence and their good luck (*Aem.* 1.6); *Dion–Brutus* examines how philosopher-statesmen had to struggle with the unmanageable reality of political life (*Dion* 1.2–2.2); *Pelopidas–Marcellus* explores the tension between courage and recklessness (*Pel.* 2.9–11); and *Pericles–Fabius Maximus* investigates sublime mildness, justice, and imperturbability in the turmoil of political affairs (*Per.* 2.5). Such proems, *mutatis mutandis*, constitute the counterpart of the question raised in a philosophical *zetema*, in that they bring the issue up for discussion. At the same time, they provide the reader with a first, rudimentary answer, since Plutarch here already anticipates a few core results of the elaborate comparison that will follow. This first clue is then problematized at length in the two subsequent *Lives*. Those provide two new perspectives on the issue, the latter usually complicating the former, and in this respect recall the ascending structure of a philosophical *zetema*.[38] This implies that *both* of the *Lives* contain interesting insights and that the second one – while often being more complicated and nuanced – may also obscure issues that are clearer in the first one.

---

[37] See Duff 1999b: 249–52; Desideri 1992b: 4475–6; Larmour 2014: 409. Philopoemen and Flamininus were contemporaries and even opponents, and it was precisely this opposition that yielded rich opportunities to view the same matters from two different points of view.

[38] See above, n. 13. In the *Lives of Agis, Cleomenes, and the Gracchi*, Plutarch even provides four different perspectives on the same issue: see Roskam 2011a.

In a formal comparison (*synkrisis*) of the two heroes, Plutarch finally works towards an overall retrospective evaluation. On the basis of a few general criteria (such as military and political qualities, the death of the hero, his power base, and so on), he assesses the similarities and, especially, the differences between the two protagonists, sometimes preferring the Greek, at other times the Roman, and usually ending up with a fair balance between the two. This concluding evaluation, however, often comes as a surprise, shows less nuance, and repeatedly even flatly contradicts what has been said in the previous *Lives*. As a result, these *synkriseis* have often been regarded as mere products of the rhetorical school[39] and have been criticized as unduly trivializing conclusions.[40] Duff has proposed a more generous reading, by relating the *synkriseis* to Plutarch's problematizing moralism. In his view, they raise new questions, destabilize the reader's judgement, and thus invite the reader to further reflection. In that sense, they are part and parcel of the moral programme of the *Parallel Lives*.[41] Such an interpretation does more justice to Plutarch's zetetic moralism. Here as well, a comparison with the *zetemata* of the *Moralia* may help us in understanding the peculiarities and oddities of the *synkriseis*.

To begin with, what Duff calls their 'closural dissonance' should no longer come as a surprise.[42] Most *zetemata* in fact show a similar internal inconsistency, collecting as they do irreconcilable answers that all throw light on a part of the truth. In the same way, the *synkriseis* reveal their part of the truth. Their perspective adds to the previous answers elaborated in the *Lives*, repeating several of their insights but also challenging or questioning them through new observations. Secondly, we have seen that Plutarch usually places the alternative which he prefers at the end of the list. The implication, of course, is that his preference likewise lies with the view presented in the *synkrisis*. This has indeed been argued more than once. Boulogne, for instance, sees the *synkriseis* as Plutarch's attempt to outline an ideal politician by combining the qualities of both heroes.[43] For Nikolaidis, they are, together with the proems and some digressions, 'the parts of the *Lives* where a more authentic Plutarch is revealed; the parts where we

---

[39] See, e.g., Russell 1966: 150; Tatum 2010: 10–14; Duff 1999b: 286; Larmour 2014: 407–8.
[40] E.g. Barrow 1967: 59; Lamberton 2001: 65 and 115; Pelling 2002: 360.
[41] Duff 1999b: 243–86.
[42] Duff 1999b: 261, 263, and 257–86 *passim*, and 2011a: 74–5.
[43] Boulogne 2000.

can be almost sure that Plutarch speaks for himself and not through his sources'.[44] Verdegem correctly objects that Plutarch was no slave of his sources in the *Lives*.[45] And, indeed, we have seen that the last alternative in a philosophical *zetema* should not be considered as Plutarch's own final word on the issue. Similarly, the truth of the *synkriseis* is only a partial truth, to be supplemented with the equally partial truths presented in the two *Lives* and even in the proem. Nevertheless, this partial truth should be taken seriously.[46]

There still remains a further problem. Pelling observes that some of the *synkriseis* are 'thought-diminishing rather than thought-provoking',[47] and even Duff agrees that Plutarch is prepared in these *synkriseis* to 'speak much more in the black-and-white terms of virtue and vice'.[48] These are interesting observations: they suggest that, in such cases, the last perspective is not the most nuanced one. Should we, then, retrace our steps and regard the *synkriseis* as uncritical addenda after all? Not necessarily. We should rather appreciate them as products of a different thinking process. Reading the *Lives* requires a process of ἀναθεωρεῖν: it involves careful reflection while *going through* the events (*Aem.* 1.2; cf. *Reg. et imp. apophth.* 172E). The *synkriseis*, on the other hand, are the fruit of ἀποθεωρεῖν:[49] at this stage, the reader has finished reading the detailed accounts and is now able to look back *from a distance* at what they have read. They can ponder anew over the two men's lives and weigh their decisions against one another by means of more general criteria. This obviously opens up new opportunities, but also implies bracketing concrete historical details. To a certain extent, the perspective of the *synkriseis* switches from particular historical events to more philosophical issues, from τί to οἷα. Their ἀποθεώρησις often results in a more straightforwardly philosophical reading of history. This reading still makes use of history as the matter of philosophy, but the philosophical perspective now comes to the fore and this difference of emphasis entails dissonance and new evaluation. But here as well, Plutarch carefully refrains from speaking the last word and rather urges his readers to pass their own judgement.[50]

---

[44] Nikolaidis 2014: 359.
[45] Verdegem 2010a: 36.
[46] Duff 1999b: 200–4 and 252–86, and 2011a: 74–5.
[47] Pelling 2002: 360.
[48] Duff 1999b: 271.
[49] See *Comp. Ag., Cleom. et Gracch.* 1.1; *Comp. Ages. et Pomp.* 4.7. See also *Reg. et imp. apophth.* 172D; Roskam 2011a: 221–3 and 2014a: 188 and 190–1.

3. The characterization of the heroes

Plutarch refers to the protagonists of the *Parallel Lives* as rulers, lawgivers, and generals (*Reg. et imp. apophth.* 172D). We may wonder in passing why he did not rather write biographies of philosophers. He would have easily found distinguished figures who eminently qualified as moral paradigms: Plato, no doubt, and several of his followers, but also Pythagoras, Socrates,[51] Aristotle, and, as a negative example, the infamous Epicurus. The obvious problem, of course, was that they spent much of their lives in their schools and thus met with fewer difficult practical dilemmas.[52] As a result, their lives were probably less interesting for a project of zetetic moralism such as we find in the *Parallel Lives*.[53]

Plutarch, then, preferred writing about famous politicians and generals, but he wrote about them as a philosopher. Indeed, the general view of humanity that informs the *Parallel Lives* rests on the same philosophical foundations as the ethical thinking in the *Moralia* (see above, Chapter IV). In both cases, the theoretical basis is a dichotomy in the soul between reason and the passions, as elaborated in *On moral virtue*.[54] This is the philosophical lens through which Plutarch views the careers of the protagonists of history and which shapes the moralism of the *Lives*. Every hero had to wage his own struggle with his passions and try to overcome them time and again by the powers of his reason. The *Parallel Lives* contain a kaleidoscope of human passions. Prominent among them, of course, is love of honour (φιλοτιμία), the tireless gadfly of nearly every Plutarchan hero,[55] but many other passions follow in its wake: Nicias is superstitious, Philopoemen contentious, Coriolanus prone to anger, Crassus greedy, Pelopidas reckless, Dion wilful, Demetrius and Antony lovers of pleasure, and so on.

Furthermore, Plutarch's heroes are 'great natures', with potential for great vices and great virtues (*Demetr.* 1.7).[56] If they succeed in bringing

---

[50] *Comp. Ag., Cleom. et Gracch.* 5.7. See also Pelling 2002: 273–5; Duff 2004: 286–7 and 2011a.

[51] See Beck 2014b on the Socratic paradigm in the *Lives*.

[52] Although Plutarch stresses the political accomplishments of many philosophers, including the Stoics; on this, see Roskam 2009b: 31–65.

[53] Cf. Duff 1999b: 66.

[54] On the soul of the Plutarchan hero, see esp. Duff 1999b: 72–98 and Beneker 2012: 9–17.

[55] Russell 1972: 106; Wardman 1974: 115–24; Frazier 1988 and 2014; Pelling 2002: 242–7 and 292–7; Roskam *et al.* 2012.

[56] See esp. Duff 1999a (pointing to the Platonic antecedents of the theory; *Resp.* 491e1–492a5) and 1999b: 47–9, 60–5, and *passim*; also Bucher-Isler 1972: 80–1.

their passions under rational control, they are capable of the most brilliant virtuous achievements, whereas their failure to do so ends in utter disaster. Everything depends on how strong a grip the hero's reason has on the irrational powers of his soul. No wonder, then, that Plutarch shows a keen interest in his heroes' attitude towards philosophy in general and notably in their collaboration with philosophers. Many of the heroes were known to have associated with famous thinkers of their day: Pericles with Anaxagoras (*Per.* 4.5–5.1; 16.8–9; *Them.* 2.5), Alexander the Great with Aristotle (*Alex.* 7.2–8.4), Philopoemen with the Academics Ecdemus and Megalophanes (*Phil.* 1.5), Cleomenes with Sphaerus (*Ag./Cleom.* 23.2–3; 32.4), Tiberius Gracchus with Blossius of Cumae (*TG/CG* 8.6; 17.5; 20.5–6), Pompey with Cratippus (*Pomp.* 75.4–5), and – *cause célèbre* – Alcibiades with Socrates (*Alc.* 4.1–4; 6.1; 6.5). Dion was an alumnus of the Academy (*Dion* 1.2; 17.1; 47.4), just like Phocion (*Phoc.* 4.2; 14.7) and Cicero (*Cic.* 3.1; 4.1–3; *Luc.* 42.3), and Lucullus (*Luc.* 42.3) and Brutus (*Brut.* 2.2–3; cf. *Dion* 1.2) also expressed their preference for the Old Academy. The heroes' education is another recurrent motif, especially in the Roman *Lives*: the misbehaviour of Coriolanus (*Cor.* 1.3–6; 15.4–5), Flamininus (*Flam.* 1.4), and Marius (*Mar.* 2.2) can be explained by their lack of an appropriate *paideia*, whereas Marcellus (*Marc.* 1.3; 21.4; 21.7) and Lucullus (*Luc.* 1.6; 42.4) illustrate what can be gained from an adequate Greek education.[57]

All of this raises the question to what extent Plutarch's moralizing agenda in the *Parallel Lives* enables him to do justice to the individual nature of his heroes. The *Lives* are no moral treatises, of course,[58] nor general sermons on particular vices,[59] but they do not lay bare all the idiosyncratic peculiarities of the different protagonists either. In other words, these protagonists are staged as characters rather than personalities.[60] Plutarch sees them as moral agents with a relatively fixed set of qualities and failures, and he likes to exemplify key aspects of their character (ἦθος) through well-chosen anecdotes which contain a snapshot of their basic nature.[61] They are not simplified stereotypes,

---

[57] On the importance of *paideia* in the *Parallel Lives*, see above, Chapter IV, §4, with n. 31.
[58] Den Boer 1985: 379 goes too far in stating that the *Lives* 'could better be called ethical essays rather than biographies'.
[59] *Contra* Russell 1972: 106.
[60] See esp. Gill 1983; also Bucher-Isler 1972: 61, 79, 83, and 92; Beneker 2012: 84.

however, but 'integrated characters' that are gradually coloured in as the *Life* goes on, though without ending up as lifelike, psychologically complicated personalities.[62]

Nevertheless, Plutarch's heroes do have distinctive individual features.[63] For surely there was only one Alcibiades. And how could there be a second Sulla, or Alexander, or Antony?[64] On the one hand, their idiosyncrasies are seen from a general, Platonic point of view. *Individuum est ineffabile.* If we really want to learn from their lives, we need to have at least some things in common with them. Therefore, a more generalizing, philosophical perspective is a necessary condition. On the other hand, Plutarch's zetetic moralism can only bear full fruit when due attention is given to particularities, to the peculiarity of the historical context but also to the singularity of every hero and to their mutual differences. Only then can we adequately consider whether Pericles' mildness is entirely the same as that of Fabius Maximus, or in which respects it is different (cf. the passage from *Mul. virt.* 243B–C quoted above). Only then can we obtain a deeper insight into the specificity of their moral decisions. Moreover, the heroes' individual character traits interfere with a simple, thoughtless imitation of them – it is evidently not possible to clone Aristides, Timoleon, or Tiberius Gracchus – and thus again stimulate more in-depth moral reflection. In that sense, a discussion of the hero's individual characteristics and nature significantly contributes to the process of moral *zetesis*. This brings us to the next point.

4. Plutarch's view of historical truth

If the *Parallel Lives* should be regarded as an essentially moral project, and if the work's central comparative approach and the characterization of the protagonists is thoroughly conditioned by this moral goal, the question remains what this implies for Plutarch's attitude towards

---

[61] On Plutarch's sophisticated use of anecdotes, see Stadter 1996; Beck 1999, 2000, and 2005; Duff 2003; Schmitt Pantel 2008. On the protagonists as moral agents with a fixed set of qualities, exemplified through well-chosen anecdotes revealing their nature, Duff 2008a is particularly relevant.

[62] Pelling 2002: 287–97 and 315–21.

[63] See Nikolaidis 2014: 362–4; Aloumpi 2017: 193; Zadorojnyi 2018: 222–8.

[64] Yet Plutarch repeatedly employs pluralized names: the Cimons (*Per.* 16.3), the Marii (*Brut.* 29.6), even the Alcibiadeses (*De Al. Magn. fort.* 328C; *Flam.* 11.5). See Zadorojnyi 2018 on such 'biographical synecdoche'.

historical truth. If he uses history as the mere matter of philosophy, does he adapt this matter at his own discretion to the demands of his philosophy? How, in short, does Plutarch the philosopher relate to Plutarch the historian?

Many scholars have argued that Plutarch's account is often quite unreliable,[65] that Plutarch simply did not wish to be a historian,[66] and that the *Parallel Lives* should be understood as a philosophical project.[67] Yet he has his defenders too. Badian, for instance, states that 'Plutarch, when he set his mind to it, could be a critical historian superior to many of the professedly historical writers.'[68] Indeed, Plutarch was not blind to the bias of his sources (see, e.g., *Per.* 13.16; *Pomp.* 10.9; *Arat.* 38.11–12) and frequently mentions alternative views. Furthermore, he attaches great importance to the plausibility (εἰκότης or πιθανόν) of his account. There is no shortage of passages where he appears as a critical author displaying a sincere concern for the historical truth.

In order to better understand Plutarch's attitude towards historical truth, we may again consider it against the backdrop of the zetetic moralism of the *Parallel Lives*. To begin with, such zetetic moralism is in principle open to historical facts, whatever they may be. We have repeatedly seen that Plutarch's zetetic philosophy in general enables him to deal with the most diverse aspects of a given problem, including those that are unwelcome from a Platonic point of view. The same basic open-mindedness can be found in the *Parallel Lives*. In trying to recover what had happened, Plutarch usually saw little need to distort the facts for the sake of a simplifying moralism. Such distortion would sometimes even be counterproductive and would in any case run counter to the spirit of genuine zetetic moralism. A project of zetetic moralism rather presupposes correct and reliable information which can then be questioned and considered from a moral point of view. In other words, zetetic moralism presupposes and includes zetetic historical criticism.

---

[65] See, among many others, Ameling 1985; Worthington 1985; Schütrumpf 1987; Tritle 1987; Bosworth 1992: 80; Bloedow 1996; Schepens 2000: 351; Bresson 2002; Verdegem 2004/5: 149; Binder 2008: 26.

[66] Barigazzi 1994: 291: 'In realtà Plutarco non volle essere uno storico. Qualcuno si ostina a considerarlo soltanto uno storico, ma egli esplicitamente nega a se stesso tale qualifica' ('In reality Plutarch did not want to be a historian. Some insist on considering him only a historian, but he explicitly denies himself this title').

[67] See Schneeweiss 1979: 382 (arguing that, in the *Parallel Lives*, Plutarch transfers Plato's doctrine of Ideas to the field of history) and Wolman 1972 (on the Roman *Lives*).

[68] Badian 2003: 44; see also Shipley 1997: 5; Nikolaidis 1997b: 341; Schmitt Pantel 2008: 249.

Thus, Plutarch did not want to gloss over his heroes' mistakes and weaknesses. On the contrary, such flaws often raise interesting moral questions.[69] They should not be overemphasized, though. In the proem to the *Cimon–Lucullus*, Plutarch explains that he regards them rather as 'shortcomings in some virtue than as vile products of vice' (*Cim.* 2.5). Elsewhere, he is willing to evaluate them in the light of their time (*Comp. Sol. et Publ.* 4.4; *Cam.* 1.2). Nevertheless, they are mentioned and criticized.[70]

Sometimes, the same events are understood differently in different *Lives*. For instance, Cleomenes' proposal to give Megalopolis back to its citizens is praised as a reasonable and humane offer in *Ag./Cleom.* 45.8 but unmasked as a clever trick to seize the city in *Phil.* 5.3–4. Again, Plutarch denies that Cimon turned to demagogical practices (*Cim.* 10.8) but elsewhere argues that Pericles was outdone by Cimon's demagogy (καταδημαγωγούμενος, *Per.* 9.2). His evaluation of Athens' foreign policy considerably differs in the *Life of Phocion* and in the *Life of Demosthenes*, and so on.[71] These are neither inconsistencies nor distortions of the historical truth, but zetetic attempts to take into account the perspective of the different heroes and the complexity of the historical situation which could be faced from different – even opposite – angles.

Furthermore, in writing the *Parallel Lives*, Plutarch came across numerous historical situations in which justice was diametrically opposed to efficiency and expediency. Such historical matter is embarrassing for an oversimplifying moralism that without further ado equates justice with usefulness, but it is particularly interesting for a more problematizing zetetic moralism. Typically enough, Plutarch devotes several pairs to this issue[72] and makes no attempt at an intellectual justification of the heroes' morally problematic decisions,[73] simply allowing the facts to speak for themselves and leaving further judgement to his readers. Similarly, quite some attention is given to the influence of fortune and providence on historical events,

---

[69] Plutarch even decided to add a pair of biographies in which the negative character traits were at the forefront, the *Demetrius–Antony*; see above, n. 19.

[70] Cf. Stadter 2015b: 237–43.

[71] See Duff 1999b: 133–4. More examples can be found in Buszard 2008: 187 and Duff 2011a: 73–4.

[72] E.g. *Lysander–Sulla* and *Phocion–Cato Minor*; see the rich analyses of Duff 1999b: 131–204. On this topic, see also Pérez Jiménez 2004.

[73] See Frazier 1995: 157; see also Leão 2019b on the *Life of Solon*.

again an issue with potentially far-reaching philosophical overtones.[74] Brenk points to a dichotomy between Plutarch's philosophical convictions about the omnipresent working of providence, on the one hand, and his historical writings, which give a much more significant part to fortune, on the other hand, and even goes so far as to call Plutarch 'a schizophrenic when it comes to *tyche*'.[75] I would rather appreciate this tension as one more telling illustration of Plutarch's intellectual honesty. He essentially stuck to the facts and preferred to deal with them for what they were rather than explaining them away from an ivory tower philosophical perspective. All this shows that his moral goals and interests did not interfere with the demands of history and that he had no problem at all in combining concern for moral truth with respect for historical truth.

This, however, is only one side of the picture. Its other side is that zetetic moralism also conditions the historian's outlook and determines his selection and evaluation of his material. And this, in turn, can entail blind spots. For instance, although Plutarch does not entirely ignore economic and social matters, he repeatedly underestimates their importance and overemphasizes the impact of the heroes' individual decisions. Similarly, military matters are seldom treated in detail, although many battles are mentioned in the *Parallel Lives*. Plutarch's interest lay primarily in the character and career of his heroes and this posed new problems. Information about their days of glory was not difficult to find, but Plutarch all too often faced gaps in the available sources concerning their childhoods. These he tried to fill through 'creative reconstruction', evoking an image of the young hero on the basis of a few well-chosen anecdotes.[76] As a rule, gross distortions of the historical truth are avoided and Plutarch's reconstructions of the childhood remain within the boundaries of what he would call εὐστόχως λέγειν ('successful guesswork'; *Phoc.* 17.6). Finally, the comparative approach can entail reconstructions of a different kind, which may exaggerate minor similarities between the heroes' character or experiences (see below, Chapter VI, for concrete examples). Again, Plutarch was willing to 'help his truth along a little'.[77] In all of these

---

[74] It is central to the *Aemilius–Timoleon* pair. On this topic, see Swain 1989b; Hershbell 1997: 241–3; Frazier and Leão 2010; Opsomer 2011; Titchener 2014.

[75] Brenk 1977: 163.

[76] The term is borrowed from Pelling 2002: 154; see also 310.

[77] Thus Pelling 2002: 150. Cf. *Cim.* 2.4 with Kaesser 2004.

cases, the relation between zetetic moralism and its philosophical truth, on the one hand, and historical truth, on the other, is a complicated one.

The same holds true concerning matters of chronology. A notorious case is Plutarch's version of the famous story of Solon's encounter with Croesus (*Sol.* 27.1):

As for Solon's meeting with Croesus, some think to prove by chronology that it is fictitious. But when a story is so famous and so well-attested, and, what is more to the point, when it comports so well with the character of Solon, and is so worthy of his magnanimity and wisdom, I do not propose to reject it out of deference to any chronological canons, so called, which thousands keep revising, without to this day being able to bring their contradictions into any general agreement.[78]

Prima facie, this passage suggests that Plutarch here deliberately sacrifices historical to moral truth. On closer inspection, though, the matter is not so simple. To begin with, he at least *mentions* the chronological problem. If he had only eye for the rich moral message of the story, he could have ignored chronology altogether. Secondly, his position is not unreasonable, given the great dissension among specialists in chronology. In light of these disagreements, simply dismissing the story on chronological grounds does not show careful historical criticism either. In fact, there also appear to be many witnesses who support the story – although Plutarch gives no names; moreover, the story corroborates what we know about Solon's character, an observation that is relevant for the historian and the moralist alike. In that sense, Plutarch's decision to accept the story shows neither complete lack of historical criticism nor an occasional lack of interest in historical truth.[79] It rather reveals his sense of the limits of historical truth claims and his justified caution (εὐλάβεια) vis-à-vis exaggerated confidence in dubious chronology. His decision to adopt a 'benefit of the doubt' approach in such circumstances is far from uncritical and unreasonable.

A similar case concerns the relation of Numa and Pythagoras. Here, too, Plutarch is aware of chronological difficulties. In the first chapter of the *Life of Numa*, he refers to the view of those who say that Pythagoras lived as many as five generations after Numa (*Num.* 1.4). This

---

[78] For Plutarch's reception of Herodotus' famous story, see Muñoz Gallarte 2010–11; see also Pelling 2011b: 41–3; Leão 2020: 286–8.

[79] Cf. Pelling 2002: 143: 'This, perhaps, is one instance where Plutarch shows less concern to investigate historical truth than we should like.'

chronological observation is counterbalanced, however, by a lengthy discussion of the many clear correspondences between Pythagoras' convictions and those of Numa (8.5–20). Plutarch's course thus closely resembles the one he took in the *Life of Solon*: while again mentioning the chronological problem very clearly and right at the start, he does not hesitate to examine the parallels in detail, while adding, at the end of this discussion, that trying to decide the controversial question of Numa's acquaintance with Pythagoras would show youthful contentiousness (μειρακιώδους φιλονεικίας, 8.21). Thus the note of caution sounded at the outset resounds with even more effect at the end.

Plutarch returns once more to the issue at the end of the *Life* (*Num.* 22.5), arguing that 'we may well be quite indulgent (συγγνώμην ἔχειν πολλήν) with those who are eager (φιλοτιμουμένοις) to prove, on the basis of so many resemblances between them, that Numa was acquainted with Pythagoras'. This, if anything, is a strategically well-considered and subtle judgement. The term φιλοτιμουμένοις recalls, albeit in a slightly more positive register, the youthful contentiousness of the over-enthusiastic believers, and the phrase συγγνώμην ἔχειν suggests not merely that Plutarch bears in mind the demands of chronology but even that the hypothesis of the believers is problematic if not false. At the same time, his argument vindicates the lengthy treatment of the many correspondences. This is, once again, a telling way of both having and eating both one's historical and one's moral cake.

5. Heuristics and method of working

The previous section has shown that zetetic moralism goes hand in hand with careful historical criticism. It also presupposes meticulous heuristics, which leads us to the question of Plutarch's sources.[80] What did Plutarch read?

He read an awful lot. The *Parallel Lives* illustrate his erudition no less than the polymathic works of the *Moralia* (see above, Chapter III). He never limited himself to the most obvious sources but actively looked for interesting new material. In the proem to *Nicias–Crassus*, he says (*Nic.* 1.5):

---

[80] This is a much discussed topic. Nearly every commentary on a *Life* or a pair contains a section on the sources which Plutarch used. General studies include Peter 1865; Theander 1951; Scardigli 1979; Desideri 1992a; Schettino 2014.

Those deeds which Thucydides and Philistus have set forth – since I cannot entirely pass them by, above all when they indicate the nature of my hero and the disposition which lay hidden beneath his many great sufferings – I have run over briefly, and with no unnecessary detail, in order to escape the reputation of utter carelessness and sloth; but those details which have escaped most writers, and which others have mentioned casually (εἰρημένα σποράδην), or which are found on ancient votive offerings or in public decrees, these I have tried to collect, not massing together useless material of research (ἱστορίαν), but handing on such as furthers the appreciation of character and temperament (κατανόησιν ἤθους καὶ τρόπου).

As usual, the proem should be understood against the background of the following *Life*, yet it also throws light on a more general problem. The main events in Greek and Roman history had been extensively related by excellent writers before Plutarch. For the *Life of Nicias*, he could fall back on Thucydides and Philistus; for other Greek *Lives*, he could rely on Herodotus, Xenophon, Polybius, Ephorus, and Theopompus. All of these were major sources for Plutarch and in one way or another he had to distinguish himself from them. He specifies that his emulation is not of a literary kind – as Thucydides is anyhow beyond imitation (*Nic.* 1.1; 1.4–5) – but concerns the understanding of the hero's character. In this, he claims, he could still add to authors as inimitable as Thucydides.

To that purpose, he also used other sources and, to find these, he was willing to go more than one extra mile. In the above passage he mentions decrees and inscriptions,[81] but he also benefited from other contemporary sources, including the writings of the protagonists themselves.[82] Whenever possible, he supplemented his material through autopsy and hearsay.[83] Furthermore, for his Roman *Lives*, he took pains to read Latin sources as well.[84] In short, all this reveals

---

[81] Plutarch's use of inscriptions is discussed in Liddel 2008.

[82] E.g. Cicero's Περὶ ὑπατείας (*Crass.* 13.4, *Caes.* 8.4, and probably the main source for *Cic.* 10–23: see Lendle 1967; Pelling 2002: 45–9) and his *Cato*, as well as Caesar's *Anti-Cato* (*Cic.* 39.5, *Caes.* 3.2 and 54.2–3; see also *Ca. Mi.* 11.4 and 36.3); the *Memoirs* of Aratus (*Arat.* 3.3, 32.5, 33.3, 38.6; *Agis/Cleom.* 15.4, 37.4–5, 38.4, 40.4: see Stadter 2015a: 163–5) and of Sulla (*Sull.* 6.8 and 37.1; *Mar.* 35.4: see Russo 2002); the verses of Solon; and the *Letters of Alexander* (Hamilton 1969, lix–lx).

[83] See esp. Buckler 1992; also Theander 1951: 2–32; Frost 1980: 50–2; Muccioli 2012: 78–89.

[84] Plutarch's knowledge of Latin is another much discussed topic. The *locus classicus* on this issue is *Dem.* 2.2–4, where Plutarch claims that his familiarity with the subject matter enables him to understand his Latin sources, but that he cannot appreciate the beauty of the Latin style. The *communis opinio* has it that Plutarch's claims in this passage are largely justified. See, e.g., Rose 1924: 11–19; C. Jones 1971: 81–7; De Rosalia 1991; Moya del Baño and Carrasco Reija 1991; Strobach 1997: 33–9; Setaioli 2007; Stadter 2015b: 133–7 and 2016.

painstaking research, inspired by the zetetic spirit, in finding the sources.

This *zetesis* especially comes to the fore in Plutarch's attention to the σποράδην εἰρημένα: not the great outlines of the story that everybody knows from Thucydides but the tiny details, anecdotes, and sayings mentioned in passing by only one author, which provide such interesting material for moral reflection. These fill many pages of the *Parallel Lives* and also found their way into separate collections like the *Sayings of kings and commanders* and the *Spartan sayings*.

The precise relation between these collections of sayings and the *Parallel Lives* is a matter of scholarly debate. According to Stadter, the *Spartan sayings* were part of a greater collection which Plutarch used as a source for the *Parallel Lives*, whereas the *Sayings of kings and commanders* are a later, edited selection of the big collection.[85] Pelling, on the other hand, focuses on the *Sayings of kings and commanders*, which he regards as a fruit of the provisional drafts of the *Parallel Lives*.[86] However that may be, the collections of sayings have their own profile, as appears from the dedication letter to Trajan at the outset of the *Sayings of kings and commanders*.[87] There, Plutarch says that the collection aims at an understanding of the characters and fundamental choices of leading men (κατανόησιν ἠθῶν καὶ προαιρέσεων ἡγεμονικῶν; 172C). This strikingly resembles his statement in the proem to *Nicias–Crassus* quoted above. The goal of the collections of sayings, then, is exactly the same as that of the *Parallel Lives*: they are a project of zetetic moralism. But the collections are also presented as a kind of shortcut. Whereas the reading of the *Parallel Lives* requires considerable time, the collections of sayings directly focus on the heroes' pithy statements, which constitute the very core, the 'samples and seeds of their lives' (δείγματα τῶν βίων καὶ σπέρματα; 172E). The difference between the collections of sayings and the *Parallel Lives*, then, lies neither in their moral purpose nor in Plutarch's general attitude towards the relevant material – in both cases, history is regarded as the matter of philosophy – but rather has to do with the selection of the material.

---

[85] Stadter 2014.

[86] Pelling 2002: 65–90.

[87] The authenticity of the letter (and of the collection as a whole) has long been doubted, but has been convincingly defended by Flacelière 1976: 100–3 and Beck 2002; see also Roskam 2014a: 190–1.

Yet this selection does have important implications for the goal of the collections of sayings. Trajan can ruminate on these anecdotes in his rare moments of leisure. He can carefully ponder about and learn from them, come to his conclusions, and take inspiration from them, but the short anecdotes do not allow for the same detailed zetetic reflections as the *Parallel Lives*. They provide little information about the historical background, about alternative, opposite reactions to the same event, or about negative behaviour. Plutarch's selection thus omits much material that stimulates genuine and nuanced *zetesis*. He provides his busy reader with a ready-made package of anecdotes that stimulates reflection (ἀναθεώρησιν; 172E) but lacks the depth of the *Parallel Lives*. In short, the collections of sayings aim at zetetic moralism in its light version.

Back to the *Parallel Lives* and to Plutarch's method of working. In all likelihood, Plutarch read all the main sources before he began the composition of a *Life*.[88] He read them very carefully, paying attention to relevant details,[89] and taking notes while reading. These notes probably did not contain the basic outlines of the historical events – which Plutarch knew or easily remembered – but it was precisely the casual mentions (σποράδην εἰρημένα) that caught his eye. His careful zetetic heuristics was thus matched by an equally painstaking *zetesis* in reading the sources.

After Plutarch had finished his reading, he usually selected one principal source. Some *Lives* largely rest on this main source (like the *Life of Nicias* or the *Life of Coriolanus*, respectively based on Thucydides and Dionysius of Halicarnassus[90]), but usually different main sources are used for different sections of a *Life*.[91] Relying on this (or these) source(s), he then composed a provisional draft

---

[88] This is the hypothesis of Pelling, who distinguishes between three phases in the composition process, viz. the preliminary reading of the sources, the production of a first draft, and the writing of the final version; Pelling 1988: 31–3 and 2011a: 36–42; see also Stadter 1989: xliv–li; Heftner 1995: 12–13; Verdegem 2010b: 76–7. Reading for one *Life* also provided Plutarch with material for other *Lives*, and it is likely that several *Lives* were indeed prepared simultaneously; thus Pelling 2002: 2–11 (on the *Lives of Pompey*, *Cato the Younger*, *Crassus*, *Caesar*, *Brutus*, and *Antony*, as different from the earlier *Cicero* and *Lucullus*). See also Nikolaidis 2005: *passim*; Verdegem 2010b: 93 and 402 (on *Alcibiades* and *Nicias*); Moles 2017: 11 (on the pairs *Dion–Brutus*, *Aemilius–Timoleon*, and *Alexander–Caesar*).

[89] See *De gen. Socr.* 575C–D, with Beneker 2012: 81.

[90] See Pelling 2002: 118–22 and 2011a: 40 n. 90 (on the *Life of Nicias*); and Russell 1963 and Ahlrichs 2005 (on the *Life of Coriolanus*).

[91] Occasionally, Plutarch even combines many sources, so that it is no longer possible to trace back larger sections to specific sources. A case in point is the *Life of Alexander*: see Hamilton 1969: xlix–lxii.

(a ὑπόμνημα).[92] Whatever was less relevant for his project of zetetic moralism was omitted or shortened, while other material was transposed or added from different sources, sometimes resulting in learned digressions.[93] This substantial and thorough transformation of the source(s) never became a mechanical process in the hands of the experienced biographer but always required a process of searching reflection. The lens of zetetic moralism is no mere glaze on historical earthenware but entails a new perspective on the hero's career.[94] Even though the moral interest of the story is seldom made explicit, the underlying zetetic and moralizing spirit still conditions Plutarch's overall interpretation and evaluation of his material. His solid *zetesis* in finding and reading the sources was thus completed by a painstaking *zetesis* in transforming them.

While the provisional version in all likelihood already contained the core of Plutarch's view of the hero, it was still a great step to the published version. That step not only required final structuring and literary polishing (*dispositio* and *elocutio*) but probably also included the pairing of the two heroes. This obviously necessitated a new process of reflection with further expansion and/or abridgement of the provisional draft. The final result was a product of intensive *zetesis* inviting further *zetesis*, well written and well considered, based on careful historical research and nuanced moral reflections, providing attractive and entertaining reading, as well as inspired and inspiring food for thinking.

6. Conclusion

This chapter has only touched on a few important aspects of the *Parallel Lives*: their moral purpose and comparative approach, Plutarch's dealing with his heroes, and his attitude towards historical truth. There is so much more to say. The ancient historian would certainly

---

[92] This hypothesis (see above, n. 88) is supported by interesting information about the ancients' working methods that can be found in other authors: see esp. Lucian, *Hist. conscr.* 48; Ammonius, *In Arist. Cat.* 4.6–13 Busse; Philoponus, *In Arist. Cat.* 3.29–4.10 Busse; Olympiodorus, *In Arist. Cat.* 6.25–35 Busse. See also Avenarius 1956: 85–104; Dorandi 1991: 13 and 2000: 111. On Plutarch's ὑπομνήματα, see also above, Chapter III, §5, with n. 53.

[93] Plutarch's adaptation of his source material has often been discussed. Again, Pelling paved the way: Pelling 1988: 33–6, 2002: 1–63 and 91–115, and 2011a: 56–8. See also Moles 1988: 36–8; Stadter 1989: xlviii–li; Larmour 1992: 4165–74; Konrad 1994: xxxix–xli; Heftner 1995: 14–19; Ahlrichs 2005: 41–2 and *passim*; Binder 2008: 22–3; Verdegem 2010b: 62–3 and 405–9.

[94] Cf. Beneker 2012: 59–64.

want to learn more about Plutarch's reception of the previous historical and biographical tradition; about his historical method and to what extent it differs from, or corresponds to the methodological principles he laid down himself in *On the malice of Herodotus* (see above, Chapter III, §4); or about his view of Greece and Rome and his treatment of different Greek cities and powers. The philosopher would like to explore the Platonic inspiration of the *Parallel Lives* in further detail, as it appears from the many links with Plutarch's ethical and political philosophy (including the ideal of the philosopher-king) but also from digressions about epistemological and theological matters and from his view of the working of providence and fortune in the course of history. The literary scholar would find rich opportunities for a narratological study of the *Parallel Lives*, for an enquiry into their rhetoric, their imagery, their intertextuality, and their relationship with the 'Second Sophistic'.

Reading the *Parallel Lives* is like walking in a gallery full of precious statues, being overwhelmed by their variegated beauty and not knowing where to look first. Every statue is unique and repays accurate observation, and their comparison adds a further dimension to the spectator's experience. This comparison between the *Parallel Lives* and statues was made by Plutarch himself, but he also points to an important difference (*Cim.* 2.2): 'We believe that a portrait which reveals character and habits is far more beautiful than one which merely copies body and countenance.' He had it right: the statues of his *Parallel Lives* are living indeed. It was Plutarch himself who breathed life into them. His breath of life was that of zetetic moralism. This enabled the lively statues of the *Parallel Lives* to interact with one another, beyond the spatial and temporal boundaries of their historical existence. In turn it enabled them to interact with Plutarch's readers and, indeed, with all of us.

VI. A CLOSE ENCOUNTER WITH THE *PARALLEL LIVES*: TWO CASE STUDIES

At the outset of Plato's *Timaeus*, Socrates briefly recalls the discussion of the ideal state which he had the day before with his companions (*Tim.* 17c1–19b2). Looking back at it, he experiences what people often experience when they see beautiful creatures in repose: he wants to see them in motion (19b3–c2). This is precisely the goal of the present chapter. The previous one has provided a general overview of several essential themes and characteristics of the *Parallel Lives*. Now, it is time to see them 'in motion'.

To that end, I shall take a closer look at two books of the *Lives*. These case studies complement the previous chapter in different ways. They give a better and more concrete idea of how zetetic moralism actually works, of how the comparison between the two heroes informs and complicates the reflection on their characters and the moral value of their decisions. They also give due attention to the great versatility of the *Parallel Lives*. As a matter of fact, every pair raises its own questions, connected with the particular careers of its two protagonists. Zetetic moralism as discussed in the previous chapter may be the fundamental unifying factor between all the *Lives*, but their specific focus can be very different, as the two case studies will indeed illustrate. Finally, they may also throw some more light on Plutarch's narrative technique. Of course, the enthralling stories of the *Parallel Lives* can only be fully appreciated and enjoyed by reading them in their entirety, and the following case studies are in this respect no more than a second sailing that fails to replace such a full reading and cannot even exhaustively lay bare the wealth of the two respective pairs. Yet they may at least provide a few samples of Plutarch's captivating biographical art.

1. Themistocles–Camillus

The pair *Themistocles–Camillus* is a good touchstone for the general interpretation of the *Parallel Lives* presented in the previous chapter. For Pelling, the *Life of Themistocles* is a fairly historical life and 'not on the whole one of Plutarch's most thoughtful or incisive Lives',[1]

---

[1] Pelling 2002: 132.

while *Themistocles–Camillus* as a whole is 'hardly the most successful of Plutarch's pairs'.[2] As to the *Life of Camillus*, Stadter comments that 'Plutarch has not been able to transform the historical narrative which was his source into a moral biography.'[3] If all this is true, we may well wonder whether traces of zetetic moralism can be found in this pair.

The *Life of Themistocles* opens with some information about the hero's descent,[4] nature, and character.[5] For Plutarch – as for Thucydides, his principal source of inspiration (1.138.3) – Themistocles' two main characteristics were cleverness (τῇ φύσει συνετός, 'clever by nature', 2.1) and great ambition (τῇ φιλοτιμίᾳ πάντας ὑπερέβαλεν, 'in ambition he surpassed everyone', 5.3; τῇ φύσει φιλοτιμότατος, 'most ambitious by nature', 18.1).[6] Moreover, he placed his trust in his natural capacities in particular. He was not interested in education that aimed at character formation but rather preferred practical instruction (2.3).[7] This, in Plutarch, is not a promising beginning. Here already, the tension is anticipated between Themistocles' great practical ambitions and the moral restrictions that may impede them. Thus, we are prepared for one of the most important themes of the pair: that is, the question of how far ambition can go, both in private and in public life. What should one do if useful decisions come into conflict with moral concerns?

The first moment when this conflict arises comes early in Themistocles' career. Unlike the Athenians, he foresees the danger of Darius and the Persians, but he realizes that he cannot convince his fellow citizens at this stage to spend the revenues of the silver mines in Laurium on the building of a new fleet that can be used against the Persians. Therefore, he cleverly uses the war against Aigina as a pretext for building a hundred triremes (4.1–3).[8] This cunning strategy obviously yielded interesting results, yet not everybody was enthusiastic about it. None other than Plato blames Themistocles for having turned

---

[2] Pelling 2002: 133.

[3] Stadter 1984: 359.

[4] Duff 2008b: 159–68.

[5] The pair lacks a proem, but this could be lost, as the *Life of Themistocles* begins with a δέ; see Duff 2008b: 176–9.

[6] Cf. H. Martin 1961.

[7] Duff 2008a: 3–11 and 2009.

[8] Frost 1980: 83 argues that the historical reality was probably different and that the Athenians were conscious of the Persian threat and the intentions of Themistocles' proposal.

the Athenians into seafarers (*Leg.* 4, 706b7–d2) and Plutarch quotes Plato's criticism (4.4), but he adds (4.5):

Now, whether by accomplishing this he did injury to the integrity and purity of public life or not, let the philosopher rather investigate (ἔστω φιλοσοφώτερον ἐπισκοπεῖν). But that the salvation which the Hellenes achieved at that time came from the sea, and that it was those very triremes which restored again the city of Athens, Xerxes himself bore witness, not to speak of other proofs.

This is not a straightforward rejection of Plato's criticism:[9] for Plutarch, the philosophical point of view is surely valuable and interesting, but it is only one side of the coin. No-one can deny that Themistocles' policy proved particularly useful at Salamis, and this deserves to be underlined, even against Plato. Yet it is far less certain whether such fair recognition necessarily implies an overall acceptance of Themistocles' course. The question remains open, but the confrontation of the two different points of view at least gives interesting food for thought.

Thus a refrain appears that will sound throughout Themistocles' entire career. Time and again he does not hesitate to use (morally) problematic means to reach his goals.[10] He bribes the incompetent Epicydes (6.1–2), buys the loyalty of Architeles (7.6–7), does not even hesitate to use the gods (10.1–3; 10.7),[11] and cheats the enemy (12.4–5, the so-called Sicinnus affair). This series culminates in Chapter 13: before the Battle of Salamis, the seer Euphrastides tells Themistocles to sacrifice three Persian prisoners to Dionysus Carnivorous. Themistocles' reaction characterizes him very well (13.4):

Themistocles was terrified, feeling that the word of the seer was monstrous and shocking; but the multitude, who, as is wont to be the case in great struggles and severe crises, hoped for safety rather from unreasonable than from reasonable measures, invoked the god with one voice, dragged the prisoners to the altar, and compelled the fulfilment of the sacrifice, as the seer commanded.

Plutarch does not say that Themistocles himself bears direct responsibility for the awful sacrifice (contrast *Pel.* 21.3), yet the hero did nothing to avoid it either. He apparently complied with the irrational wish of the people and it is perfectly possible to adduce this

---

[9] Thus correctly Zadorojnyi 2006: 263 against the common interpretation of the passage.

[10] Larmour 1992: 4187–9. On Plutarch's position on the question whether the end justifies the means, see esp. Nikolaidis 1995; also Duff 1999b: 131–3; Frazier 2016: 217–24.

[11] Tuci 2006.

passage as one more example of Themistocles' pragmatic sly cleverness (*synesis*).[12] Thus this anecdote brings the moral question to a head: how far can a man go in contriving and enforcing actions for the sake of the public interest? By pointing to Themistocles' shocked reaction, Plutarch clearly indicates what is morally at stake here, but omits any further explicit comment. Throughout the first part of the *Life*, he has repeatedly raised the question, has now brought it to a first climax, and then leaves the judgement to his readers. A fine example of zetetic moralism indeed.

More is to come, for in the remainder of the *Life*, the theme keeps returning. Themistocles again sends a false message to Xerxes and thus persuades him to leave Greece (16.5), a ruse that is praised by Plutarch as a sample of *phronesis* (prudence; 16.6). He misleads the Athenian citizens (18.1) and bribes or deceives the Spartan ephors (19.1). In the end, he comes into collision with his fellow citizens, who are overcome with envy – a recurrent theme in the pair and in the *Parallel Lives* as a whole.[13] Ostracism follows (22.4) and even a charge of high treason (23.1). This marks a break in Themistocles' life, though not in his character, for Themistocles always remains Themistocles. He succeeds in getting the support of Admetus, the king of the Molossians and his former enemy, by cleverly using the Molossians' customs of supplication (24.2–5) and puts pressure upon the captain of the ship that is bringing him to Asia (25.2). The last stage in his journey to the Persian king is noteworthy (26.4–6):

Most barbarous nations, and the Persians in particular, are savage and harsh by nature in their jealous watchfulness over their women. Not only their wedded wives, but also their bought slaves and concubines are strictly guarded, so that they are seen by no outsiders, but live at home in complete seclusion, and even on their journeys are carried in tents enclosing them on all sides and set upon four-wheeled wagons. Such a vehicle was made ready for Themistocles, and safely ensconced in this he made his journey, while his attendants replied in every case to those who met them with enquiries, that they were conducting a little Hellenic woman from Ionia to one of the King's courtiers.

This is Themistocles all over. How far one can fall! The great victor of Salamis is now carried as an ordinary courtesan. Away with *decorum*, away with glory...but not with success, for the smart trick brings Themistocles precisely where he wants to be, at the court of the Persian king.

---

[12] Cf. Larmour 1992: 4194.
[13] H. Martin 1961: 331–4; Larmour 1992: 4196–8; Duff 2010: 46 and 54–6. See also Wardman 1974: 69–78; Verdegem 2005.

This leads to yet another climax in Chapter 27, where Plutarch tells how Themistocles asks for an audience with the king. The Chiliarch replies that this is possible, provided that Themistocles observes the local customs, including the obeisance (27.3–5). But this is by no means simple: Greeks do not prostrate themselves before kings and a well-known episode from Alexander's life illustrates how delicate the matter was. When Alexander wanted to introduce the Persian custom of such *proskynesis* among the Macedonians, he met with vigorous opposition (*Alex.* 54.2–6; 74.2–3; cf. 45.1; 51.5). A true Greek refuses to demean himself like this. Or does he? Themistocles, the conqueror of the barbarians, sees no problem (*Them.* 27.6), but readily adapts himself and gives obeisance, not once (28.1) but later too (πάλιν προσκυνήσαντος, 'having once again paid obeisance'; 29.3). As usual, Plutarch adds no further comment, but his passing reference to the renewed obeisance illustrates the relevance of the theme and stimulates further reflection. Rejecting Themistocles' un-Greek behaviour may seem the obvious reaction, yet it would also be a premature and oversimplifying one. In any case, Themistocles' decision once again yields a useful result, as it enables him to gain personal security and even reputation among the Persians, and to enjoy the pleasures of a luxurious life (29.6–10; 31.3).

The whole *Life*, then, illustrates that Themistocles was πανοῦργος, ready to do anything that suited his purposes (see 1.3; *Arist.* 2.2). The idiosyncratic combination of his cleverness and ambition, not checked by any moral concern, made him willing to accomplish whatever could bring him benefit. And, indeed, this attitude yielded many great successes, for Greece, Athens, and himself.[14] Yet the picture is more nuanced than that. Themistocles also acted as an impartial arbitrator (5.6) – although this, of course, added to his good reputation among the people. He once warned Simonides that he had to obey the law (5.6), a statement that suggests a noble stance, even though it remains unclear how consistent he was in such matters.[15] Particularly revealing is his opposition to Aristides, surnamed 'the Just' (*Arist.* 6.1–2). The two had characters that were diametrically opposed (*Them.* 3.3; *Arist.* 2.2). Accordingly, Themistocles had Aristides

---

[14] Duff 2008b: 165–7 and 2010: 53–4 and 57–8. Themistocles' attitude towards money (*Them.* 25.3; cf. 5.1) is discussed by Zadorojnyi 2006: 270–85 (who aptly links him to Plato's timocratic man).

[15] Contrast Timocreon's sharp attack on Themistocles (21.3–7); Zadorojnyi 2006: 279–81.

ostracized but later wrote a decree to call him back (*Them.* 11.1) and thus showed himself open to reconciliation and collaboration.[16] Plutarch appreciates this as a great deed but, again, this reconciliatory course is not opposed to Themistocles' *synesis*. We may well wonder whether, in such cases, Themistocles' apparent devotion to what is honourable (τὸ καλόν) is not the servant of his cleverness.

The course of events, however, repeatedly thwarts his plans, and Chapter 20 is especially interesting in this respect. Plutarch there relates how Themistocles divulges to Aristides his secret plan to destroy the fleet of the Greeks. Aristides then tells the Athenians that, in his view, no plan could be either more useful or more unjust (20.2; cf. *Arist.* 22.3). Again, we encounter a situation in which the general theme of the *Life* is brought to a head. Significantly, the historicity of the event is by no means certain,[17] yet Plutarch has inserted the anecdote because it is especially relevant for the overarching philosophical theme of the *Life*. Aristides' judgement was correct, no doubt; more interestingly, he left the final decision to the Athenians, thus inviting his fellow citizens to deliberate on the matter in a way that recalls the well-considered zetetic moralism typical of Plutarch himself. The Athenians decided to abandon the plan, thus preferring justice to usefulness (*Them.* 20.2; cf. *Arist.* 22.4). This decision will prove interesting in light of the *Life of Camillus*, where the Romans face a similar dilemma.

Finally, in the *Life of Themistocles* Plutarch points to the tension between short-term and long-term usefulness. So far, we have seen that Themistocles' decisions usually yielded great profit in the short term, yet it is not evident whether they would always prove advantageous in the long run as well. Themistocles himself was not blind to the problem. His decision to abandon Athens, for instance, was undoubtedly problematic when one only takes into account its direct consequences. The city risked plundering and utter destruction. In a moving scene, Plutarch evokes the departure from Athens (10.8–10):

When the city was thus putting out to sea, the sight provoked pity in some, and in others astonishment at the boldness of the step; for they were sending off their families in one direction, while they themselves, unmoved by the lamentations and tears and embraces of their parents, were crossing over to the island. Besides, many who were

---

[16] See Duff 2010: 53.
[17] See Flacelière *et al.* 1961: 94; Marr 1998: 123.

left behind on account of their great age invited pity also, and much affecting fondness was shown by the tame domestic animals, which ran along with yearning cries of distress by the side of their masters as they embarked. A story is told of one of these, the dog of Xanthippus the father of Pericles, how he could not endure to be abandoned by him, and so sprang into the sea, swam across the strait by the side of his master's trireme, and staggered out on Salamis, only to faint and die straightway. They say that the spot which is pointed out to this day as 'Dog's Mound' is his tomb.[18]

Themistocles, then, did not always go for immediate success but also had an eye for the more distant future. Nevertheless, in most cases his policy aimed at short-term success but later turned out to be problematic if not detrimental. For instance, the initial dilemma raised in Chapter 4 returns in Chapter 19, where Plutarch argues that Themistocles filled the common people with boldness (19.5–6),[19] thus echoing Plato's criticism in a moment of φιλοσοφώτερον ἐπισκοπεῖν. Moreover, Themistocles reaped what he had sown. He was often willing to do whatever served his personal interest, but as soon as a price was put on his head, he became the prey of equally unscrupulous opportunists (26.1). Finally, his contrivances ultimately led to his death. He had promised the Persian king to assist him in dealing with Greek affairs, but when the king reminded him of his promise, he contemplated suicide as his last resort (31.5),

neither embittered by anything like anger against his former fellow citizens, nor lifted up by the great honour and power he was to have in the war, but possibly thinking his task not even approachable, both because Hellas had other great generals at that time, and especially because Cimon was so marvellously successful in his campaigns; yet most of all out of regard for the reputation of his own achievements and the trophies of those early years.

Sic transit gloria mundi. Themistocles finally finds himself in a situation which precludes both cunning wiles and honourable conduct. The difficulty with which he is now confronted is the last consequence of his previous career and decisions, and he does not shrink from facing facts unflinchingly.[20] Plutarch adds that the king admired Themistocles when he heard about his death (31.7). This is certainly one possible perspective on the hero's end – although it is here attributed to a

---

[18] On this passage, see Graninger 2010 (who regards the scene as an example of 'creative reconstruction' on the basis of Thucydides' account of the departure of the Sicilian expedition; cf. Flacelière *et al.* 1961: 100–1).

[19] See Duff 2008b: 171–2 and 2010: 55–6.

[20] Duff 2010: 56–8.

barbarian. Alternative views are conceivable too, yet Plutarch leaves it at that. Readers should arrive at their own conclusion, but do well to turn first to the *Life of Camillus*, where they will become acquainted with a different course that may further deepen their understanding and judgement.

★★★

The *Life of Camillus* immediately sets the tone through a fine characterization of its protagonist as a man full of moderation (*metriotes*) and prudence (*phronesis*) (1.4). This combination strikingly differs from Themistocles' dominant character traits. This *Life* will not contain the story of excessive ambition and knavery but of moderate restraint in exercising power and of a cleverness that can be called virtuous prudence rather than sly cleverness (*synesis*).[21]

That is not to say, however, that Camillus lacks ambition and cleverness. His ambition especially appears from an episode early in his career, when he celebrates a pompous triumph (7.1–2), whereas his cleverness is illustrated by the many ingenious tricks which he uses throughout his career. He allows his soldiers to plunder the city of Veii (7.7), although he has vowed a tenth of the booty to Apollo, and later comes up with 'the absurdest of all explanations' (τὸν ἀτοπώτατον τῶν λόγων), viz. that he has simply forgotten his vow (8.2). He smartly uses the war against the Falerians as a means to distract attention from internal problems (9.2–3). In the lawsuit against Manlius, he transfers the court outside the city, away from the Capitol, so that it becomes easier to forget Manlius' former bravery (36.7).[22] He feigns sickness when confronted with serious political difficulties (39.4). Aside from all that, he repeatedly shows himself as an extremely competent general, always able to assess what the particular situation requires (see 35.3: ὀρθῶς λογισάμενος, 'having reasoned correctly'), and accumulating victories for Rome. All of these successes were the rewards of his cleverness and vigour (τῇ δεινότητι καὶ τῷ δραστηρίῳ; 36.1). These are certainly features which he shares with Themistocles, yet he is led by entirely different concerns.

Those concerns become clear early in his life, after the sack of Veii. Camillus' reaction to it is far from triumphalist. He addresses the gods

---

[21] On the difference between *phronesis* and *synesis* in Plutarch, see Frazier 2016: 283–4.
[22] Duff 2010: 63 with 77–8 n. 109, points to the parallel in *Them.* 19.6 about the Thirty changing the orientation of the Pnyx.

and argues that the assault of the Romans is not unjust but simply necessary (οὐ παρὰ δίκην, ἀλλὰ κατ᾽ ἀνάγκην), an act of self-defence (5.7). Themistocles usually had far fewer problems with injustice and mainly considered the exigencies of the moment. Camillus, in contrast, tries to reconcile the two.

The same concern for justice reappears during the siege of Falerii. When a local schoolteacher betrays his city and hands his pupils over to Camillus, the latter is given an excellent chance to force the Falerians to their knees. Themistocles, who used the Persian Sicinnus against Darius, would probably not have hesitated to make use of this opportunity. Camillus, however, sends the traitor back to the city, with the comment that 'even wars have certain laws which good men will respect' (10.5), and the Falerians later declare that Camillus has indeed honoured justice before victory (10.7). Camillus thus begins to resemble the righteous Aristides much more than the wily Themistocles;[23] what is more, his strategy pays off, for he obtains the city without bloodshed.

Yet Camillus, just like Themistocles, then comes into conflict with his fellow citizens and, when he is indicted and risks condemnation, he curses the city and goes into exile (11.1–13.1).[24] What follows is a lengthy account of the Gallic invasion of Italy, and Camillus disappears from the scene for many chapters. This long section has been regarded as evidence of Plutarch's historical interests,[25] but it also develops the central issue of the pair. When Clusium is attacked by the Gauls and turns to the Romans for help, the latter send envoys to Brennus, the king of the Gauls, and ask what wrong they have suffered from the Clusians. Brennus replies (17.3–5):

The Clusians wrong us in that, being able to till only a small parcel of the earth, they yet are bent on holding a large one, and will not share it with us, who are strangers, many in number and poor. This is the wrong which you too suffered, Romans, formerly at the hands of the Albans, Fidenates, and Ardeates, and now lately at the hands of the Veientines, Capenates, and many of the Faliscans and Volscians. You march against these peoples, and if they will not share their goods with you, you enslave them and despoil them and raze their cities to the ground; not that in so doing you are in any wise cruel or unjust, nay, you are but obeying the most ancient of the laws which gives to the stronger the goods of the weaker, beginning with God himself and ending

---

[23] See Larmour 1992: 4184; Pelling 2005: 335; Duff 2010: 62.
[24] Duff 2010: 59–61.
[25] Stadter 1984: 359; Pelling 2005: 335–6.

with the world of the beasts. For these too are so endowed by nature that the stronger seeks to have more than the weaker.

This is a splendid piece of rhetoric, built on a quite embarrassing and sarcastic *argumentum ad hominem*. It characterizes Brennus very well, but also problematizes the view of other people, mentioned earlier in the *Life* (6.3), that Rome would never have become so famous and powerful without divine assistance. Brennus takes a very different stand on this issue and such confrontation of alternative perspectives obviously contributes to the zetetic dynamics of this *Life*. Moreover, Brennus' reply shows with merciless precision that the Romans had themselves few scruples or moral concerns in their past history. Their pragmatic policy indeed recalls a Themistoclean attitude.

This is confirmed by the sequel of the conversation. The Roman envoys see that their attempts are to no avail and therefore decide to incite the Clusians against the Gauls and even participate in the fight (17.6–7). In condemning such inappropriate behaviour (17.8), Brennus has a point – ambassadors should not take up arms – as even the Roman Senate has to acknowledge (18.1). The people, however, pay no heed to such concerns (18.3). The Gauls attack Rome and the Romans soon get into serious trouble. After a long siege, they finally agree to buy their freedom for a thousand pounds of gold, but the Gauls tamper with the scales and Brennus scornfully abuses his military preponderance. The Romans are at a loss (28.7):

Some of the Romans were incensed and thought they ought to go back again with their gold and endure the siege. Others urged acquiescence in the mild injustice. Their shame lay, they argued, not in giving more, but in giving at all. This they consented to do because of the emergency; it was not honourable, but it was necessary (οὐ καλῶς ἀλλ᾽ ἀναγκαίως).

Here we encounter the same motif of conflict between a more principled attitude and a willingness to set aside concerns for what is honourable. Here, too, the Roman people are prepared to prefer the useful to the noble course and thus adopt a basically Themistoclean approach. However, this also constitutes an interesting reversal of the pattern described in the *Life of Themistocles*. There, it was the protagonist who had a distinct preference for pragmatic decisions, whereas the Athenian people were more concerned with justice. Here, it is not Camillus but the people who are more prone to focus on what is useful (see also 7.6). In this light, the whole section about the Gallic invasion has a moral relevance, developing as it does the central moral issue of the pair. Furthermore, the contrast between the pragmatic behaviour of both Gauls and Romans, on the one hand, and Camillus' policy, on the other, throws additional light on the latter's decisions and character.

During the Gallic invasion, Camillus at first lives a quiet and sequestered life in Ardea, although he has not turned his back on Rome (23.2) – contrary to Themistocles, who sought refuge with the Persian king. He assumes the command of the Ardeans and gains a victory over the Gauls (23.3–7). As a result, many Romans join his side and ask him to take the command (24.1–3). Themistocles would have welcomed their offer with open arms. But Camillus is no Themistocles: he declines and declares that the citizens on the Capitol should first legally elect him as their commander (24.3). Is this stubbornness? Coriolanus-like rancour? Or sweet revenge? Plutarch rather presents it as a telling example of caution (*eulabeia*) and nobleness (*kalokagathia*) that wins general admiration (24.4). Even when obtaining such a great opportunity to rescue Rome, Camillus insists on obedience to the laws. Again, this reminds us more of Aristides than of Themistocles.

Yet Camillus' policy, honourable though it may be, raises an obvious difficulty: it is far from easy to reach the citizens on the Capitol (24.4). The problem is solved by the ambitious Pontius Cominius, who ventures the extremely dangerous journey to Rome and succeeds in mounting the Capitoline hill and delivering Camillus' message to the Senate.[26] When the Senate has indeed appointed Camillus dictator, Pontius repeats his gallant deed, again steals through the lines of the Gauls, and reports the decision of the Senate to Camillus (25.1–5). This interesting episode is not without significant moral relevance, as it shows that the pragmatic Themistoclean course is not a *conditio sine qua non* of success. An alternative *prohairesis* (fundamental choice) that respects the demands of justice may require more boldness and be much more dangerous, but turns out equally successful.

---

[26] Duff 2010: 63 points out that Pontius' ambition recalls that of Themistocles: 'The brief parallel might be read as a reminder that ambition, although it can get out of hand and become dangerous, is necessary for the performance of great exploits: men like Themistocles and Cominius are needed at such times of crises.' We may add that Pontius' boldness, while recalling that of Themistocles, is not opposed to Camillus' vigour (τῷ δραστηρίῳ; 36.1) either.

Or does it? Simplifying moral conclusions are seldom correct in Plutarch and, here as well, reality proves to be more complex. The Gauls find the route that Pontius has taken and at night climb the hill. At that critical moment, Rome is about to be destroyed. The watchers are sleeping, the Gauls ready to take the citadel, with neither man nor dog being aware of their approach, but (27.2–3)

there were some sacred geese near the temple of Juno, which were usually fed without stint, but at that time, since provisions barely sufficed for the garrison alone, they were neglected and in evil plight. The creature is naturally sharp of hearing and afraid of every noise, and these, being specially wakeful and restless by reason of their hunger, quickly perceived the approach of the Gauls, dashed at them with loud cries, and so awakened all the garrison.

The attack of the Gauls is repelled, and somewhat later Camillus arrives with his army, just in time to prevent the ignoble ransom. After all the perils, his way of dealing with the situation bears fruit at last, since he can now act as the legitimate ruler of Rome and overrule all those willing to compromise and preferring the necessary to the honourable (29.3).

And thus Rome is saved. All's well that ends well? Yes indeed, though not immediately so, for there remains another difficult problem that has to be solved first. Rome is in ruins and needs to be almost completely rebuilt. But why take all this trouble, when Veii is close by and provides everything the exhausted Roman people need (31.2)? Camillus would not be Camillus if he did not opt for the more difficult and noble path and plead for the reconstruction of Rome. And once again, he gains unexpected support. When Lucius Lucretius is about to declare his opinion (32.2–3),

it chanced that a centurion with a squad of the day watch passed by outside, and calling with a loud voice on the standard-bearer, bade him halt and plant his standard there, for that was the best place to settle down and stay in. The utterance fell at the crisis of their anxious thought for the uncertain future, and Lucretius said, with a devout obeisance, that he cast his vote with the god. The rest, one by one, followed his example.

Mere coincidence or evidence of providential care? Arguments for both positions could be adduced, but Plutarch leaves the question open and continues his account. Rome will be rebuilt and Camillus will gain several other important victories (33.1–41.7) which all illustrate his military talents but which need not further detain us here.

★★★

The *Themistocles–Camillus* pair lacks a concluding *synkrisis*, but the book as a whole illustrates Plutarch's project of zetetic moralism very well.[27] Apart from the clear outline of the protagonist's characters at the outset of each *Life*, Plutarch's account contains relatively few explicit and straightforward moral comments, yet the entire book thematizes and examines the moral problem of the difficult relation between usefulness and justice by juxtaposing the different policies of the two heroes. Plutarch's overall sympathy seems to lie with Camillus, but the reader looks in vain for clear-cut and definitive answers. Themistocles' choices enabled him to save Greece: a great achievement that should not be underestimated,[28] even if the means to that end were often problematic from a moral point of view. In the long run, however, his pragmatic course ended in demeaning himself before the Persian king, and suicide. Camillus resembles Aristides instead in his persistent concern for justice. This is praiseworthy, no doubt, yet he comes into no less conflict with his people, and later his honourable decisions entail the greatest dangers and difficulties. The success of such a course is far from certain: in fact, without sacred geese and a passing centurion, it would have ended in utter disaster. In this respect, Themistocles had a better control over the direct course of events, although Camillus' policy proved more advantageous in the long run.

The pair, then, clearly stimulate nuanced moral reflection, and the parallel between Themistocles and Camillus serves this end particularly well. The two heroes belong to different periods and cultures, have different characters, and often make opposite choices, yet their careers also contain several striking similarities[29] that enable Plutarch to raise in their respective *Lives* the same basic philosophical problem, to deal with it in two different ways, and thus to examine its different dimensions and perspectives. This, in short, is ingenious parallelism in the service of zetetic moralism, providing much food for moral reflection...and imitation.

It should be clear by now precisely what this imitation means. The reader should not slavishly copy Themistocles or Camillus. This would not be possible, since they will never find themself in exactly

---

[27] The most likely hypothesis is that the *synkrisis* is lost: see Swain 1992: 111; Duff 1999b: 253; Larmour 2014: 410; *contra* Pelling 2002: 377–82. Discussions also in Erbse 1956: 403–6; Larmour 1992: 4175–7; Duff 2011b: 258–9.

[28] Cf. Duff 2008b: 165–6 and 2010: 53 on the recurrence of the motif of greatness in the *Life of Themistocles*.

[29] See esp. Larmour 1992: 4176–8.

the same situation. History repeats itself, no doubt, but always with significant variations. The readers should therefore remain who they are, but their careful reading of this pair can help them in understanding the relation between virtue and usefulness in all its complexity. Readers can ask themselves what Themistocles or Camillus would have done in their situation (cf. *De prof. in virt.* 85A–B) and then, inspired by the heroes' decisions, translate their new insights into well-considered deeds.

2. Sertorius–Eumenes

Sertorius–Eumenes is one of the few books in which the Roman hero comes first. Several scholars have argued that Plutarch shows Sertorius in the best possible light, which seems to suggest a fairly straightforward, unproblematizing moralism.[30] Eumenes seems to receive less sympathy and his *Life* is also less appreciated among modern scholars.[31] Moreover, we are here dealing with two generals. As early as the first chapter, Sertorius is included among the most warlike (πολεμικώτατοι) of generals (*Sert.* 1.8) and the parallel between the two heroes rests on their military careers (1.11–12):

Both were born to command and given to wars of stratagem; both were exiled from their own countries; commanded foreign soldiers, and in their deaths experienced a fortune (τύχη) that was harsh and unjust; for both were the victims of plots (ἐπιβουλευθέντες), and were slain by the very men with whom they were conquering their foes.

This book, then, will contain fascinating stories of military tricks, endless fighting, and brilliant generalship, but what has all this to do with zetetic moralism? On closer inspection, it raises interesting moral questions which are already anticipated by two key terms in Plutarch's explanation of the parallel. Both heroes were often confronted with external circumstances that forced decisions upon them: *tyche* (fortune), then, and the necessity it involves, is a major issue in this book. Another one is that of confidence and loyalty, and their limits (as hinted at in the participle ἐπιβουλευθέντες). The tension

---

[30] Konrad 1994: xxx–xxxi; García Moreno 1992: 146–52 (Sertorius as an ideal ruler); Flacelière and Chambry 1973: 2–6. On Plutarch's sources, which include both very critical and positive views of Sertorius, see esp. Konrad 1994: xli–liii; also Scardigli 1979: 98–100.

[31] Geiger 1995: 185 regards it as a 'biography so inferior to the very best in the series'; cf. García Moreno 1992: 134 and Konrad 1994: xxxii–xxxiii.

between these two issues – between loyalty and necessity – thus constitutes one of the central themes throughout this book: how far should loyalty go in situations conditioned by necessity and how genuine can such loyalty actually be? These are complicated moral issues indeed.

In the first chapters of the *Life of Sertorius*, the hero is introduced as an excellent general, combining cleverness (*synesis*) with daring (*tolme*) (3.4) and distinguishing himself as a young man in several battles (3.1–4.5). Yet even at this early stage, we may wonder whether this splendid military career really results from Sertorius' own deliberate choice. For he also had rhetorical talents and acquired some influence in this way, but, so Plutarch adds, 'his brilliant successes in war turned his ambition (φιλοτιμίαν) in this direction' (2.2). It is probably not without reason that φιλοτιμίαν is the *object* of the sentence, suggesting that Sertorius is almost in spite of himself dragged away by his own military success. This anticipates the many times when his decisions will result from events which he is unable to control.

However that may be, his great military accomplishments persuade him to make a bid for the tribunate, yet he loses the election due to Sulla's opposition (4.6) and therefore joins the party of Marius and Cinna (4.6–7).[32] This decision, logical though it may be, is the direct result of a political fiasco, which raises the question of how loyal Sertorius really is to the Marian cause. Is this not merely loyalty *faute de mieux*? That will soon come to light, when Marius proposes to serve under Cinna as a private citizen. Sertorius opposes this plan, either out of personal ambition or because he fears Marius' excessive passions (5.1). Cinna agrees with Sertorius but still has a problem, since he has himself invited Marius (5.3). Sertorius replies (5.4):

Indeed, I for my part thought that Marius came of his own accord into Italy, and so I was trying to discover what was advantageous in the matter; but in your case it was not well to deliberate at all after the arrival of one who you yourself did ask to come; nay, you should have received and employed him, since a pledge leaves room for no reasoning (τῆς πίστεως μηδενὶ λογισμῷ χώραν διδούσης).

Sertorius' answer raises an interesting problem and was probably elaborated by Plutarch precisely for this goal, viz. the issue of loyalty and its importance.[33] As long as a man has made no agreement or

---

[32] For the historical background, see Konrad 1994: 59–62; I. König 2000: 445–7.
[33] The historicity of this conversation between Sertorius and Cinna has been questioned by Katz 1983: 62.

commitment whatsoever, he is free to consider the most useful strategy, but once the demands of loyalty come into play, there is no longer room for reasoning. Thus Sertorius makes loyalty an absolute value in this context. In other words, loyalty entails necessity. For Cinna, this means self-chosen necessity: he has to take the consequences of his previous decision. Sertorius, however, is confronted with a necessity to which he has to adjust himself and this is exactly what he decides to do. Nevertheless, this enforced loyalty need not imply blind obedience. When Cinna and Marius take bitter revenge on their enemies, Sertorius does not follow them and recommends moderation (5.6), thus qualifying his previous absolute statement about loyalty by his independent conduct: loyalty is certainly important, but it does not always preclude reasonable deliberation.

This appears even more clearly after the deaths of Marius and Cinna. Sertorius sees how things risk going wrong for the Marian party and warns Scipio, to no avail. Once again, necessity proves too strong and Sertorius sees only one way out: that is, to flee to Spain in order to afford a refuge (καταφυγή) for his friends (6.4).[34] This characterizes Plutarch's Sertorius very well: his decision to leave Rome for Spain is not primarily motivated by military considerations but by his concern for loyalty to his friends and by the necessity of the situation.

Yet Sertorius' first results in Spain are rather disappointing: he meets with adversity and is forced to sail with his fleet along the Spanish coast (7.1–8.1). Then he encounters sailors who have recently returned from the so-called 'Atlantic Islands' and describe them to him in the most positive terms (8.2–5). 'When Sertorius heard this, he was seized with an amazing desire to dwell in the islands and live in quiet, freed from tyranny and wars that would never end' (9.1). This is the first occurrence of a key motif that will be of paramount importance for Plutarch's general evaluation of Sertorius' character and career. It can also be found in Sallust (*Hist.* 1, fr. 87–90 Ramsey) – probably Plutarch's principal source for this *Life* – but Plutarch gives it an interesting turn. For Sallust, such an escape to the Atlantic Islands was no more than a brief and utopian dream.[35] For Plutarch, it was a

---

[34] Plutarch here considerably abridges the events; more details about the historical background of Sertorius' decision to go to Spain can be found in Strisino 2002; cf. de Michele 2005 and Konrad 1994: 73–85.

[35] McAlhany 2016; see also García Moreno 1992: 143–6 (who connects the episode with the paradoxographical tradition).

real option and we can easily see why: Sertorius' longing for these blessed islands is perfectly in line with his character as we have come to know it so far. For we have seen how his decisions are time and again dictated by necessity. In such a light, Sertorius' supposed desire to rid himself of the endless wars is not implausible, and the ideal of a quiet life (ζῆν ἐν ἡσυχίᾳ) will from now on constitute an important voice in the counterpoint of his motivations.

Here too, however, necessity proves too strong. The sailors refuse to bring Sertorius to the Atlantic Islands and the latter begins a new campaign in Africa in order to sustain the morale of his army and keep them together (9.3).[36] He now achieves great successes (9.4–5) and shows himself as a loyal and reliable ruler, complying with the requests of those who have put their trust in him (πιστεύσαντας) (9.11). Then he is asked by the Lusitanians to become their leader.[37] Their confidence in him is explained in a kind of 'second introduction', containing a lengthy discussion of Sertorius' many qualities.[38] His military talents are again underlined – his daring, his insight, his willingness to turn to ruse whenever necessary – but the positive traits of his character are also listed anew: his moderation and generosity and his insensibility to pleasure and fear (10.2–4). Sertorius incarnates the ideal ruler – or nearly so... (10.5–7):

And yet, in the last part of his life, the savage and vindictive treatment which he bestowed on his hostages would seem to show that his mildness was not natural to him, but was worn as a garment, from calculation (λογισμῷ), as necessity required (διὰ τὴν ἀνάγκην). In my opinion (ἐμοὶ δὲ...δοκεῖ), however, a virtue that is sincere and based upon reason (ἀρετὴν μὲν εἰλικρινῆ καὶ κατὰ λόγον συνεστῶσαν) could never by any fortune (τύχη) be converted into its opposite, although it is true that excellent principles and natures (προαιρέσεις καὶ φύσεις), when impaired by great and undeserved calamities, may possibly change their character (ἦθος) as the guiding genius changes. And this, I think, was the case with Sertorius when fortune at last began to forsake him; as his case grew hopeless he became harsh toward those who did him wrong.

This is a much discussed passage,[39] which raises the interesting philosophical question of the possibility of character change. Plutarch's answer is nuanced and typically enough considers two

---

[36] Konrad 1994: 111: 'P.'s explanation here shows the levelheaded, calculating, risk-taking soldier we encountered in chapters 3–6; surely it is correct.'

[37] On the role played by Sertorius' friends in Spain, see *Sert.* 22.10 and Konrad 1987.

[38] Beneker 2010: 108.

[39] See, e.g., Brenk 1977: 177–9; Wardman 1974: 132–40 (esp. 134–6); Gill 1983; Swain 1989a.

alternative views. According to the first, Sertorius' nature did not undergo any change at all: his mildness was merely dictated by necessity. This view is not a priori wrong: Plutarch endorses it in other contexts concerning other figures (see esp. *Arat.* 51.4 on Philip of Macedonia; *Sull.* 30.6 on Sulla) and it also suits the specific case of Sertorius, who, as we have seen, was continuously pursued by adversity and necessity, and who was certainly capable of such calculation. This first explanation, then, should not be dismissed too quickly and may well contain at least a kernel of truth. Yet there is also a second one, introduced by an emphatic ἐμοὶ δὲ...δοκεῖ, according to which Sertorius' nature *did* change. Plutarch there makes a clear distinction between perfect virtue and its necessary conditions. The former marks the end of a long process of moral progress; once it has finally been reached, it can no longer be lost, even under the most adverse circumstances. This conviction echoes a philosophical position that Plutarch defends elsewhere too.[40] The presence of a good nature and a correct fundamental choice (*prohairesis*), on the other hand, though an important *conditio sine qua non* of moral virtue, is not in and of itself virtue. It obviously has a decisive influence on one's character (*ēthos*), but even a good *ēthos* should not simply be equated with perfect virtue.[41] As long as this perfect virtue is not yet reached, a reversal is always possible,[42] and this is what actually happened in Sertorius' later career.

This passage thus provides a fine illustration of Plutarch's general zetetic approach in the *Parallel Lives*. Theoretical philosophical ideals about perfect virtue (ἀρετὴν εἰλικρινῆ καὶ κατὰ λόγον συνεστῶσαν) are confronted with and challenged by concrete reality. The heroes never completely embody the high philosophical ideals, nor do the *Parallel Lives* contain samples of such perfect virtue. In the famous proem to the *Cimon–Lucullus* pair, Plutarch explicitly deplores the fact that no human character is absolutely good and indisputably set towards virtue (*Cim.* 2.5). This applies to Sertorius as well: he was a noble man, no doubt, but he was not perfect and thus his cruel behaviour at the end of his life should not be explained in terms of losing

---

[40] E.g. in moral works such as *On fortune* and *Is vice a sufficient cause for unhappiness?*; see also *De tranq. an.* 475B–476A; *De virt. et vit.* 101D–E.

[41] We can improve our character (βελτιουμένῳ τὸ ἦθος, *De prof. in virt.* 85C) but we improve *towards* virtue (βελτιουμένου πρὸς ἀρετήν, 75B).

[42] Cf. *De prof. in virt.* 76C–78A on intermissions and retrogressions during the process of moral improvement; Roskam 2005b: 247–55.

virtue but as a change in his nature, *prohairesis*, and character, influenced by misfortune.

Moreover, these reflections do not come out of the blue but are closely connected to the overall theme of the book. The disloyalty shown by Sertorius' former allies, the merciless influence of necessity (ἀνάγκη), and the motif of fortune abandoning Sertorius all constitute key issues that return in this passage. The fundamental question of how all this affects Sertorius' character is a natural one and Plutarch answers it in a sensible and nuanced way. In short, this is a characteristic example of careful zetetic moralism fed by the warp and weft of history.

The next section of the *Life* presents Sertorius as an excellent general and thus confirms the correct assessment of the Lusitanians. He far surpasses his opponent Metellus (12.5–13.12; 18.1; 22.1–4), displays his cleverness in the war against the Characitani (17.1–13), and even outgenerals Pompey at Lauron (18.5–11) and after the Battle of Saguntum (21.7–8). In all these instances, his military skills bring the greatest and most capable Roman generals into serious difficulties (21.9). This is the connecting thread throughout this section of the *Life*. Sertorius is simply a particularly clever tactician and strategist. If need be, he can be very warlike (πολεμικώτατος) indeed. Furthermore, Plutarch dwells at length on the way in which Sertorius knew how to gain and keep the loyalty of the Lusitanians. After all, it is not obvious that a foreign people would be willing to be led by a Roman general. Many were attracted by Sertorius' mildness and efficiency (11.2),[43] others were deceived by his cunning tricks. He made clever use of a white doe in order to take advantage of the barbarians' superstition (11.3–8; 20.1–5). But he also converted their forces into a well-ordered army, gave them a beautiful array, and provided the sons of their most distinguished families with a Greek and Roman education (14.1–4).[44] All this results in an ambivalent picture of Sertorius. On the one hand, he takes diligent care of the troops which fortune has granted him, almost like a loving father. On the other hand, this loving father is also a clever manipulator. His concern for well-equipped and well-ordered barbarian troops of course suits his own purposes as well, and, while telling (λόγῳ) the barbarians that he educates their sons, he in reality (ἔργῳ) makes hostages of them

---

[43] On this balance between mildness and efficiency, see also *Sert.* 6.9 and 18.11.

[44] The last of these topics is discussed by Scherr 2015; cf. Konrad 1994: 141–4; Payen 2002: 106–8.

(14.3). We begin to wonder how sincere his loyalty actually is (the more so in light of Plutarch's comments in Chapter 10).

Who, then, is the real Sertorius and where does his loyalty really lie? The answer to this pressing question is elaborated in the following chapters, where he appears as a magnanimous man (22.5; 23.1) and a true patriot (ἀνὴρ φιλόπατρις; 22.7). This, again, is by no means obvious: as the commander of the Lusitanians, he can be regarded as the public enemy of Rome.[45] Plutarch, however, underlines Sertorius' great loyalty to Rome. The general creates a new Senate in Spain, consisting of Roman senators who have joined his cause (22.5), and his aim is not to strengthen the barbarians against Rome but rather to regain freedom for the Romans (22.6). This echoes Plutarch's earlier statement that Sertorius has fled to Spain in order to afford a refuge (καταφυγή) for his friends (6.4). From the later passages we can see that he has not forgotten his intentions, and thus follows a perfectly consistent policy. Yet this unfaltering loyalty towards his friends and fatherland also generates questions about his loyalty towards the Lusitanians, whom he apparently uses as mere means for his own goal. This impression is corroborated by his proposal to Metellus and Pompey (22.7–8):

> as a victor he sent to Metellus and Pompey expressing his readiness to lay down his arms and lead the life of a private citizen if he could get the privilege of returning home, since, as he said, he preferred to live in Rome as her meanest citizen rather than to live in exile from his country and be called supreme ruler of all the rest of the world together.

Once again, this gives a good idea of what kind of person Sertorius really is, and it is no coincidence that in such a context the ideal of a quiet life reappears (22.12). Sertorius is not a man who pursues the greatest ambitions, and his military accomplishments are essentially engendered by necessity.[46] He would freely give all of them away for a peaceful life. Yet this attitude problematizes his loyalty to the Lusitanians even further. Indeed, abandoning his present life and military power would mean leaving his barbarian allies and his Roman friends to fend for themselves.

---

[45] I. König 2000.

[46] His preference for a simple, anonymous life in Rome is diametrically opposed to that of Caesar (*Caes.* 11.4). See Konrad 1994: 189; Beneker 2010: 114–15.

Moreover, Sertorius decides to make a treaty with Mithridates, Rome's arch-enemy. Here as well, Plutarch presents Sertorius' policy in the best possible light, as one more example of his magnanimity (23.1). For indeed, Sertorius is not prepared to unquestioningly accept Mithridates' proposals, even though his entourage eagerly supports the plan, but flatly refuses to hand over a Roman province to the king (23.2–7). And his principled course bears fruit, because Mithridates consents to Sertorius' alternative proposal and a treaty is finally made (24.1–3). Once again, Sertorius succeeds in using the support of the barbarians without compromising his high Roman ideals. He sends his general Marcus Marius to Asia and, when the latter conquers several cities, Mithridates voluntarily follows him as his vassal (24.4).

The final chapters of the *Life* show us the precariousness of a loyalty that basically rests on necessity. We have seen so far that Sertorius pursues the interests of his Roman friends, providing them with a safe refuge (καταφυγή), even if this course is only an inferior option (a δεύτερος πλοῦς as Plato put it) enforced by necessity, since the ultimate ideal of a tranquil life is beyond reach. Yet it will be these friends who betray Sertorius' confidence. The villain in this case is Perpenna, repeatedly characterized as a worthless and conceited fellow (15.2; 25.2). He begins to set the senators and the men of equal rank in Sertorius' circle against the general, pointing to their paradoxical situation. They have come to Spain, so he argues, because they refused to obey the omnipotent Sulla and preferred to live as free men, but they have now of their own free will become the slaves of Sertorius the exile (25.3). Perpenna may be wicked and his disloyalty may be blamed, yet he does make an interesting point. What, after all, has remained of Sertorius' honourable ideal? And what will be their fate if Sertorius is allowed to lead a carefree, quiet life? These are challenging questions indeed, concealed behind the sophistic rationalization of Perpenna's wickedness.

Subsequently, the loyalty of the barbarians is put to the test as well. The conspirators repeatedly maltreat them and provoke rebellion (25.4), which entails Sertorius' cruel reaction anticipated in Chapter 10: he kills the sons of the Iberians who are being educated in Osca and sells others into slavery (25.6). Plutarch adds no further comment but the reader can now reconsider the issue in light of new evidence.[47]

---

[47] The moral evaluation of Sertorius' deed has been discussed in *Sert.* 10.5–7 and is recalled in the brief phrase ἐκ τῆς προτέρας ἐπιεικείας καὶ πραότητος μεταβαλόντα ('having laid aside his former clemency and mildness'; 25.6).

In fact, Sertorius' loyalty to the barbarians is here further questioned. It turns out to be a mere means for his own purposes, which makes us wonder whether the first explanation proposed in Chapter 10 is not, after all, the correct one!

Perpenna's conspiracy will lead to Sertorius' death: he is killed at a symposium, without associates and trusting his friends (26.8–11; cf. *Comp. Sert. et Eum.* 2.6). Yet that is not the end of the story. The last chapter of the *Life* briefly deals with the fate of the conspirators. Perpenna, worthless as ever, is defeated by Pompey and promises to show him Sertorius' private correspondence (27.3). Thus the motif of loyalty returns for the last time: by being prepared to betray Sertorius' powerful friends in Rome, Perpenna even proves perfidious after Sertorius' death. Yet he is brought to justice for this perfidy (27.4–5):

Pompey, then, did not act in this emergency like a young man, but like one whose understanding was very well matured and disciplined, and so freed Rome from great revolutionary terrors. For he got together those letters and all the papers of Sertorius and burned them, without reading them himself or allowing anyone else to do so; and Perpenna himself he speedily put to death, through fear that seditions and disturbances might arise if the names of the correspondents of Sertorius were communicated to anybody.

Pompey's action is praised as wise statesmanship (cf. also *Pomp.* 20.6–8) but it also provides a telling conclusion to the theme of loyalty explored in this *Life*. Pompey, Sertorius' most formidable opponent, is the one who ultimately proves most loyal to him after his death. Here at last, loyalty towards Sertorius and his friends is combined with genuine loyalty towards Rome.

The very last words of the *Life* recall Sertorius' ideal of a quiet life. Such an ideal is finally reached by Aufidius, the only one of the conspirators who has managed to escape, but there is little reason for envy here. In fact, his situation is diametrically opposed to Sertorius' ideal. Whereas Sertorius dreamt of living a tranquil life as a respected citizen in Rome, Aufidius grows old in a barbarian village, as a poor and hated man (27.7).

★★★

In the *Life of Eumenes*, Plutarch further explores the same moral questions. From the very beginning, Eumenes is introduced as one of the cleverest (συνέσει) and most loyal (πίστει) friends of Alexander

(1.4). His *synesis* resembles that of Sertorius and will bring him great military success. His *pistis* to Alexander reintroduces the central theme of loyalty, which thus becomes one of the most important leitmotifs in the entire book. In the *Life of Eumenes*, the hero's loyalty to the Macedonian royal house will often be underlined and equally often be questioned. For Eumenes, loyalty never means blind obedience. This already appears in the first chapters, where Plutarch tells how Eumenes more than once comes into collision with Alexander (2.1–10). Moreover, these conflicts are caused by Eumenes' greed, so much so that Plutarch even characterizes the hero as πανοῦργος and πιθανός: a persuasive rogue willing to do anything (2.10). This label henceforth puts his behaviour into perspective. Eumenes' loyalty, then, is always somewhat suspect.

This first impression is soon confirmed. In the conflict between the heavy infantry and the officers, Eumenes does not commit himself and assumes the role of reconciler (3.1–2). At first sight, such a course has much to be commended, even more so since Plutarch actually advises his young friend Menemachus to follow such a conciliatory policy if need be (*Praec. ger. reip.* 824B). Yet, in Eumenes' case, it also implies a wily dissimulation of his own sincere convictions. Eumenes clearly sides with the officers (3.1) but strategically conceals this loyalty, which results in a conflict between his true view and his words.[48] This, then, is a typical action of Eumenes the *panourgos*. Moreover, he cleverly takes advantage of his status as a foreigner (ξένος): he claims that, being an outsider, he should not intervene in a conflict among Macedonians (3.1). Here we come across a motif that will become very important in later chapters of the *Life*. For the time being, this approach does not harm Eumenes, to say the least: when the conflict is settled, he is appointed satrap of Cappadocia, Paphlagonia, and the southern coast of the Pontic Sea as far as Trapezus (3.3).

Somewhat later, Leonnatus tells Eumenes in confidence (πιστεύσας) that he intends to lay claim to Macedonia, and asks for his collaboration (3.6–9). Eumenes, however, declines the invitation, flees to Perdiccas, tells him everything, and accordingly gains great influence (3.10–12). Again, this episode leaves the reader with mixed feelings. By refusing Leonnatus' offer, Eumenes confirms his reputation as a loyal friend.

---

[48] See *Eum.* 3.1: τῇ μὲν γνώμῃ...τῷ δὲ λόγῳ ('in his opinion...but in what he said...'). Caesar is similarly criticized for his cunning reconciliation of Pompey and Crassus (*Pomp.* 47.2). On Solon's compromising between the poor and the rich, see *Sol.* 14.1–2; Leão 2003–4: 54.

He sticks to his word and, as is explicitly underlined at the end of the chapter, does not wish to be separated from the kings (τῶν βασιλέων ἀπολείπεσθαι μὴ βουλόμενος; 3.14). Yet the question remains to what extent his decision rests on genuine loyalty. In fact, Plutarch mentions two possible motivations behind Eumenes' course and neither has anything to do with loyalty: either he was afraid of Antipater or he was sceptical of Leonnatus' capacities. Eumenes, then, is primarily a clever man concerned with his own interest.

Nevertheless, from this moment on, Eumenes' loyalty gradually comes to the fore. Perdiccas uses him as an efficient and faithful guardian (δραστηρίου τε καὶ πιστοῦ φύλακος; 4.1). Eumenes prepares a military campaign against Craterus and Antipater and shows himself as a competent general (5.1–5). Craterus and Antipater then propose that he should come over to their side. Their offer is certainly a very attractive one: Eumenes will be confirmed as satrap and will even receive more resources and a better position (5.6). Yet he refuses: he is willing to reconcile Craterus and Perdiccas but not to compromise his honour (5.7–8). Again, Eumenes plays the part of the noble reconciler, but this time the accent is more on his loyalty to Perdiccas than on his concern for personal benefit. Plutarch begins to present Eumenes in a more positive light: the *panourgos* becomes more and more *pistos*.

When a confrontation between Eumenes and Craterus becomes unavoidable, the former once again shows his great talents as a clever strategist. He makes the appropriate preparations and decides to keep his Macedonians out of the battle, for fear that they would defect to the enemy (7.1–2). Eumenes knows perfectly well how to secure his soldiers' loyalty but, at this stage of his career, he deems it safer not to overestimate the dedication of the Macedonians, which is a wise decision indeed. Thus, the theme of loyalty has become more complex than in the *Life of Sertorius*. There, the barbarians were outsiders in a conflict between two Roman factions and there was no evident reason why the Lusitanians would desert to Pompey and Metellus. They only began to revolt after much provocation. Eumenes, on the other hand, is himself the outsider. He commands as a *xenos* (3.1) Macedonian troops that fight against Macedonians. Under such circumstances, it is far less obvious how to keep the army obedient (see also 5.3; 6.2–3; 6.6), and this will be a recurrent motif in the remainder of the *Life*.

After a fierce battle, Eumenes emerges victorious and Craterus dies on the battlefield (7.13):

When Eumenes learned of the fate of Craterus and had ridden up to where he lay, and saw that he was still alive and conscious, he dismounted, wept bitterly, clasped his hand, and had many words of abuse for Neoptolemus, and many words of pity for Craterus in his evil fortune (τῆς τύχης), and for himself in the necessity (τῆς ἀνάγκης) which had brought him into a conflict with a friend and comrade (ἀνδρὶ φίλῳ καὶ συνήθει), where he must suffer or do this harm.

Thus the clash between necessity and loyalty, the leitmotif of the *Life of Sertorius*, reappears but also gains a new dimension. Faithfulness is now closely connected with friendship, for Eumenes and Craterus have a common history as companions of Alexander. This motif will repeatedly return in the *Life of Eumenes*, since all the wars that are related in it are wars between former friends. The problem of loyalty is thus defined and examined from a new perspective, but necessity, too, plays its inexorable role.

The result of Eumenes' victory over Craterus is fame and envy – a recurrent motif in many books of the *Parallel Lives*. Remarkably enough, both friends and enemies agree that he has made use of the Macedonians to slay their best man (8.1). Eumenes' precarious position as a stranger keeps popping up. According to Plutarch's interpretation of the facts, Sertorius was loyal to Rome until his last day, but can such a principled loyalty be expected from a *xenos* like Eumenes? We have seen that his loyalty has gradually been emphasized in the previous chapters, but his non-Macedonian descent remains his Achilles heel and the consensus among both friends and enemies surely makes the question even more pressing. Yet Eumenes succeeds in gaining the goodwill of his soldiers by giving them their pay (8.9–11) and, when a price is set on his head, his Macedonians form a bodyguard for him (8.11). For the time being, then, the Macedonians are faithful to their foreign commander, although their loyalty rests on money rather than on common Macedonian origin.

After Craterus' death, Eumenes has to fight Antigonus. In this campaign, he faces several difficulties (9.1):

Now prosperity lifts even men of inferior natures to higher thoughts, so that they appear to be invested with a certain greatness and majesty as they look down from their lofty state; but the truly magnanimous and constant man reveals himself rather in his behaviour under disasters and misfortunes. And so it was with Eumenes.

This recalls the key Chapter 10 from the *Life of Sertorius*, where Plutarch tells how the noble Sertorius later degenerated when confronted with adversity. In this respect, Eumenes, initially characterized as a suspect *panourgos*, proves to be superior in the long run. When he is defeated by Antigonus (through treachery), he punishes the traitor and returns to bury his dead. Even Antigonus admires his boldness (τὸ θάρσος) and steadfastness (τὴν εὐστάθειαν) (9.5). Eumenes again shows himself as a bold general and a reliable friend. Even when he is betrayed, he remains faithful to his soldiers who have given their lives for him, and he takes care of their burial.

At this point of the *Life*, then, Eumenes proves superior to Sertorius in his loyalty to his soldiers. Yet the *panourgos* has not entirely disappeared. At a certain moment, Eumenes has an excellent opportunity to seize Antigonus' baggage, but he understands that this would harm rather than benefit him, as the booty would restrict his freedom of movement. Since he is unable to stop his Macedonians, he sends a secret message to Menander, the commander of Antigonus' baggage, and warns him to withdraw to the hills, as if being concerned for him as an old friend and comrade (ὡς κηδόμενος αὐτοῦ φίλου γεγονότος καὶ συνήθους; 9.8). This sounds honourable indeed and Eumenes is even praised for his deed among Antigonus' Macedonians (9.11), but Antigonus himself easily understands Eumenes' true intentions and explains that the latter's supposed loyalty only serves his own interests (9.12). This is no unequivocal example of true friendship but rather one of wily calculation. Moreover, Eumenes now persuades his own soldiers to abandon him and sends several of his friends away (10.1–2).[49] His motivation to do so is ambivalent, to say the least: he shows concern and friendship but also pursues his own advantage. A conference with Antigonus follows. The two embrace each other as old friends (10.5), yet Eumenes makes high demands. He is not content with his safety but requires that he should be confirmed as a satrap and recover his possessions. Those present, so Plutarch adds, admire his lofty spirit (φρόνημα) and courage (εὐτολμίαν) (10.6). This, however, is only one side of the picture. It also recalls Eumenes the *panourgos*, always concerned with his own interests. Tellingly, not the slightest reference is made to the theme of Eumenes' loyalty to the Macedonian royal house, which therefore seems irrelevant in the present situation. Moreover, Eumenes' behaviour is in striking contrast with that of Sertorius, who was prepared to accept a quiet life.[50] Here, loyalty primarily comes from Antigonus: he keeps to his

---

[49] At least, this is how Plutarch presents the matter. In reality, many soldiers simply deserted to the enemy: see Bosworth 1992: 79.

[50] Plutarch will make this point in the concluding comparison: *Comp. Sert. et Eum.* 2.1–5.

word and even protects Eumenes with his own body against his soldiers (10.8).

The *Life of Eumenes* is thus characterized by a fluctuating movement in which the protagonist's loyalty is alternately questioned and confirmed. In the previous scene, we have encountered Eumenes the *panourgos*; in the next scene Eumenes the *pistos* will take over again. Antigonus makes a new attempt to win Eumenes over and proposes a treaty with an oath in which the kings are hardly mentioned. Eumenes, however, adds the names of Olympias and the kings and proposes his new version to the Macedonians, who consider his alternative the more just one (12.2–7). In this way, Eumenes' loyalty to the Macedonian kings is once more emphasized. He refuses Antigonus' offer, even though he foresees difficulties, and consequently stands by his principles, keeping faithful to the legitimate kings, although it implies that he will have to flee. This account, however, is a misrepresentation of what actually happened. In all likelihood, Eumenes did accept Antigonus' proposal and even became his ally for some time, until he received a mandate from the royal family.[51] Plutarch therefore replaces the historical *panourgos* with an honourable and principled *pistos*. Interestingly, this adaptation further implies that a comparison with Sertorius once again works out in Eumenes' favour. Sertorius likewise changed Mithridates' proposal, yet he in the end decided to make a treaty with the enemy of Rome. Eumenes is less prepared to accept such questionable agreements and consequently remains loyal to the legitimate royal family.

It is not surprising in such a perspective that Polysperchon and King Philip grant Eumenes authority to fight against Antigonus and provide him with financial means and new troops (13.1–2). This is the beginning of a new military campaign for Eumenes, who again faces the difficulty of winning the loyalty of his army. He succeeds in winning the generals of the Silver Shields by taking advantage of their superstition. He tells them how Alexander has appeared to him in a dream and promised him to attend their deliberations and assist them when they meet in a royal tent with a throne reserved for him (13.4–8). Eumenes' clever trick recalls Sertorius' equally clever use of the white doe, but Eumenes also employs the generals' loyalty towards Alexander. Cleverness and loyalty are thus again combined and Eumenes the *panourgos* joins Eumenes the *pistos*. He

---

[51] See, e.g., Anson 1977; Bosworth 1992: 66–7; Hadley 2001: 18–20.

also buys the loyalty of his opponents, by borrowing large amounts of money – yet another clever trick (13.12–13). The soldiers, however, trust his military talents and want only him as their commander (14.1–16.1), so that other generals become envious – the usual refrain – and conspire against Eumenes. When the latter hears about this, he makes his will and destroys his personal documents because he does not want to get his friends into trouble (16.4). Sertorius was not given this chance and depended post mortem on the goodwill and understanding of his enemy Pompey. Eumenes is luckier, and shows his loyal concern for his friends even in the face of death.

In the battle that follows, he gains an overwhelming victory but loses his baggage, due to the lax fighting of his officer Peucestas (16.9). Antigonus then proposes to Teutamus, the commander of the Silver Shields, that he should restore the baggage to them and he offers to treat them kindly, provided they hand over Eumenes to him (17.1–2). This time, his invitation to betrayal proves successful, for the Silver Shields accept the offer, arrest Eumenes, and send him to Antigonus. When he is led through the Macedonians, Eumenes is allowed to address his troops for the last time (17.6–11):

'What trophy, you basest of Macedonians, could Antigonus have so much desired to set up over your defeat, as this which you yourselves are now erecting by delivering up your general as a prisoner? Was it not a dreadful thing, then, that in the hour of your victory you should acknowledge yourselves defeated for the sake of your baggage, implying that victory lies in your possessions and not in your arms, but you must also send your leader as a ransom for that baggage? As for me, then, you lead me away undefeated, a victor over my enemies, a victim of my fellow-soldiers; but as for you, by Zeus the god of armies and by the gods who hallow oaths, I bid you slay me here with your own hands. Even should I be slain there, it will be wholly your work. Nor will Antigonus find any fault; for he wants a dead and not a living Eumenes. And if you would spare your own hands, one of mine, if released, will suffice to do the business. And if you cannot trust me with a sword (οὐ πιστεύετέ μοι ξίφος), cast me under the feet of your elephants, all bound as I am. If you do this, I will absolve you from your guilt towards me, holding that you have shown yourselves most pious and righteous in your dealings with your own general.'

This is an impressive piece of rhetoric, swollen with true *pathos*, but also containing a challenging message. The full emphasis is on the perfidy of the Macedonians, who go so far as to hand over their own general for the sake of their baggage. Look how low they have sunk! But no less emphasis falls on Eumenes' loyalty. Even if they kill him (in whatever way they please), he claims that he will not find fault with them but rather consider their deed as most devout and just. Justin adds that Eumenes became angry when he failed to convince the Macedonians and that he even cursed them (14.4.10–14). Plutarch keeps silent about this and prefers to underscore Eumenes' loyalty to the very end. Thus, he again contrasts the hero with his counterpart Sertorius, who cruelly took revenge on his allies at the end of his life. Here too, Eumenes, the *pistos*, appears in a better light.

As a result of Eumenes' moving speech, many are dejected, but the Silver Shields dismiss his words as nonsense (φλυαροῦντι) (18.2):

It was not so dreadful a thing, they said, that a pest (ὄλεθρος) from the Chersonesus should come to grief for having harassed Macedonians with infinite wars, as that the best of the soldiers of Philip and Alexander, after all their toils, should in their old age be robbed of their rewards and get their support from others, and that their wives should sleep the third night now with their enemies.

This is a completely different perspective, which completes another important motif of this *Life*.[52] Until the very end, Eumenes has remained the *xenos* who commands Macedonian troops, the outsider who has caused so much trouble for the Macedonians, the ὄλεθρος from the Chersonesus.[53] How can such a foreigner lay credible claims to loyalty? From their perspective, Eumenes is indeed no more than a *panourgos*.

This confrontation of two diametrically opposed perspectives, inspired by the zetetic spirit that permeates the whole book, is completed by the addition of a third one, viz. that of Antigonus. His reaction brings out the intricacy of the whole matter. He cannot endure to see Eumenes because of their former friendship and he is long in doubt as to what he should do (18.4–6). His doubts indirectly reveal the value of the different perspectives. An ὄλεθρος deserves to be killed without further ado; a friend should be embraced and pardoned. But what about a friendly ὄλεθρος? Antigonus cannot sit on the fence, and his final decision is not to run with the hare and hunt with the hounds but to kill both the hare and the hounds. In the end, the claims of friendship prove too weak and Antigonus decides to kill his former friend, while allowing his friends to burn the body, place the ashes in a silver urn, and return it to Eumenes' wife and children (19.1–2).

---

[52] In all likelihood, Plutarch developed this perspective *ad hoc*, for the majority of the Silver Shields were probably not led by concerns for ethnicity: see Roisman 2011: 72–3.

[53] See Bosworth 1992: 64–5 on the parallel with *Sert.* 6.6.

Yet the Silver Shields fare no better. Although Antigonus promised to treat them well, he does not keep his word but sends them to Arachosia, requesting its governor to destroy them in every possible way. Of all the conspirators against Sertorius, only one man survived, albeit in the most ignoble circumstances, but, of the Silver Shields, not one man 'would ever return to Macedonia or behold the Grecian sea' (19.3).

★★★

The penetrating internal comparison of Sertorius and Eumenes throughout the book is completed by a short but thought-provoking formal *synkrisis*. Its first part focuses on a few external similarities and differences in their careers. Both commanded great armies as strangers, but Eumenes had to cope with more opposition (*Comp. Sert. et Eum.* 1.1–9). Plutarch here recalls some obvious matters of fact, but these, of course, are also relevant for moral reflection. We have seen how Sertorius' and Eumenes' position as strangers raised interesting moral questions and how Eumenes' case was more complicated than that of Sertorius. Plutarch's evaluation in the *synkrisis* is thus basically in line with his account in the two *Lives*.

Of course, Plutarch could have added many more correspondences between the two heroes (with respect to details too), yet that would perhaps have resulted in a tedious and pedantic list. The attentive reader is more than able to do this themself if they wish. All those correspondences make the book *Sertorius–Eumenes* a very successful pair. Plutarch generally had a keen eye for parallels. He saw the many opportunities and did not hesitate to fashion two heroes after one another if that would further his comparative purposes. In this book, he has gone far in this approach. The result is an in-depth exploration of the different dimensions of challenging moral questions.

This moral interest more directly surfaces in the second part of the *synkrisis*. Eumenes there appears as fond of war (φιλοπόλεμος) and contentious (φιλόνικος) (2.1). Plutarch argues that, if he had been content with second place, Antigonus would gladly have given that to him, but he was always eager for power and even led by greed (2.2–3; 2.5). Thus the concluding comparison returns to Eumenes the *panourgos*: this is how he is introduced at the very outset of his *Life* and this is how he appears at the very end. It is striking that his loyalty to the Macedonian royal family – whether real or feigned – is not even mentioned here. The *Life* is certainly more detailed in this respect, but this straightforward evaluation is, in a sense, no less problematizing, inviting the reader to return to the essential question of where Eumenes' real loyalty lay.

In Sertorius' case, the answer to this question is easier: he loved a quiet life (ἡσυχία) and regarded war as a dire necessity (2.1–5). This motif has been important in the *Life of Sertorius* and is now underlined once more. Again, Plutarch no longer raises the question of Sertorius' (alleged or real) loyalty to Rome and to the barbarians. At this moment, he is rather interested in the ultimate motivations of his heroes, in a movement of searching ἀποθεώρησις ('distanced reflection'). This, of course, is not a denial of the nuanced and more detailed story of the preceding *Lives*, but a new horizon against which the story can be reconsidered and reassessed.

Finally, Plutarch briefly compares the deaths of Sertorius and Eumenes. The former died unawares, because he trusted his friends (2.6); the latter tried to escape and even supplicated, thus making his enemy master not only of his body but of his soul as well (2.6; 2.8). This is a severe Platonic verdict that is somewhat discordant with the account of the *Life of Eumenes*,[54] although it is consistent with the general view of Eumenes in the *synkrisis*, which focuses on Eumenes the *panourgos* rather than the *pistos*. This assessment seems to support the view that Plutarch ultimately preferred Sertorius to Eumenes on moral grounds.[55] This is not impossible, yet perhaps the matter is less simple than that. A careful reading of the two *Lives* shows that Eumenes was superior to Sertorius in several respects, on moral grounds as well as others. It would certainly be an oversimplification to tip the scale now in favour of Sertorius in every respect, and Plutarch definitely does not do this himself in the *synkrisis*.

What, then, can Plutarch's readers learn from this book? Will they become better generals by reading it?[56] Although it cannot be denied that they can pick up an inspiring idea here and there, that is probably not Plutarch's first goal. A straightforward imitation of models like Sertorius and Eumenes is far too simplistic. In this book, Plutarch is interested in a much more fundamental, philosophical reflection about complicated moral problems. Together with his readers, he pursues deeper insight into loyalty at different levels, into the relation

---

[54] Duff 1999b: 275.

[55] Thus, e.g., Bosworth 1992: 56–7; García Moreno 1992: 134.

[56] This is the view of Jacobs 2018, who sees the *Parallel Lives* as pragmatic biography (see above, Chapter V, §1).

between goal and means, into the heroes' fundamental decision (*prohairesis*) and its stability in adverse circumstances. These are huge questions indeed and the readers never receive easy, ready-made answers. They do, however, receive much interesting food for thought. And thus, the pair *Sertorius–Eumenes* exemplifies zetetic moralism at its best.

VII. REASON AS A MYSTAGOGUE: PLUTARCH'S VIEW OF GOD

It is not only Alexander alone who has the right to be proud because he rules over many men, but no less right to be proud have they who have true notions concerning the gods.

This quotation from a letter of Aristotle to Antipater (fr. 664 Rose) repeatedly occurs in the Plutarchan corpus.[1] Plutarch clearly agreed. He regarded rational thinking about the gods as a human's most divine possession and as the most decisive influence on their happiness (*De Is. et Os.* 378C–D), and, as we have already seen, he adopted the Platonic phrase of ὁμοίωσις θεῷ (κατὰ τὸ δυνατόν) ('assimilation to God [as far as possible]') as the final end of life (see above, Chapter II, §1).[2] In several ways, then, God is, as it were, the keystone that lends bearing power to the whole vault of Plutarch's philosophical thinking. A correct understanding of his thought therefore presupposes a deeper insight into his conception of God.

1. A god of philosophers

This, however, is by no means easy. There is no extant work by Plutarch that contains a systematic and comprehensive discussion of his view of God.[3] Thus, his image of God has to be inferred from specific arguments, isolated passages, and *obiter dicta* that are scattered all over his work, at the risk of unjustified generalizations. Nevertheless, the gist of his view of God is clear.[4]

Essentially, Plutarch's God is the Demiurge of Plato's *Timaeus*. In that sense, his idiosyncratic interpretation of this dialogue (see above,

---

[1] *De prof. in virt.* 78D–E; *De tranq. an.* 472E; *De se ipsum laud.* 545A; cf. Van der Stockt 1999b.

[2] Such assimilation to God can be reached through knowledge (*De Is. et Os.* 351C and 351E; *fr.* 143) or virtue (*De sera num.* 550D; *Ad princ. iner.* 781A; *Arist.* 6.5).

[3] *On the E at Delphi*, and notably its last section, is often considered as the key source for Plutarch's thinking about God. This view, however, has recently been challenged, and rightly so; see below, §7.

[4] On Plutarch's view of God, see, e.g., Latzarus 1920; Valgiglio 1988; Ferrari 1995: 231–69 and *passim*, 1996 (on *Platonic question* 2), and 2005a; Dillon 2002; Hirsch-Luipold 2005b and 2014; Brenk 2012. Different aspects of his religious thinking are also discussed in García Valdés 1994; Gallo 1996; Frazier and Leão 2010; Van der Stockt *et al.* 2010; Roig Lanzillotta and Muñoz Gallarte 2012; Hirsch-Luipold and Roig Lanzillotta 2021.

Chapter II, §3.1) is an important source of information for his thinking about God. Plutarch considers the highest God to be the father and maker of all things (*Quaest. conv.* 718A; *Quaest. Plat.* 1000E–1001C). This God dwells at the level of intelligible being, far removed from matter.[5] He is self-sufficient (*De def. or.* 413F; *Comp. Arist. et Ca. Ma.* 4.2) and perfectly good, and indeed lacks none of the virtues (*De def. or.* 423D).[6] This also implies that he cannot possibly be regarded as the cause of any evil.[7]

Moreover, God is a providential God and, although he strictly stays in his intelligible realm, far away from our corporeal world, the gap between the two levels is somehow bridged.[8] Plutarch indeed repeatedly insists that God carefully observes all the details of our earthly existence (*Sept. sap. conv.* 161F; *De sera num.* 560B and 562D). The working of this divine providence consists in overseeing and directing (ἐφορᾶν καὶ κατευθύνειν), by providing everything with its first rational principles and seeds (ἀρχὰς καὶ σπέρματα καὶ λόγους) (*De def. or.* 426A). Such an understanding of providence perfectly squares with the role of the Demiurge, who likewise brings rational order to pre-existent matter. The impact of this ordering providence can also be detected in the course of human history, especially at decisive moments or in great evolutions like the rise of Roman power or the fall of the Roman Republic.[9] Yet it also affects the life of every single individual, as appears from *On the slowness of divine punishments*.

This dialogue opens on a note of consternation. 'Epicurus' has quite aggressively attacked the doctrine of divine providence with a series of incoherent arguments and then left the company without waiting for a reply. The rest of the group need a few moments to recover, after which they decide to refute the attack by focusing in particular on the problem of God's delay in punishing criminals.[10] For Patrocleas, such delay

---

[5] See, e.g., *De Is. et Os.* 382A–C and 382F; *Ad princ. iner.* 781F; see also *De Is. et Os.* 383A and *De def. or.* 414E. On *De def. or.* 413C, see Brouillette 2010.

[6] His justice is frequently underlined (Pérez Jiménez 2005), as are his kindness and humanity: see *De sup.* 167F; *De Pyth. or.* 402A; *De sera num.* 550F and 551C; *Ad princ. iner.* 781A.

[7] *De aud. poet.* 34A–B; *De ad. et am.* 63F; *De Is. et Os.* 369A–B; *De an. procr.* 1015C; *Non posse* 1102D–E.

[8] See Opsomer 1997 and Roskam 2015a.

[9] Swain 1989b.

[10] Plutarch's choice of words in introducing the central question is not without importance. Patrocleas points to the slowness and delay of the god (τοῦ δαιμονίου) in his punishment of the wicked. This may suggest that the actual punishment is not the work of the highest God but of *daimones*, and a few other passages seem to corroborate this suggestion (552F and 555D; cf. 567C in the eschatological myth). Yet things are far more complicated. Olympichus returns to

actually emboldens criminals (548C–549B) and Olympichus adds that it undermines belief in providence without benefiting criminals at all (549B–E). 'Plutarch', who appears as the main character in this dialogue, begins by underlining the need for caution. Given our human limitations, plausibility concerning such matters is the best we can hope for (549F; 550C–D). He then argues that, by postponing punishment, God acts as an example of mildness for us. The classic ideal of ὁμοίωσις θεῷ is thus the starting point of the whole argument (550D–551C). Next, he points out that a delay of punishment makes room for moral improvement and other benefits (551C–553D) and that it ensures that the penalty comes at the right moment and in the appropriate way (553D–F).

'Plutarch' then introduces a new perspective by explicitly questioning the implicit presuppositions of all his previous arguments. Whereas these all assume that the punishment is delayed, he now shows that criminals are punished as soon as they have gone wrong. He rhetorically elaborates on the criminals' fears, sorrows, pangs of remorse, and so on, which make the rest of their lives one prolonged punishment (553F–556E):

Plato says of Herodicus of Selymbria, who contracted consumption, an incurable disease, and became the first person to combine medicine and exercise, that he devised for himself and others with the same ailment a protracted death; likewise all those criminals who seem to have avoided instantaneous catastrophe are in fact paying a more protracted, not more delayed penalty: they are not punished *after* a longer time, but *for* a longer time; they have not been punished on growing old, but have grown old in punishment (οὐδὲ γηράσαντες ἐκολάσθησαν, ἀλλ᾽ ἐγήρασαν κολαζόμενοι). (554C–D)[11]

This, of course, is a quite different perspective. We are dealing, as it were, with two different solutions to the same *zetema*. Both offer aspects of the truth but neither exhausts the subject, and, while being

---

Patrocleas' problem and points out the tardiness and delay of the divine (τοῦ θείου) (549B). The impersonal τὸ θεῖον also occurs in 557A, and 'Plutarch' connects τὰ θεῖα καὶ τὰ δαιμόνια at the beginning of his reply (549F). Furthermore, justified and useful punishment is associated throughout the work with God (ὁ θεός), who acts as a kind of doctor, curing the disease of wickedness (551B–C; 553A; 560B; 562D; cf. 550A; 562A–B). Sometimes, even the plural form (θεοί) occurs (550C), although usually in proverbial expressions or poetic quotations (549E; 556E; 562F; we may add 557E on the anger of the gods [αἱ τῶν θεῶν ὀργαί] – a notion that is diametrically opposed to Plutarch's Platonic view of the divine).

[11] Trans. Waterfield and Kidd 1992.

compatible to a certain extent, they cannot simply be fused together into one comprehensive account.[12]

Timon then brings on the 'third wave' (a clear allusion to Plato, *Resp.* 472a3–4), raising the question of children who are punished for their parents' crimes (556E–557E). Again, 'Plutarch' insists that, with this argument about God, he enters an obscure labyrinth and that he can at best claim some plausibility (τὸ εἰκὸς καὶ πιθανόν) (558D). He then reminds his listeners of the contagiousness of vice throughout the generations and emphasizes that cities and families are a single whole (558D–560A). Furthermore, we can be confident that criminals will be punished after death and suffer even more when they see that their offspring are in a sorry plight through their fault (560C–561B). Finally, God sometimes curtails wicked intentions before they are translated into bad actions (561C–563B). The arguments of 'Plutarch', and the dialogue as a whole, are then crowned by the myth of Aridaeus/Thespesius (see above, Chapter II, §2).

On the slowness of divine punishments contains Plutarch's attempt at a theodicy and gives us a good idea of his considered approach towards the difficult problem of divine providence. It is characterized by a remarkable intellectual honesty. Plutarch knew well enough that he was groping in the dark and did not conceal it from his readers, hence his repeated disclaimers and his insistence on plausibility rather than certainty. Notwithstanding this caution, his view is in line with his Platonic conception of God. All aspects of God's providential working can be explained by his justice, mildness, and concern for what is good. Again, God is not the cause of evil; for Plutarch, all his decisions are perfectly justifiable in a rational way.

2. In search of a middle course

The above discussion has shown that Plutarch basically believes in one God.[13] This God, moreover, is impersonal: he is connected with true being (τὸ ὄντως ὄν), with the Good (τὸ καλόν), and so on. Yet he has

---

[12] This zetetic approach may help in explaining the difficult structure of the work. Plutarch's general argument in *On the slowness of divine punishments* is also analysed in detail in Opsomer 2016 and Frazier 2019. See also Helmig 2005, who underlines the *ad hominem* character of Plutarch's argument, and Baldassarri 1994 for the philosophical background of the discussion.

[13] There are a few traces of a distinction between two levels in the divine realm (thus Donini 1992 and 2011b: 75–82; Dillon 2002: 226) but the importance of these passages should not be

some personal features as well, for the Demiurge is a father figure who takes care of the world and of man. In short, τὸ θεῖον ('the divine') and ὁ θεός ('God') are often interwoven and mixed up.[14] However that may be, the essence of Plutarch's Platonic conception of God is obviously at odds with certain aspects of traditional religion.[15] For the Homeric Olympus is crowded by many gods who often struggle with one another, who help their favourites and spitefully ruin their opponents. Moreover, many traditional rites imply a philosophically problematic view of God, in that they often attempt to prevent or placate the wrath of the gods. All of this is anathema to Plutarch, irreconcilable with his high-minded view of God.[16]

No wonder, then, that Plutarch frequently rejects traditional stories about the gods as myths and false fabrications.[17] An interesting work in this respect is *On superstition*, a spirited attack on superstition or δεισιδαιμονία, literally 'fear of the gods'. And this is precisely what is rejected: the erroneous conviction that the gods are the cause of pain and harm (165B). This conviction, which engenders continuous fears that mar one's whole life, ignores one of the most fundamental insights of Plutarch's thinking of God, viz. that the gods are benevolent and beneficent (166D–E; 167D–E). Everyone who disregards this insight necessarily goes wrong. In that sense, Platonic metaphysics provides us with a very important criterion for our attitude towards the gods.

This also appears from the comparison between superstition and atheism that is a connecting thread in Plutarch's argument. Atheism, too, evidently ignores the insights of Platonic metaphysics and is therefore no less problematic. Plutarch unambiguously rejects it as an intellectual mistake (a bad judgement or κρίσις φαύλη, 165B). Yet, in this work, superstition is seen as even worse, since it involves passions and irrational behaviour. Thus (169F–170A),

---

overemphasized (cf. Ferrari 2005a: 18–20; Thum 2013: 358–61). The basic distinction is that between gods and demons, for which see below, §4.

[14] See esp. Massaro 1996; cf. Brouillette 2014: 105–13.

[15] Nevertheless, Plutarch claims that it is in line with the common conceptions. All people, he argues, conceive God as blessed and incorruptible (*De Is. et Os.* 358E; cf. *De sup.* 165B). In *Arist.* 6.3, he lists incorruption, power, and virtue as the three distinctive characteristics of the divine; in *De comm. not.* 1075E, he lists immortality, blessedness, humanity, care, and beneficence (cf. *De Stoic. rep.* 1051F on Antipater's view of God).

[16] See Roig Lanzillotta 2012 on Plutarch's polemic against Herodotus on this point.

[17] See, e.g., *De Is. et Os.* 358F; *De sera num.* 557F; *De sup.* 170A–B (on erroneous convictions regarding Artemis and other Olympians), *De Pyth. or.* 402A (on a wrong representation of Apollo); also *De Is. et Os.* 378D and *fr.* 157.2.

for my part, I should prefer that men should say about me that I have never been born at all, and there is no Plutarch, rather than that they should say 'Plutarch is an inconstant fickle person, quick-tempered, vindictive over little accidents, pained at trifles. If you invite others to dinner and leave him out, or if you haven't the time and don't go to call on him, or fail to speak to him when you see him, he will set his teeth into your body and bite it through, or he will get hold of your little child and beat him to death, or he will turn the beast that he owns into your crops and spoil your harvest.'

The irrational and ridiculous conduct of the superstitious man is described in a lively, sometimes slightly ironic way. We learn how he is tormented by uninterrupted fears, caused by bad dreams (165D–166C). Neither death (166F–167A) nor joyful occasions like participation in the rites (169D–E) bring relief. Moreover, the superstitious man does not even ask for help but simply resigns himself to his miserable situation (168C; 168E–F) and loses himself in ignoble behaviour: he is thoroughly fumigated and smeared all over, while old crones hang on him, as on a peg, whatever they happen to find (168D–E). This evocative description of the 'ludicrous actions and passions of superstition' (τῆς δεισιδαιμονίας ἔργα καὶ πάθη καταγέλαστα, 171A) recalls the κρίσις component of Plutarch's psychotherapeutic writings (see above, Chapter IV, §3). It contains a particularly vivid and eye-opening diagnosis that should start off a process of improvement.

On superstition has often been regarded as a youthful work of a rationalistic Plutarch who only became interested in religion and mystery in a later period of his life.[18] This hypothesis, however, has now been generally abandoned, and rightly so, for, as a matter of fact, the attack on both superstition and atheism is one of the leitmotifs that recur in Plutarch's whole oeuvre.[19] There are a few tensions between his position in *On superstition* and what he defends elsewhere,[20] but they can usually be explained by the difference in context.[21] Be that as it may, *On superstition* illustrates several important aspects of Plutarch's attitude towards the religious tradition: (1) the importance of Platonic metaphysics as normative criterion for a correct view of God; (2) a certain sobermindedness and rationalism, averse from

---

[18] See, e.g., Ziegler 1951: 826; Moellering 1963: 20; Klaerr in Defradas *et al.* 1985: 243–6.
[19] See, e.g., *De Is. et Os.* 355C–D and 378A; *Non posse* 1101B–C; *Cam.* 6.6. See further Brenk 1977 and 1987b: 256.
[20] Moellering 1963: 106–47.
[21] On Plutarch's inconsistencies, see esp. Nikolaidis 1991.

excessive credulity;[22] and (3) a well-balanced middle course that rejects both superstition and atheism. It is no accident that the final word of the work is piety (*eusebeia*).

3. Plutarch's exegetical principles

Such a piety implies that traditional religion is not completely rejected. On the contrary, many of its components can easily stand the test of Platonic philosophy. Even more, the 'faith of the fathers', the *patrios pistis*, as expressed in myths and rites, should be considered a rich source of the truth. In *That the Pythia now does not give her oracles in verse*, for instance, Sarapion insists that we should not abandon pious ancestral belief but rather look for solutions for seemingly problematic issues (402E; cf. also *De sup.* 166B and *Amatorius* 756B). Next to Platonic metaphysics, the *patrios pistis* can significantly contribute to a deeper insight into the divine.

Yet metaphysics and ancestral faith are not on the same level. The former, as said above, yields the normative criterion for the correct interpretation of myths and rites and thus has philosophical primacy over the latter: the *patrios pistis* should only be adopted when it expresses a philosophical truth. In other words, traditional myths and rites should always be examined for compatibility with Platonic metaphysics. This rule reflects one of the most fundamental principles of Plutarch's exegesis: everything should be carried back to reason (ἐπὶ τὸν λόγον ἀνοιστέον ἅπαντα; *De Is. et Os.* 378B). We should never accept myth in a thoughtless and unconsidered way (ἀπερισκέπτως καὶ ἀλογίστως; *De sup.* 171E–F) but use reason as our mystagogue (*De Is. et Os.* 378A) and derive from established religious customs what is useful and what symbolizes philosophical truth (cf. *De Is. et Os.* 380F). This will also entail a solemn view of God: *semnotes* ('solemnity') is a term that repeatedly occurs in Plutarch's thinking about God and that apparently yields an additional criterion for a correct understanding of the divine.[23]

Moreover, we should not easily connect one entire myth with one philosophical insight but carefully ponder different details: 'We must

---

[22] This also appears from more general discussions of Plutarch's approach towards religion, as in Brenk 1977 and Veyne 1999.

[23] See, e.g., *De sup.* 167E; *De def. or.* 414E and 426C; Ingenkamp 1984: 80 and 1985: 40–1; Opsomer 1998: 131–2.

not treat myths as if they were rational accounts at all, but we should adopt that which is appropriate in each myth in accordance with its verisimilitude' (*De Is. et Os.* 374E). This exegetic principle illustrates both the thoroughness that the interpretation of myth requires and the mutual relation between myth and *logos*. What we find here is essentially a philosophical deconstruction of myth. Indeed, traditional myth should be dismantled into its separate components, which should then, if possible, be connected with (coherent or disconnected) philosophical truths.

Such a philosophical deconstruction makes it possible to integrate the *patrios pistis* to a great extent into Platonic philosophy, even more so since this *patrios pistis* is itself open to philosophical adaptation and refiguration. It shows a remarkable plasticity that mainly rests on its historical dimension.[24] For indeed, the ancestral faith can be traced back to primitive sages who, long ago, expressed their natural philosophy in myths and in a theology such as is found in mystery ceremonies (μυστηριώδης θεολογία).[25] Myths and rites therefore contain many seeds of the truth, though usually veiled, in the form of riddles and symbols.[26]

Plutarch's general thinking about God and religion thus shows a delicate balance between the fundamental primacy of Platonic philosophy and the great importance of the ancestral tradition. In this balance, we find the beating heart of his Academic philosophy. It is based on an attitude that is very often mentioned in his works, that is, εὐλάβεια πρὸς τὸ θεῖον. In the *Lives*, this 'caution towards the divine' usually refers to pious respect for the gods.[27] In *De sera num.*, Plutarch connects it explicitly with the Academy (549E–F), acknowledging that we cannot reach certain knowledge about the gods and that plausibility (τὸ εἰκὸς καὶ πιθανόν; 558D) is the best we can obtain in such matters (cf. 550C; 561B). This epistemological limitation, however, precisely stimulates creative thinking and careful questioning of the religious tradition. We should become skilled trackers of the truth (*Amatorius* 762A). In short, we should adopt a zetetic attitude towards the *patrios pistis*, while being aware that definitive certainty is beyond reach.

---

[24] Van Nuffelen 2011: 48–71.
[25] *Fr.* 157.1; on this fragment, see Van Nuffelen 2011: 50–5; Scannapieco 2012. See also *De Is. et Os.* 378F–379D; *De E* 385A; *Amatorius* 763C.
[26] Cf. Hirsch-Luipold 2002 and 2005a: 144–52.
[27] *Cam.* 21.3; *Aem.* 3.3; *Cor.* 25.7; *Num.* 22.11.

This, however, is only one side of Academic 'caution towards the divine'. The recognition of our human limitation does not exclude the possibility that at least some certainty can be reached. When hearing myths about the base conduct of the gods, we should 'spit and cleanse the mouth' (*De Is. et Os.* 358E, with reference to Aeschylus, *TrGF* 3.354).

One should not timorously, or as though under the spell of superstition in a holy place, shiver with awe at everything, and fall prostrate, but should rather acquire the habit of exclaiming with confidence 'wrong' and 'improper' no less than 'right' and 'proper'. (*De aud. poet.* 26B)

Such passages interestingly show that Academic caution towards the divine can perfectly be reconciled with a certain confidence. God does move in a mysterious way, yet there can be no doubt about the fact that he has nothing at all to do with evil. At least a limited secure insight can be reached through Platonic metaphysics.

4. Demonology

Even on such fundamental issues, Academic *eulabeia* ('caution') prevents unjustified overconfidence. For here we encounter a particularly difficult problem: the ancestral tradition overflows with stories about the bad behaviour of the gods. If we have to prune all of them away, we risk ending up with a drastically mutilated *patrios pistis*. If we really want to take the ancestral tradition seriously as a source of wisdom, we should take pains to throw light on these aspects as well (see *De Pyth. or.* 402E). Covering all this up is not really an example of penetrating *zetesis* and it is to Plutarch's credit that he does not shy away from the problem but tries to find plausible solutions.

One such solution is provided by an elaborate theory of *daimones*.[28] This theory gives him a particularly interesting way to explain the wicked actions of malicious gods without contradicting his own Platonic view of God. Along the lines of this demonological approach, the wicked deeds that the tradition attributes to the gods should be ascribed to bad demons, intermediate beings that possess divine powers

---

[28] Plutarch's demonology has often been discussed in scholarly literature. Seminal contributions are Soury 1942; Moellering 1963: 119–38; Brenk 1973, 1977, and 1987b: 275–94; Dillon 1977: 216–24; Froidefond 1987: 205–8; Vernière 1989; Van Nuffelen 2011: 164–7; Timotin 2012: 164–201 and 244–59.

but also share in human passions.[29] That Plutarch did not a priori rule out the existence of such bad demons is suggested by several famous passages from the *Lives of Dion and Brutus*.[30] At the outset of this pair, he recalls that both heroes saw an apparition shortly before their death (*Dion* 2.3–6). Dion saw a great woman like a tragic Fury (55.1–3). Brutus, for his part, saw a dreadful figure that was standing silently by his side and that subsequently identified itself as 'I am your evil demon (ὁ σὸς δαίμων κακός) and you'll see me at Philippi' (*Brut.* 36.6–7; cf. 48.1; *Caes.* 69.9–11). Although Plutarch shows a certain reluctance in accepting the truth of these stories,[31] this reluctance should be regarded as one more example of the Academic *eulabeia* that does not fall into the trap of excessive credulity. In fact, there are enough indications that Plutarch took seriously the explanations offered by the demonological interpretation.[32]

Plutarch's demonology yields two important advantages: it enables him to make sense of several elements of the *patrios pistis* – that is, demonology has a *conservative* function; and it enables him to keep his view of God pure – demonology also has a *cathartic* function. This also explains why the demonological interpretation usually comes quite early in a zetetic structure. In such interpretations, Plutarch develops a cathartic perspective that makes room for further, more positive speculations about the divine. At the same time, this demonological perspective plays an important part in the argumentative dynamics of the *zetema*: its purifying role is part and parcel of Plutarch's position and is never taken back.

This, however, is only half of the story. Alongside such bad demons, there also exist good ones. The most important source about the latter is one of Plutarch's best works, *On Socrates' divine sign*. This literary dialogue contains an account of the liberation of Thebes in 379 BC. Plutarch tells how a group of conspirators make preparations to deliver their city from Spartan occupation and how they eventually succeed in their mission. Now and then, the action is interrupted by philosophical

---

[29] The *locus classicus* is Cleombrotus' view in *De def. or.* 414F–415A and 417E–418C; see also *De Is. et Os.* 360D–363D. The chthonic gods can also be understood from this perspective; see Van der Stockt 2005.

[30] Cf. Moles 2017: 314–27; Mossman 2019.

[31] See Brenk 1973: 3–5; 1977: 62–3; 1987b: 277 and 281–2; Van Nuffelen 2011: 166.

[32] Cleombrotus' explanation is never rejected in *In the obsolescence of oracles* (see Babut 1992: 216–20 and Brouillette 2014: 156–68). On the demonological interpretation of *On Isis and Osiris*, see Roskam 2017c: 207–11.

discussions, so that the whole work shows a sophisticated combination of *logoi* and *praxeis*.[33] The most important topic for discussion concerns Socrates' notorious divine sign. In a kind of embedded *zetema* that is smoothly integrated into the rest of the work, several characters look for an explanation of this *daimonion*. According to the seer Theocritus, it was a kind of vision (580C–F), whereas Galaxidorus understands it as a trivial occurrence such as a sneeze or a random utterance that shows the way in a situation of equality between two propositions (580F–581A; 581F–582C). Simmias then develops an interesting physicalist explanation: Socrates' pure mind was able to perceive the wordless messages of demons (588C–589F).[34] He then tells the myth of Timarchus (see above, Chapter II, §2), which identifies a demon with the *nous* (589F–592F). Finally, Theanor argues that demons are disembodied souls that assist other souls that have reached the end of the cycle of metempsychosis (593A–594A).

Again, we are given a salient example of painstaking *zetesis* in which various perspectives are used, step by step, in order to throw light on the different dimensions of this complex problem. Here as well, demonology yields an interesting interpretative key to approach the tradition, albeit in a different, complementary sense. Alongside its conservative and cathartic function, it also provides positive insights into our human nature and into the communication between God and man. As such, it is part and parcel of Plutarch's philosophy.

5. The Pythian dialogues

Unlike Socrates, most people have no direct access to the unuttered messages of demons and need the mediation of oracles. Thus we arrive at another important aspect of Plutarch's thinking about God. In the so-called Pythian dialogues,[35] Plutarch, who served Apollo as his priest

---

[33] This has entailed much scholarly discussion about the unity of the work; see, e.g., Riley 1977; Babut 1984; Barigazzi 1988; Georgiadou 1995; Brenk 1996; Effe 2008; Bonazzi 2020. Excellent studies of *On Socrates' divine sign* include Corlu 1970; Nesselrath 2010; Donini 2017.

[34] Simmias' theory is discussed in detail by Long 2006; see also Corlu 1970: 53–60 and Döring 1984.

[35] The name actually stems from Plutarch himself; *De E* 384E. These works have received much scholarly attention. Apart from the studies mentioned in the next notes, see esp. the seminal article of Babut 1992 on the thematic unity and structure of these works. A comprehensive philosophical interpretation can be found in Brouillette 2014. Simonetti 2017 examines the issue of oracular divination in these works.

in Delphi (see above, Chapter I, §3), discusses several questions that are directly related to the Delphic shrine.

On the E at Delphi deals with the meaning of the mysterious E that had been dedicated in Apollo's temple at Delphi.[36] The dialogue contains an extensive account of a conversation that Plutarch had in his youth, when he frequented Ammonius' circle. This account, however, is prefaced by an interesting introduction that places the work into its proper philosophical perspective. Plutarch argues that, while Apollo solves the problems of our lives by his oracles, he raises other problems that challenge our reasoning capacities, thus stimulating a yearning for the truth (384F). This conviction thus constitutes the starting point of the conversation itself. Ammonius claims that Apollo is no less a philosopher than a seer, for riddles like the E cause wonder and thus stimulate enquiry (ζητεῖν), which is the beginning of philosophy (385B–C; a clear reference to Plato, *Tht.* 155d2–4; cf. *Quaest. conv.* 680C–D). Thus we again find the dynamics of zetetic thinking with which we are familiar by now: the philosophical dialogue which follows is once again introduced as a vehicle for an open-minded search for the truth.

Six speakers then put forward divergent interpretations. According to Lamprias, the E should be understood as the number five: it was dedicated by the five Wise Men (Chilon, Thales, Solon, Bias, and Pittacus) in order to make clear that they were only five in number and that Cleobulus and Periander were mere impostors (385D–386A). An unnamed member of the company recalls the theory of a Chaldaean visitor, that epsilon is the second vowel and the sun the second planet. The two therefore belong together, since nearly all the Greeks identify the sun with Apollo (386A–B). Nicander the priest adopts the *communis opinio* that is also endorsed by the guides of the shrine: the E means 'if' – understanding E as EI, an old spelling – and introduces the questions of those who consult the god (inquiring 'if' they should do something) as well as their wishes (beginning with εἰ γάρ or εἴθε) (386B–D). Nicander's criticism of the logicians naturally entails a reaction from Theon, who emphasizes the importance of the copulative conjunction 'if' that forms the basis of the hypothetical syllogism and as such has a crucial part to play in the philosophical search for the truth (386D–387D). Next,

---

[36] The best starting point for a study of the dialogue are the recent commentary of Obsieger 2013 and the outstanding study of Thum 2013; see also Moreschini 1997 and Boulogne *et al.* 2006.

Eustrophus suggests that the E is a symbol of the pempad and invites the young 'Plutarch' to develop this view. The latter enthusiastically sings the praise of the number five (387D–391E).

Finally, Ammonius proposes a metaphysical interpretation (392A):

It is an address and salutation to the god, complete in itself, which, by being spoken, brings him who utters it to thoughts of the god's power. For the god addresses each one of us as we approach him here with the words 'Know Thyself,' as a form of welcome, which certainly is in no wise of less import than 'Hail'; and we in turn reply to the god 'Thou art,' as rendering unto him a form of address which is truthful, free from deception, and the only one befitting him only, the assertion of being.

For, as Ammonius goes on, we human beings belong to the world of becoming and are in a permanent Heraclitean flux, whereas the god exists in all eternity, belonging to the realm of motionless, timeless being, of τὸ ὄντως ὄν (392A–394C). His speech thus forms an illustrative example of Plutarch's general strategy of placing a metaphysical outlook above the ancestral tradition. The two domains retain their own autonomy and the interplay between them is a very complex one. Strictly speaking, Ammonius never explicitly *identifies* Apollo with being.[37] His metaphysical speculations throw light on a significant aspect of the god. They do not, however, exhaustively lay bare Apollo's *essence* but rather his power (τῆς τοῦ θεοῦ δυνάμεως; 392A) or his *mode of being* (ὡς ὄντα διὰ παντός; 394A). In short, Ammonius uses one element of the tradition (viz. the puzzling E) as an interesting source that reveals a philosophical truth concerning the god.

In *That the Pythia now does not give her oracles in verse*, we follow a group of learned men on a guided tour of the Delphic sanctuary and witness their philosophical reactions to different monuments.[38] When the company finally arrive at Apollo's temple, they sit down on its steps in order to investigate why the oracles are no longer given in verse. In a lengthy speech, Theon develops several considerations that at least partly complement each other. In his view, Apollo makes use of the Pythia as his instrument (ὄργανον). This human instrument,

---

[37] This claim needs a detailed interpretation of the different steps in Ammonius' argumentation, which is beyond the scope of this book. Chapter 19 is entirely about being; in the next chapter, Ammonius turns to the god (ὁ θεός; 393A). From that moment on, the two perspectives alternate without, however, merging into one single point of view. On 393A (εἷς ὤν), see Obsieger 2013: 346 and Thum 2013: 249–55.

[38] Every reader of *That the Pythia...* will benefit from the thorough commentary of Schröder 1990; cf. also Valgiglio 1992b.

however, also has its own characteristics which the god cannot simply ignore. Apollo acts upon the Pythia's soul through an external impulse, but the specific nature of the Pythia's soul plays its part too. Thus, we should not expect grandiloquent verse from a pure but uncultivated young woman.

This well-balanced ὄργανον theory enables Theon to do full justice to the divine origin of the Delphic oracle while at the same time taking into account its human aspects, and most of his speech concerns the latter.[39] He insists on the importance of historical evolutions and circumstances, and thus adopts a strikingly down-to-earth approach towards the whole issue. Such an attitude obviously has nothing to do with naïve, unreflecting devotion to the god, nor does it suggest any scepticism or disbelief regarding Apollo's active involvement in the oracular process. The goal of Theon's speech is aptly characterized in its very last words: it is an attempt to reach the god's thought through reasoning (ἐξικνεῖσθαι τῷ λογισμῷ πρὸς τὴν τοῦ θεοῦ διάνοιαν; 409D).

On the obsolescence of oracles contains a similarly meandering conversation among learned men.[40] The principal topic, interrupted by several lengthy digressions, concerns the question of why so many oracle sites have been abandoned in Plutarch's day. As usual, different solutions are proposed. Didymus points to the universal wickedness that has caused the departure of the gods (412F–413B), while Ammonius explains the situation by the general depopulation of Greece (413F–414C). These answers basically resemble the approach in *That the Pythia now does not give her oracles in verse* of giving due attention to both the god's role and the relevance of historical circumstances. Cleombrotus then argues at length that the oracles are not administered by the gods but by demons. When one of these decides to depart, his oracle obviously falls silent (414E–418D). Finally, Lamprias suggests that the soul itself has a prophetic capacity, which is stimulated by vapours and streams coming from the earth. Since these vapours sometimes disappear in one place and come to the surface elsewhere, the oracles inevitably lose their power (431D–434C).

Up to this point, we can easily detect the usual zetetic structure behind the façade of the literary dialogue. Indeed, the lively conversation hardly

---

[39] The philosophical background of the theory is disputed: Schröder 1990: 25–59 and 1994–5 traces it back to Stoic philosophy, Holzhausen 1993 and Simonetti 2017 to Plato's *Timaeus*.

[40] This dialogue is the least studied of the three Pythian dialogues, although that does not mean that it is understudied. A good point of departure is the detailed commentary by Rescigno 1995.

conceals a series of juxtaposed alternative solutions. Yet Lamprias' final contribution now raises a powerful objection from Ammonius (435A–B):

A little while ago, we somehow managed to let the argument shift the responsibility for prophecy from the gods to certain *daimones*; and now we seem to be expelling these also from the oracle and the tripod here, by resolving the principle, or rather the very essence and force of prophecy, into a matter of 'spirits', vapours, and exhalations. For the more these balances and warmings and temperings are bound up with physical causes, the more they turn our thoughts away from the gods.[41]

Why, then, should we still sacrifice to the gods and perform the rites before consulting the oracle, if our soul turns out to possess the prophetic power itself and if its inspiration can indeed be explained by purely physical factors? Ammonius here puts his finger on a tricky problem. We have seen before that *zetemata* usually show an ascending structure in which the more plausible solutions are placed at the end. In this case, however, the god progressively disappears from sight and we end up with a purely material explanation. Should this, then, be considered the most plausible view?

Lamprias recognizes the problem and is forced to situate his point of view in a broader perspective, that is, the theory of two causes. By distinguishing between a material and a divine cause, he is able to maintain his physical explanation (436E–F) while simultaneously ascribing a role to demons (436F–437A) and acknowledging the presence of the god (437A–C). Thus he arrives at a (partial) fusion of the different perspectives, something that we only occasionally find in Plutarch's works. This rare attempt at a comprehensive synthesis is probably Plutarch's way of preventing or correcting the unjustified inference that the descending structure of the argument (from god over demons to the human soul and material causes) also implies an ascending structure with regard to plausibility. A solution that ignores the divine cause is as one-sided as the one that neglects the material cause (436D–E).

Does this imply that, for once, the philosophical enquiry has yielded a definitive solution? Not at all. Typically enough, Lamprias emphasizes that his view is open to many objections and he invites his friends to re-examine the issue frequently (438D–E). The last word, then, is not one of triumph or even self-confidence, but one of caution and willingness to continue the search for the truth.

---

[41] Trans. Russell 1993a.

6. Wisdom from abroad: delving into the Egyptian lore

The leitmotif of the picture so far is Plutarch's continuous search for a delicate balance between the ancestral religious tradition and philosophical insight, between *nomos* and *logos*. A similar circumspect approach returns in his reception of the myths and rites of non-Greek people.[42] This appears especially in *On Isis and Osiris*. This lengthy treatise, dedicated to his friend Clea, a priestess at Delphi,[43] gives a good idea of his attitude towards Egyptian religion in both its breadth and its depth.[44]

After a programmatic introduction (351C–355D)[45] and the account of the myth (355D–359D), Plutarch proposes four different interpretations. According to the euhemeristic point of view, Osiris was originally a king (359D–360D), whereas the demonological interpretation considers Osiris and Isis as demons who became gods through their virtue (360D–363D). Along the lines of a physical allegory, Osiris can also be understood as the general principle and power of moisture, while Typhon is associated with everything dry and fiery (363D–369A). All of these interpretations throw interesting light on several aspects of the Egyptian myth and rites, although none of them is entirely unproblematic. The last interpretation deals with the matter from a metaphysical point of view. Everything that is orderly and good should be honoured as the image of Osiris (371A–B; 377A). The god is far removed from the earth, is the first intelligible principle (382C), and shows some features of the Platonic Idea of the Good (383A). Isis is understood as the receptive power that longs for the order of Osiris but who also leaves room for Typhon, the origin of everything that is harmful and bad.

Thus, the zetetic dynamics of Plutarch's thinking once again yield a particularly rich and multifaceted interpretation that lays bare the different dimensions (and tensions) of the Egyptian myth. The fundamental exegetical principles on which the treatise is based are

---

[42] See Graf 1996 on Roman religion. For Plutarch's view of the Jews, see, e.g., Feldman 1996; Brenk 1997: 100–4; Muñoz Gallarte 2008; Geiger 2010. On the figure of the Scythian sage Anacharsis in Plutarch, see Leão 2019a.

[43] On Clea, see Puech 1992: 4842–3 (with previous literature).

[44] Much material that is indispensable for a correct understanding of the work is collected in the commentaries by Hopfner 1941 and Griffiths 1970, and in the important monograph by Hani 1976. Interesting new insights are reached in the interdisciplinary edited volume Erler and Stadler 2017. See also Richter 2001; Petrucci 2016a and 2016b.

[45] Analysed in Roskam 2014b.

neatly summarized in the following passage, taken from the last part of the work (377F–378A):

> Nor do we think of the gods as different gods among different peoples, nor as barbarian gods and Greek gods, nor as southern and northern gods; but, just as the sun and the moon and the heavens and the earth and the sea are common to all, but are called by different names by different peoples, so for that one rationality which keeps these things in order and the one Providence which watches over them and the ancillary powers that are set over all, there have arisen among different peoples, in accordance with their customs, different honours and appellations. Thus men make use of consecrated symbols, some employing symbols that are obscure, but others those that are clearer, in guiding the intelligence toward things divine, though not without a certain hazard. For some go completely astray and become engulfed in superstition; and others, while they fly from superstition as from a quagmire, on the other hand unwittingly fall, as it were, over a precipice into atheism.

The diversity of divine names and religious customs can thus be traced back to a more fundamental unity. This conviction enables Plutarch to reconcile gods like Osiris and Isis unproblematically with the *fait primitif* of the *patrios pistis*. In *On superstition* he warns against dishonouring and transgressing 'the divine and ancestral dignity of piety' (τὸ θεῖον καὶ πάτριον ἀξίωμα τῆς εὐσεβείας) by using barbarian phrases (166B).[46] A similar note of caution appears at the end of the passage quoted above, where he likewise points to the dangers of both superstition and atheism (see also 355C–D). Yet Plutarch also shows the way in which these dangers can be overcome.

In his view, the religious tradition should be regarded as a rich source of symbols that lead thought to the divine (τὰ θεῖα). The same conviction occurs elsewhere in the treatise as well. Egyptian theology is called a riddling wisdom (αἰνιγματώδη σοφίαν; 354C) that contains reflections and refractions of the truth (*ibid.*) and that needs philosophical reason as a mystagogue (378A).[47] This philosophical *logos* provides interpretative beacons, for not everything conduces to a deeper insight into the truth about the gods. Plutarch explicitly says that he omits several 'useless and superfluous' parts of the myth

---

[46] The qualification 'barbarian' usually implies a negative evaluation (as in this phrase too); see esp. the detailed study of Schmidt 1999; cf. Nikolaidis 1986. Yet Plutarch also recognizes instances of barbarian wisdom, the case of *On Isis and Osiris* being the most obvious example (next to the lost *Barbarian questions*); see Schmidt 1999: 258–62.

[47] Such imagery from mystery cults often occurs in Plutarch's writings; see esp. Pérez Jiménez and Casadesús Bordoy 2001. We may recall that Plutarch and his wife were initiated into the mysteries of Dionysus (*Cons. ad ux.* 611D).

(355D; cf. 358E). In the present passage, he even reduces all the different traditions to their very essence, that is, the one rationality and the one providence with its ancillary powers. Thus, he once again looks at religious customs from the perspective of his Platonic philosophy. This obviously implies an *interpretatio graeca* of Egyptian religion: for Plutarch, Isis is a Greek word (351F)[48] and the whole story about the Egyptian gods basically represents Plato's account of the generation of the universe in the *Timaeus*.

Does this also imply that Plutarch ultimately failed to do justice to the Egyptian perspective by forcing it into the straitjacket of Greek philosophical thinking? To a certain extent it does,[49] although we should add that he deals with Egyptian religion as with his own *patrios pistis*. In both cases, the same exegetical rules apply. Moreover, Plutarch really took seriously the Egyptian lore and his characterization of it as a riddling wisdom is no empty term. Indeed, it is remarkable how many elements from Egyptian wisdom are discussed in the treatise. Not only the myth in all its details but also many rites and customs are mentioned and interpreted. All this should be appreciated as precious paths to the truth.[50] In the end, however, the input of philosophy is decisive: the true votary of Isis is not the one who confines himself or herself to external aspects of her cult but who philosophically investigates the truth it contains (352C). Here, as ever, *zetesis* has the last word.

7. The gods of the *patrios pistis*

We have seen how Plutarch succeeds in reconciling many components of the *patrios pistis* with his Platonic conception of God through a many-sided and thorough zetetic reinterpretation. The interpretative horizon of his thinking is his conception of one intelligible God. The key passage from *On Isis and Osiris* discussed above (§6) suggests a monotheistic point of view. Such a position is obviously opposed to ancestral polytheism. Many negative aspects of the behaviour of the traditional gods can be explained away through a demonological interpretation, of course, but we now have to face a much more radical

---

[48] See Strobach 1997: 116–36 for Plutarch's etymological explanations of Egyptian words (122–4 on Isis).

[49] See Richter 2001 and Roskam 2004b.

[50] See also Plutarch's frequent use of the Egyptian tradition in the *Table Talk*; Meeusen 2017.

suggestion: should we not completely abandon the traditional belief in many gods and replace it by a philosophically justified belief in the one truly existent and perfect God?

This is not the impression we get when reading Plutarch's works, where polytheism is often endorsed without any problem. Plutarch recognizes that different gods have their own domains (*De tranq. an.* 472A–B) and are associated with different rituals (*Adv. Col.* 1119E–F). He also refers to many traditional surnames of the gods.[51] All this, however, entails a crucial question: what is the relation between the highest God, father and maker of the universe, the Demiurge of Plato's *Timaeus*, on the one hand, and the hotchpotch of all too human Olympians, on the other hand?

A Jove principium. There is no doubt that Plutarch, in line with tradition, considers Zeus as the supreme deity.[52] He is characterized by Thrasyllus as 'the great leader in heaven' (*Quaest. conv.* 722D: ὁ μέγας ἡγεμὼν ἐν οὐρανῷ; cf. *Non posse* 1102E). In Crete, so Plutarch says, there is a statue of Zeus without ears, which makes sense since 'it is not fitting for the ruler and lord of all to listen to anyone'.[53] Zeus's superiority rests on his knowledge and wisdom (*De Is. et Os.* 351D–E; see also *De aud. poet.* 32A). Not everything the poets tell us about the gods is correct (*De aud. poet.* 17A and 25F) but they sometimes offer helpful insights. Pindar's characterization of Zeus as the 'best of artificers' is entirely fitting for a providential Demiurge;[54] and the early tragic poet Thespis' view of the god is perfectly in line with Plato's (*De aud. poet.* 36B–C). We thus see the same exegetical method at work again: problematic aspects of the traditional image of Zeus are either rejected as offensive and wrong, or simply ignored as useless, whereas other elements are strategically selected and reoriented towards a philosophical perspective.

From father Zeus to his son Apollo. Plutarch's view of the oracular god has received far more attention.[55] Scholars focus especially on the dialogue *On the E at Delphi*, which is not merely regarded as the

---

[51] See the lengthy list in Valgiglio 1988: 131–271. See also Burkert 1996 and Sfameni Gasparro 1996.

[52] Much material is to be found in López Férez 2007.

[53] *De Is. et Os.* 381E; see Brenk 2007 and Harrison and Francis 2008: 796–7.

[54] *De sera num.* 550A; *Quaest. conv.* 618B; *De facie* 927B; *De comm. not.* 1065E; cf. *Praec. ger. reip.* 807C. The Pindar quote is part of a cluster of recurrent material, as shown by Van der Stockt 2002.

[55] See esp. Boulet 2008 and Nikolaidis 2009, and the literature dealing with *On the E at Delphi* quoted above, n. 36.

most important source for Plutarch's understanding of Apollo but even for his conception of God.[56] The awkward implication of this view is that Apollo, rather than Zeus, occupies the highest position in Plutarch's pantheon, which has reasonably surprised several scholars.[57] Yet, although the dialogue, and notably Ammonius' contribution, is definitely interesting, we should not overemphasize its importance.[58] We should not forget that Ammonius' view is strongly conditioned by the specific matter under discussion: the mysterious E. This letter reveals one important aspect of the god, no doubt, but not his complete essence (see above, §5). The traditional Apollo is much more than τὸ ὄντως ὄν or the One.[59] Several aspects of Apollo are indeed ignored by Ammonius, although Plutarch no doubt considered them relevant.[60] Moreover, the caveat of Academic *eulabeia* towards the divine remains relevant for Ammonius' explanation as well.[61] In short, his speech illustrates the rich opportunities that a Platonic interpretation of the traditional god Apollo offers, but reveals only one aspect of the truth, which is rooted in the specific focus of the context. It would be rash to conclude on the basis of this speech that Apollo has, for Plutarch, taken the place of Zeus.

A similar approach can be found in the *Dialogue on love*, where Eros appears as a great god. In a lengthy speech, 'Plutarch' elaborates on the god's power and benefactions (756A–766B). Eros there appropriates several essential characteristics of the Platonic Demiurge, but again, this does not imply that he replaces Zeus or Apollo or should be identified with them.[62] The same holds true for Osiris in *On Isis and Osiris*. Time and again, Plutarch looks at different gods in different contexts through the lens of his Platonic metaphysics. This results in

[56] Ferrari 1995: 38–68 and 2010: 71 and 86 even argues that the dialogue is programmatic for Plutarch's philosophy as a whole.

[57] Dillon 2002: 225 n. 8: 'The dialogue is, admittedly, concerned with Apollo, but this is still odd'; Brenk 2005: 41: 'Apollo(n) is not the logical name a Platonic philosopher would use for the highest God.'

[58] See esp. Thum 2013. Obsieger 2013: 38–46 underscores the playful aspect of Ammonius' speech, but at the same time underestimates its genuine zetetic aspect.

[59] Cf. Brenk 2012: 84: 'If Plutarch really believed the One were so important, we would expect it to figure large in his other writings, and especially in his allegorical interpretation of *On Isis and Osiris*.'

[60] Ammonius touches upon Apollo's role as oracular god at the beginning of the dialogue (*De E* 385B) but it does not constitute a part of his own metaphysical interpretation. Another aspect that is ignored (by Ammonius and by Plutarch in the rest of his oeuvre) is Apollo's role as an archer; see Nikolaidis 2009: 569.

[61] Thus Bonazzi 2008. Cf. Thum 2013: 77–9 (on *De E* 385B) and 58–9 (on *De def. or.* 426E–F).

[62] Görgemanns 2005: 186.

a sublime image of the individual gods that makes them acceptable in the context of his Platonic thinking. While it is true that all these individual gods thus begin to resemble one another, being all in turn associated with the same intelligible realm of true Being and Beauty, Plutarch nowhere says that we can extrapolate his comments on individual gods to one theologically coherent and monotheistic system.

It is no coincidence that Plutarch never clarifies the mutual relations between the different gods, since this is a real problem for his thinking. He prefers to zoom in on one individual god and deal with him (or her) from his philosophical perspective. This implies that everything that he says about the traditional gods is related to its specific context. It is also evident from one of the most prominent images of God (or particular gods) in his works, viz. the sun. Again, the traditional *patrios pistis* (which identifies Apollo with the sun[63]) there encounters Plato's metaphysics (where the sun appears as the image of the Idea of the Good; cf. Plato, *Resp.* 508b12–509b9), and there too, the latter provides the normative hermeneutic key for the interpretation of the former. Since every god is by definition good, the sun can be the image of every god: of Apollo, but no less of Zeus, Eros, Osiris, or simply of the highest God.[64]

8. Conclusion

Plutarch's thinking about God and the gods has been characterized in many ways. It has often been connected with a celebrated passage from *On the obsolescence of oracles*, where Cleombrotus' project is introduced as an enquiry (ἱστορία) to serve as material (ὕλην) for a philosophy that has theology as its goal (410B).[65] Others regard it as a 'philosophical monotheism with loopholes for polytheism',[66] as 'henotheism',[67] or as 'polylatric monotheism'.[68] Each of these labels throws light on important aspects of Plutarch's position but, to a certain extent, they also risk obscuring the dynamics of his sophisticated approach towards

---

[63] Cf. *De E* 386B; *De def. or.* 434F–435A; *De lat. viv.* 1130A.

[64] See 282B–C; 372A; 372D; 393C–D; 400D; 416D; 433D–E; 764D–E; 780F; 781F; 944E. On this topic, see Hirsch-Luipold 2002: 165–8; Roskam 2006; Brouillette 2010 and 2014: 113–25.

[65] Flacelière 1943: 109–11 and 1974; Valgiglio 1988: 74–5; Burkert 1996: 21; Sfameni Gasparro 1996: 188; Hirsch-Luipold 2002: 11, 2005b: 1–2, and 2014: 167. *Contra*, however, Russell 1972: 83; Brenk 1977: 91 n. 7; Moreschini 1996: 41; Frazier 2019.

[66] Rose 1924: 61.

[67] Boulogne 2004: 104.

[68] Hirsch-Luipold 2014: 168; cf. 2005: 154 (inclusive monotheism).

the rich religious and philosophical tradition. Its beating heart is the zetetic attitude, averse from over-systematization, characterized by a great respect for the *patrios pistis* but also by sobermindedness, a critical spirit, and *eulabeia* towards the divine. Plutarch considered myths and rites with far-reaching benevolence and mobilized all the subtleties of his philosophical thinking in order to enthrone them as precious sources of wisdom. Nevertheless, while doing so, he always observed the clear standards of reason. These guided him on a pious middle course that avoids both atheism and superstition and that entails a philosophical purification of the ancestral religious tradition. Reason is the driving force of a kind of sublimation process,[69] in which distinct features of the traditional gods are sacrificed on the altar of philosophy. Colourful figures like the Homeric Zeus or Apollo are thus clothed in the tunic of 'true Being' or the cloak of 'the Good'.

Whereas the traditional Olympians mainly inspire awe and fear, the divine in Plutarch's view now inspires admiration, even love. The lover indeed turns his regard to the divine and intelligible Beauty (*Amatorius* 766A: πρὸς τὸ θεῖον καὶ νοητὸν καλόν; cf. 765D and 765F) – the impersonal phrasing is noteworthy in this context of love. A similar process may occur after death. In the eschatological myth of *On the face that appears in the orb of the moon*, Plutarch relates how the mind (νοῦς) is separated from the soul 'by love for the image in the sun through which shines forth manifest the desirable and fair and divine and blessed (τὸ ἐφετὸν καὶ καλὸν καὶ θεῖον καὶ μακάριον) towards which all nature in one way or another yearns' (944E).

Again, the same impersonal phrasing. We could wish such a fate on Plutarch himself. We could even wish that he became a hero after his death, and then a *daimon*, and even a god.[70] But whether he really expected to encounter his 'beloved Apollo' (*De E* 384E) as a personal god after his death is far from clear. It is a question which I prefer, with due Plutarchan *eulabeia*, to leave open, while, in an equally Plutarchan vein, insisting on the need for further *zetesis*.

---

[69] Roskam 1999a.
[70] Cf. *De def. or.* 415B–C and *Rom.* 28.10. On Plutarch's thinking about the destination of the soul, see further Brenk 1994.

LIST OF PLUTARCH'S WORKS

Moralia

[*De liberis educandis*] (Περὶ παίδων ἀγωγῆς) – [*On the education of children*]	1A–14C	*De lib. educ.*
De audiendis poetis (*Quomodo adulescens poetas audire debeat*) (Πῶς δεῖ τὸν νέον ποιημάτων ἀκούειν) – *How the young man should listen to poetry*	14D–37B	*De aud. poet.*
De audiendo (*De recta ratione audiendi*) (Περὶ τοῦ ἀκούειν) – *On listening*	37C–48D	*De aud.*
De adulatore et amico (*Quomodo adulator ab amico internoscatur*) (Πῶς ἄν τις διακρίνειε τὸν κόλακα τοῦ φίλου) – *How can one tell a flatterer from a friend?*	48E–74E	*De ad. et am.*
De profectibus in virtute (*Quomodo quis suos in virtute sentiat profectus*) (Πῶς ἄν τις αἴσθοιτο ἑαυτοῦ προκόπτοντος ἐπ᾽ ἀρετῇ) – *How can one become aware of one's moral progress?*	75A–86A	*De prof. in virt.*
De capienda ex inimicis utilitate (Πῶς ἄν τις ὑπ᾽ ἐχθρῶν ὠφελοῖτο) – *How can one profit from one's enemies?*	86B–92F	*De cap. ex inim.*
De amicorum multitudine (Περὶ πολυφιλίας) – *On having many friends*	93A–97B	*De am. mult.*
De fortuna (Περὶ τύχης) – *On fortune*	97C–100A	*De fortuna*
De virtute et vitio (Περὶ ἀρετῆς καὶ κακίας) – *On virtue and vice*	100B–101E	*De virt. et vit.*
[?] *Consolatio ad Apollonium* (Παραμυθητικὸς πρὸς Ἀπολλώνιον) – *Consolation to Apollonius*	101F–122A	*Cons. ad Apoll.*
De tuenda sanitate praecepta (Ὑγιεινὰ παραγγέλματα) – *Precepts of health care*	122B–137E	*De tuenda*
Coniugalia praecepta (Γαμικὰ παραγγέλματα) – *Precepts of marriage*	138A–146A	*Con. praec.*
Septem sapientium convivium (Τῶν ἑπτὰ σοφῶν συμπόσιον) – *The banquet of the Seven Sages*	146B–164D	*Sept. sap. conv.*
De superstitione (Περὶ δεισιδαιμονίας) – *On superstition*	164E–171F	*De sup.*

Regum et imperatorum apophthegmata (Ἀποφθέγματα βασιλέων καὶ στρατηγῶν) – *Sayings of kings and commanders*	172A–208A	*Reg. et imp. apophth.*
Apophthegmata Laconica – Instituta Laconica – Lacaenarum apophthegmata (Ἀποφθέγματα Λακωνικά – Τὰ παλαιὰ τῶν Λακεδαιμονίων ἐπιτηδεύματα – Λακαινῶν ἀποφθέγματα) – *Spartan sayings – Ancient customs of the Spartans – Sayings of Spartan women*	208A–242D	*Apophth. Lac.*
Mulierum virtutes (Γυναικῶν ἀρεταί) – *Virtues of women*	242E–263C	*Mul. virt.*
Quaestiones Romanae (Αἴτια Ῥωμαϊκά) – *Roman questions*	263D–291C	*Quaest. Rom.*
Quaestiones Graecae (Αἴτια Ἑλληνικά) – *Greek questions*	291D–304F	*Quaest. Graec.*
[Parallela Graeca et Romana] (Συναγωγὴ ἱστοριῶν παραλλήλων Ἑλληνικῶν καὶ Ῥωμαϊκῶν) – *[Greek and Roman parallel stories]*	305A–316B	*Parall. Graec. et Rom.*
De fortuna Romanorum (Περὶ τῆς Ῥωμαίων τύχης) – *On the fortune of the Romans*	316C–326C	*De fort. Rom.*
De Alexandri Magni fortuna aut virtute (Περὶ τῆς Ἀλεξάνδρου τύχης ἢ ἀρετῆς λόγοι β΄) – *On the fortune or virtue of Alexander*	326D–345B	*De Al. Magn. fort.*
De gloria Atheniensium (Bellone an pace clariores fuerint Athenienses) (Πότερον Ἀθηναῖοι κατὰ πόλεμον ἢ κατὰ σοφίαν ἐνδοξότεροι) – *Were the Athenians more famous in war or in wisdom?*	345C–351B	*Bellone an pace*
De Iside et Osiride (Περὶ Ἴσιδος καὶ Ὀσίριδος) – *On Isis and Osiris*	351C–384C	*De Is. et Os.*
De E apud Delphos (De E Delphico) (Περὶ τοῦ ΕΙ τοῦ ἐν Δελφοῖς) – *On the E at Delphi*	384D–394C	*De E*
De Pythiae oraculis (Περὶ τοῦ μὴ χρᾶν ἔμμετρα νῦν τὴν Πυθίαν) – *That the Pythia now does not give her oracles in verse*	394D–409D	*De Pyth. or.*
De defectu oraculorum (Περὶ τῶν ἐκλελοιπότων χρηστηρίων) – *On the obsolescence of oracles*	409E–438E	*De def. or.*
An virtus doceri possit (Εἰ διδακτὸν ἡ ἀρετή) – *Is virtue teachable?*	439A–440C	*An virt. doc.*

De virtute morali (Περὶ τῆς ἠθικῆς ἀρετῆς) – *On moral virtue*	440D–452D	*De virt. mor.*
De cohibenda ira (Περὶ ἀοργησίας) – *On the control of anger*	452F–464D	*De coh. ira*
De tranquillitate animi (Περὶ εὐθυμίας) – *On tranquillity of mind*	464E–477F	*De tranq. an.*
De fraterno amore (Περὶ φιλαδελφίας) – *On brotherly love*	478A–492D	*De frat. am.*
De amore prolis (Περὶ τῆς εἰς τὰ ἔγγονα φιλοστοργίας) – *On affection for offspring*	493A–497E	*De am. prol.*
An vitiositas ad infelicitatem sufficiat (Εἰ αὐτάρκης ἡ κακία πρὸς κακοδαιμονίαν) – *Is vice a sufficient cause for unhappiness?*	498A–500A	*An vitiositas*
Animine an corporis affectiones sint peiores (Πότερον τὰ τῆς ψυχῆς ἢ τὰ τοῦ σώματος πάθη χείρονα) – *Are the affections of the soul worse, or those of the body?*	500B–502A	*Animine an corp.*
De garrulitate (Περὶ ἀδολεσχίας) – *On talkativeness*	502B–515A	*De gar.*
De curiositate (Περὶ πολυπραγμοσύνης) – *On curiosity*	515B–523B	*De cur.*
De cupiditate divitiarum (Περὶ φιλοπλουτίας) – *On love of wealth*	523C–528B	*De cup. div.*
De vitioso pudore (Περὶ δυσωπίας) – *On compliance*	528C–536D	*De vit. pud.*
De invidia et odio (Περὶ φθόνου καὶ μίσους) – *On envy and hate*	536E–538E	*De inv. et od.*
De se ipsum citra invidiam laudando (*De laude ipsius*) (Περὶ τοῦ ἑαυτὸν ἐπαινεῖν ἀνεπιφθόνως) – *On praising oneself inoffensively*	539A–547F	*De se ipsum laud.*
De sera numinis vindicta (Περὶ τῶν ὑπὸ τοῦ θείου βραδέως τιμωρουμένων) – *On the slowness of divine punishments*	548A–568A	*De sera num.*
[*De fato*] (Περὶ εἱμαρμένης) – [*On fate*]	568B–574F	*De fato*
De genio Socratis (*De Socratis daemonio*) (Περὶ τοῦ Σωκράτους δαιμονίου) – *On Socrates' divine sign*	575A–598F	*De genio Socr.*
De exilio (Περὶ φυγῆς) – *On exile*	599A–607F	*De exilio*
Consolatio ad uxorem (Παραμυθητικὸς πρὸς τὴν γυναῖκα) – *Consolation to his wife*	608A–612B	*Cons. ad ux.*
Quaestionum convivalium libri IX (Συμποσιακῶν βιβλία θ´) – *Table Talk*	612C–748D	*Quaest. conv.*
Amatorius (Ἐρωτικός) – *Dialogue on love*	748E–771E	*Amatorius*

[*Aqua an ignis utilior sit*] (Πότερον ὕδωρ ἢ πῦρ χρησιμώτερον) – [*Is water or fire more useful?*]	955D–958E	*Aqua an ignis*
De sollertia animalium (*Terrestriane an aquatilia animalia sint callidiora*) (Πότερα τῶν ζῴων φρονιμώτερα τὰ χερσαῖα ἢ τὰ ἔνυδρα) – *Are land or sea animals cleverer?*	959A–985C	*De soll. an.*
Gryllus (*Bruta animalia ratione uti*) (Περὶ τοῦ τὰ ἄλογα λόγῳ χρῆσθαι) – *Gryllus, or that irrational animals use reason*	985D–992E	*Gryllus*
De esu carnium (Περὶ σαρκοφαγίας λόγοι β΄) – *On the eating of flesh*	993A–999B	*De esu*
Quaestiones Platonicae (Πλατωνικὰ ζητήματα) – *Platonic questions*	999C–1011E	*Quaest. Plat.*
De animae procreatione in Timaeo (Περὶ τῆς ἐν Τιμαίῳ ψυχογονίας) – *On the generation of the soul in the Timaeus*	1012A–1030C	*De an. procr.*
Epitome libri de animae procreatione in Timaeo (Ἐπιτομὴ τοῦ περὶ τῆς ἐν Τιμαίῳ ψυχογονίας) – *On the generation of the soul in the Timaeus (abridgement)*	1030D–1032F	
De Stoicorum repugnantiis (Περὶ Στωικῶν ἐναντιωμάτων) – *On the contradictions of the Stoics*	1033A–1057C	*De Stoic. rep.*
Stoicos absurdiora poetis dicere (Σύνοψις τοῦ ὅτι παραδοξότερα οἱ Στωικοὶ τῶν ποιητῶν λέγουσιν) – *That the Stoics talk more paradoxically than the poets (epitome)*	1057C–1058D	*Stoic. absurd. poet.*
De communibus notitiis adversus Stoicos (Περὶ τῶν κοινῶν ἐννοιῶν πρὸς τοὺς Στωικούς) – *On common conceptions, against the Stoics*	1058E–1086B	*De comm. not.*
Non posse suaviter vivi secundum Epicurum (Ὅτι οὐδὲ ζῆν ἔστιν ἡδέως κατ᾽ Ἐπίκουρον) – *That it is not even possible to live pleasantly when following the doctrines of Epicurus*	1086C–1107C	*Non posse*
Adversus Colotem (Πρὸς Κωλώτην ὑπὲρ τῶν ἄλλων φιλοσόφων) – *Against Colotes in defence of the other philosophers*	1107D–1127E	*Adv. Col.*
De latenter vivendo (*An recte dicendum sit latenter esse vivendum*) (Εἰ καλῶς εἴρηται τὸ λάθε βιώσας) – *Is 'live unnoticed' well said?*	1128A–1130E	*De lat. viv.*
[*De musica*] (Περὶ μουσικῆς) – [*On music*] *Fragmenta*	1131A–1147A	*De mus. fr.*

Vitae Parallelae

Theseus – Romulus	*Thes. – Rom.*
Comparatio Thesei et Romuli	*Comp. Thes. et Rom.*
Lycurgus – Numa	*Lyc. – Num.*
Comparatio Lycurgi et Numae	*Comp. Lyc. et Num.*
Solon – Publicola	*Sol. – Publ.*
Comparatio Solonis et Publicolae	*Comp. Sol. et Publ.*
Themistocles – Camillus	*Them. – Cam.*
Aristides – Cato Maior	*Arist. – Ca. Ma.*
Comparatio Aristidis et Catonis	*Comp. Arist. et Ca. Ma.*
Cimon – Lucullus	*Cim. – Luc.*
Comparatio Cimonis et Luculli	*Comp. Cim. et Luc.*
Pericles – Fabius Maximus	*Per. – Fab.*
Comparatio Periclis et Fabii Maximi	*Comp. Per. et Fab.*
Nicias – Crassus	*Nic. – Crass.*
Comparatio Niciae et Crassi	*Comp. Nic. et Crass.*
Marcius Coriolanus – Alcibiades	*Cor. – Alc.*
Comparatio Marcii Coriolani et Alcibiadis	*Comp. Cor. et Alc.*
Lysander – Sulla	*Lys. – Sull.*
Comparatio Lysandri et Sullae	*Comp. Lys. et Sull.*
Agesilaus – Pompeius	*Ages. – Pomp.*
Comparatio Agesilai et Pompeii	*Comp. Ages. et Pomp.*
Pelopidas – Marcellus	*Pel. – Marc.*
Comparatio Pelopidae et Marcelli	*Comp. Pel. et Marc.*
Dion – Brutus	*Dion – Brut.*
Comparatio Dionis et Bruti	*Comp. Dion. et Brut.*
Aemilius Paulus – Timoleon	*Aem. – Tim.*
Comparatio Aemilii Pauli et Timoleontis	*Comp. Aem. et Tim.*
Demosthenes – Cicero	*Dem. – Cic.*
Comparatio Demosthenis et Ciceronis	*Comp. Dem. et Cic.*
Alexander – Caesar	*Alex. – Caes.*
Sertorius – Eumenes	*Sert. – Eum.*
Comparatio Sertorii et Eumenis	*Comp. Sert. et Eum.*
Phocion – Cato Minor	*Phoc. – Ca. Mi.*
Demetrius – Antonius	*Demetr. – Ant.*
Comparatio Demetrii et Antonii	*Comp. Demetr. et Ant.*
Pyrrhus – Caius Marius	*Pyrrh. – Mar.*
Agis/Cleomenes – Tiberius Gracchus/Caius Gracchus	*Agis/Cleom. – TG/CG*
Comparatio Agidis et Cleomenis cum Tiberio et Caio Graccho	*Comp. Ag., Cleom. et Gracch.*
Philopoemen – Titus Flamininus	*Phil. – Flam.*
Comparatio Philopoemenis et Titi Flaminini	*Comp. Phil. et Flam.*
Aratus	*Arat.*
Artaxerxes	*Art.*
Galba	*Galba*
Otho	*Oth.*

BIBLIOGRAPHY

Aalders, G. J. D. 1977. 'Political Thought in Plutarch's *Convivium sept[e]m sapientium*', *Mnemosyne* 30: 28–39.

―――― 1982. *Plutarch's Political Thought*. Amsterdam, Oxford, and New York, North-Holland.

―――― and de Blois, L. 1992. 'Plutarch und die politische Philosophie der Griechen', *ANRW* 2.36.5: 3384–404.

Adam, H. 1974. *Plutarchs Schrift non posse suaviter vivi secundum Epicurum. Eine Interpretation*. Amsterdam, Grüner.

Aguilar, R. M. and Alfageme, I. R. (eds.) 2006. *Ecos de Plutarco en Europa. De fortuna Plutarchi studia selecta*. Madrid, Sociedad Española de Plutarquistas.

Ahlrichs, B. 2005. '*Prüfstein der Gemüter*'. *Untersuchungen zu den ethischen Vorstellungen in den Parallelbiographien Plutarchs am Beispiel des 'Coriolan'*. Hildesheim, Zurich, and New York: Olms.

Albini, F. 1993 (ed. and trans.). *Plutarco. Non posse suaviter vivi secundum Epicurum*. Genoa, Università di Genova, Darficlet.

Alcock, S. E. 1993. *Graecia capta. The Landscapes of Roman Greece*. Cambridge, Cambridge University Press.

Alexiou, E. 2010. 'Plutarchs *Lysander* und *Alkibiades* als "Syzygie": ein Beitrag zum moralischen Programm Plutarchs', *RhM* 153: 323–52.

Algra, K. 1990. 'Chrysippus on Virtuous Abstention from Ugly Old Women (Plutarch, SR 1038E–1039A)', *CQ* 40: 450–8.

―――― 2014. 'Plutarch and the Stoic Theory of Providence', in P. D'Hoine and G. Van Riel (eds.), *Fate, Providence and Moral Responsibility in Ancient, Medieval and Early Modern Thought. Studies in Honour of Carlos Steel*. Leuven, Leuven University Press: 117–35.

Almagor, E. 2013. 'Dualism and the Self in Plutarch's Thought', in J. Rüpke and G. Woolf (eds.), *Religious Dimensions of the Self in the Second Century* CE. Tübingen, Mohr Siebeck: 3–22.

―――― 2014. 'The *Aratus* and the *Artaxerxes*', in Beck 2014a: 278–91.

Aloumpi, M. 2017. 'Shifting Boundaries: *Philotimia* in Democratic Athens and in Plutarch's *Lives*', in Georgiadou and Oikonomopoulou 2017: 191–202.

Alt, K. 1993. *Weltflucht und Weltbejahung. Zur Frage des Dualismus bei Plutarch, Numenios, Plotin*. Stuttgart, Steiner.

Ameling, W. 1985. 'Plutarch, Perikles 12–14', *Historia* 34: 47–63.

Anson, E. M. 1977. 'The Siege of Nora: A Source Conflict', *GRBS* 18: 251–6.

Ash, R. 1997. 'Severed Heads: Individual Portraits and Irrational Forces in Plutarch's *Galba* and *Otho*', in Mossman 1997a: 189–214.

———, Mossman, J., and Titchener, F. B. (eds.) 2015. *Fame and Infamy. Essays for Christopher Pelling on Characterization in Greek and Roman Biography and Historiography*. Oxford, Oxford University Press.

Auberger, J. 1993. 'Parole et silence dans les *Préceptes du mariage* de Plutarque', *LEC* 61: 297–308.

Aulotte, R. 1965. *Amyot et Plutarque. La tradition des Moralia au XVIe siècle*. Geneva, Droz.

Avenarius, G. 1956. *Lukians Schrift zur Geschichtsschreibung*. Meisenheim am Glan, Hain.

Babbitt, F. C. 1927. *Plutarch's Moralia in Sixteen Volumes. I: 1A–86A*. Loeb Classical Library 197. London and Cambridge, MA, Harvard University Press.

Babut, D. (ed. and trans.) 1969a. *Plutarque. De la vertu éthique*. Paris, Les Belles Lettres.

——— 1969b. *Plutarque et le stoïcisme*. Paris, Presses universitaires de France.

——— 1984. 'Le dialogue de Plutarque sur le démon de Socrate: essai d'interprétation', *BAGB*: 51–76.

——— 1988. 'La part du rationalisme dans la religion de Plutarque: l'exemple du *De genio Socratis*', *ICS* 13: 383–407.

——— 1992. 'La composition des *Dialogues pythiques* de Plutarque et le problème de leur unité', *JS*: 187–234.

——— 1993. 'Stoïciens et Stoïcisme dans les *Dialogues pythiques* de Plutarque', *ICS* 18: 203–27.

——— 1996. 'Plutarque, Aristote, et l'Aristotélisme', in Van der Stockt 1996: 1–28.

——— 1998. 'Polémique et philosophie dans deux écrits antistoïciens de Plutarque', *REA* 100: 11–42.

Badian, E. 2003. 'Plutarch's Unconfessed Skill: The Biographer as a Critical Historian', in T. Hantos (ed.), *Laurea internationalis. Festschrift für Jochen Bleicken zum 75. Geburtstag*. Stuttgart, Steiner: 26–44.

Baldassarri, M. (ed. and trans.) 1976a. *Plutarco. Gli opuscoli contro gli Stoici. I: Della contraddizioni degli Stoici. Gli Stoici dicono cose più assurde dei poeti*. Trento, Verifiche.

——— (ed. and trans.) 1976b. *Plutarco. Gli opuscoli contro gli Stoici. II: Delle nozioni comuni, contro gli Stoici*. Trento, Verifiche.

——— 1994. 'La difesa della provvidenza nello scritto plutarcheo *De sera numinis vindicta*', *AW* 25: 147–58.

———— 2000. 'Osservazioni sulla struttura del periodo e sulla costruzione ritmica del discorso nei *Moralia* di Plutarco', in Van der Stockt 2000b: 1–13.

Baltes, M. 1976–8. *Die Weltentstehung des Platonischen Timaios nach den antiken Interpreten*. 2 vols, Leiden, Brill.

Baltussen, H. 2009. 'Personal Grief and Public Mourning in Plutarch's *Consolation to His Wife*', *AJPh* 130: 67–98.

Barigazzi, A. 1988. 'Una nuova interpretazione del *De genio Socratis*', *ICS* 13: 409–25.

———— (ed. and trans.) 1993. *Plutarco, <Se la virtù si debba insegnare> (La fortuna, Se la virtù si possa insegnare, Se siano più gravi le malattie dell'animo o del corpo, Se il vizio sia sufficiente a rendere infelici, La virtù e il vizio)*. Naples, D'Auria.

———— 1994. *Studi su Plutarco*. Florence, Università degli studi di Firenze.

Barrow, R. H. 1967. *Plutarch and His Times*. London, Chatto and Windus.

Becchi, F. 1975. 'Aristotelismo ed antistoicismo nel *De virtute morali* di Plutarco', *Prometheus* 1: 160–80.

———— 1978. 'Aristotelismo funzionale nel *De virtute morali* di Plutarco', *Prometheus* 4: 261–75.

———— 1981. 'Platonismo medio ed etica plutarchea', *Prometheus* 7: 125–45, 263–84.

———— (ed. and trans.) 1990. *Plutarco. La virtú etica*. Naples, D'Auria.

———— 1996. 'Plutarco e la dottrina dell'ὁμοίωσις θεῷ tra Platonismo ed Aristotelismo', in Gallo 1996: 321–35.

———— 2014. 'Plutarch, Aristotle, and the Peripatetics', in Beck 2014a: 73–87.

Beck, M. 1999. 'Plato, Plutarch, and the Use and Manipulation of Anecdotes in the *Lives of Lycurgus and Agesilaus*: History of the Laconic Apophthegm', in Pérez Jiménez *et al.* 1999: 173–87.

———— 2000. 'Anecdote and the Representation of Plutarch's Ethos', in Van der Stockt 2000b: 15–32.

———— 2002. 'Plutarch to Trajan: The Dedicatory Letter and the Apophthegmata Collection', in Stadter and Van der Stockt 2002: 163–73.

———— 2005. 'The Presentation of Ideology and the Use of Subliterary Forms in Plutarch's Works', in Pérez Jiménez and Titchener 2005: 51–68.

———— (ed.) 2014a. *A Companion to Plutarch*. Malden, MA, Wiley Blackwell.

———— 2014b. 'The Socratic Paradigm', in Beck 2014a: 463–78.

Bellanti, A. 2007. 'La teoria plutarchea della virtù tra platonismo, pitagorismo e aristotelismo', in Volpe Cacciatore and Ferrari 2007: 223–64.

Beneker, J. 2005. 'Thematic Correspondences in Plutarch's *Lives* of Caesar, Pompey, and Crassus', in de Blois *et al.* 2005: 315–25.

—— 2010. '*Asēmotatos* or *Autokratōr*? Obscurity and Glory in Plutarch's *Sertorius*', in Humble 2010: 103–19.

—— 2012. *The Passionate Statesman. Eros and Politics in Plutarch's Lives.* Oxford, Oxford University Press.

—— 2016. 'The Nature of Virtue and the Need for Self-Knowledge in Plutarch's *Demosthenes–Cicero*', in Opsomer *et al.* 2016: 147–59.

Berner, U., Feldmeier, R., Heininger, B., and Hirsch-Luipold, R. (eds. and trans.) 2000. *Plutarch. Εἰ καλῶς εἴρηται τὸ λάθε βιώσας. Ist 'Lebe im Verborgenen' eine Gute Lebensregel?* Darmstadt, Wissenschaftliche Buchgesellschaft.

Bianchi, U. 1987. 'Plutarch und der Dualismus', *ANRW* 2.36.1: 350–65.

Billault, A. 1999. 'Le *Dialogue sur l'amour* de Plutarque et les *Dialogues* de Platon sur l'amour', in Pérez Jiménez *et al.* 1999: 201–13.

Binder, C. 2008. *Plutarchs Vita des Artaxerxes. Ein historischer Kommentar.* Berlin and New York, De Gruyter.

Biraud, M. 2014. 'Usages narratifs des clausules métriques et des égalités syllabiques dans l'*Eroticos* de Plutarque', *Ploutarchos* 11: 39–55.

Bloedow, E. F. 1996. '"Olympian" Thoughts: Plutarch on Pericles' Congress Decree', *OAth* 21: 7–12.

Bonazzi, M. 2003. *Academici e Platonici. Il dibattito antico sullo scetticismo di Platone.* Milan, LED.

—— 2007. 'Eudorus of Alexandria and Early Imperial Platonism', in R. W. Sharples and R. Sorabji (eds.), *Greek and Roman Philosophy 100 BC–200 AD.* 2 vols, London, Institute of Classical Studies: ii.365–77.

—— 2008. 'L'offerta di Plutarco: teologia e filosofia nel De E apud Delphos (capitoli 1–2)', *Philologus* 152: 205–11.

—— 2014. 'Plutarch and the Skeptics', in Beck 2014a: 121–34.

—— 2020. 'Demons in the Cave: Plutarch on Plato and the Limits of Politics', *Mnemosyne* 73: 63–86.

Bosworth, A. B. 1992. 'History and Artifice in Plutarch's *Eumenes*', in Stadter 1992: 56–89.

Boulet, B. 2008. 'Why Does Plutarch's Apollo Have Many Faces?', in Nikolaidis 2008: 159–69.

Boulogne, J. 1987. 'Le sens des *Questions romaines* de Plutarque', *REG* 100: 471–6.

—— 1992. 'Les "Questions romaines" de Plutarque', *ANRW* 2.33.6: 4682–708.

—— 1994. *Plutarque. Un aristocrate grec sous l'occupation romaine.* Lille, Presses universitaires de Lille.

—— 2000. 'Les συγκρίσεις de Plutarque: une rhétorique de la σύγκρασις', in Van der Stockt 2000b: 33–44.

—— 2003. *Plutarque dans le miroir d'Épicure. Analyse d'une critique systématique de l'épicurisme*. Villeneuve d'Ascq, Presses universitaires du Septentrion.

—— 2004. 'L'unité multiple de dieu chez Plutarque', *RPhA* 21: 95–106.

—— (ed.) 2005. *Les Grecs de l'antiquité et les animaux. Le cas remarquable de Plutarque*. Lille: Université Charles-de-Gaulle Lille.

—— 2008. 'Plutarque et l'hermétisme', in J. Ribeiro Ferreira, L. Van der Stockt, and M. do Céu Fialho (eds.), *Philosophy in Society. Virtues and Values in Plutarch*. Leuven and Coimbra, Coimbra University Press: 53–64.

—— 2009–10. 'La philosophie du marriage chez Plutarque', *Ploutarchos* 7: 23–34.

——, Broze, M., and Couloubaritsis, L. (eds.) 2006. *Les platonismes des premiers siècles de notre ère. Plutarque, L'E de Delphes*. Brussels, Ousia.

Bowen, A. J. (ed. and trans.) 1992. *Plutarch. The Malice of Herodotus (de Malignitate Herodoti)*. Warminster, Aris & Phillips.

Bowersock, G. W. 1969. *Greek Sophists in the Roman Empire*. Oxford, Clarendon Press.

Bowie, E. 1997. 'Hadrian, Favorinus, and Plutarch', in Mossman 1997a: 1–15.

Boys-Stones, G. 1997a. 'Plutarch on the Probable Principle of Cold: Epistemology and the *De primo frigido*', *CQ* 47: 227–38.

—— 1997b. 'Thyrsus-Bearer of the Academy or Enthusiast for Plato? Plutarch's *De Stoicorum repugnantiis*', in Mossman 1997a: 41–58.

—— 1998. 'Plutarch on κοινὸς λόγος: Towards an Architecture of *De Stoicorum repugnantiis*', *OSAPh* 16: 299–329.

—— (trans.) 2018. *Platonist Philosophy 80 BC to AD 250. An Introduction and Collection of Sources in Translation*. Cambridge, Cambridge University Press.

Bravo García, A. 1973. 'El pensamiento de Plutarco acerca de la paz y la guerra', *CFC* 5: 141–91.

Bréchet, C. 1999. 'Le *De audiendis poetis* de Plutarque et le procès platonicien de la poésie', *RPh* 73: 209–44.

—— 2010–11. 'L'*exègèsis* chez Plutarque: textes poétiques, textes philosophiques et vérité', *Ploutarchos* 8: 35–50.

Brenk, F. E. 1973. '"A most strange doctrine": Daimon in Plutarch', *CJ* 69: 1–11.

—— 1977. *In Mist Apparelled. Religious Themes in Plutarch's Moralia and Lives*. Leiden, Brill.

—— 1987a. 'From Rex to Rana: Plutarch's Treatment of Nero', in A. Ceresa-Gastaldo (ed.), *Il protagonismo nella storiografia classica*. Genoa, Università di Genova, Darficlet: 121–42.

———— 1987b. 'An Imperial Heritage: The Religious Spirit of Plutarch of Chaironeia', *ANRW* 2.36.1: 248–349.

———— 1988. 'Plutarch's *Erotikos*: The Drag Down Pulled Up', *ICS* 13: 457–71.

———— 1994. 'The Origin and the Return of the Soul in Plutarch', in García Valdés 1994: 3–24.

———— 1996. 'Time as Structure in Plutarch's *The Daimonion of Sokrates*', in Van der Stockt 1996: 29–51.

———— 1997. 'Plutarch, Judaism and Christianity', in M. Joyal (ed.), *Studies in Plato and the Platonic Tradition. Essays Presented to John Whittaker*. Aldershot, Ashgate: 97–117.

———— 2000. 'All for Love: The Rhetoric of Exaggeration in Plutarch's *Erotikos*', in Van der Stockt 2000b: 45–60.

———— 2005. 'Plutarch's Middle-Platonic God: About to Enter (or Remake) the Academy', in Hirsch-Luipold 2005b: 27–49.

———— 2007. 'Zeus' Missing Ears', *Kernos* 20: 213–15.

———— 2009. '"In learned conversation": Plutarch's Symposiac Literature and the Elusive Authorial Voice', in Ribeiro Ferreira *et al.* 2009: 51–61.

———— 2012. 'Plutarch and "Pagan Monotheism"', in Roig Lanzillotta and Muñoz Gallarte 2012: 73–84.

———— 2016. 'Plutarch's Flawed Characters: The *Personae* of the Dialogues', in Opsomer *et al.* 2016: 89–100.

———— 2019. 'Plutarch the Greek in the *Roman Questions*', in Leão and Roig Lanzillotta 2019: 240–54.

Bresson, A. 2002. 'Un "Athénien" à Sparte ou Plutarque lecteur de Xénophon', *REG* 115: 22–57.

Brittain, C. 2005. 'Common Sense: Concepts, Definition and Meaning in and out of the Stoa', in D. Frede and B. Inwood (eds.), *Language and Learning. Philosophy of Language in the Hellenistic Age. Proceedings of the Ninth Symposium Hellenisticum*. Cambridge, Cambridge University Press: 164–209.

Broecker, H. 1954. *Animadversiones ad Plutarchi libellum Περὶ εὐθυμίας*. Bonn: Habelt.

Brokate, C. 1913. *De aliquot Plutarchi libellis*. Diss. Göttingen.

Brouillette, X. 2010. 'Apollon au-delà de tout ce qui est visible: Plutarque et *République* 6, 509B', in Brouillette and Giavatto 2010: 29–48.

———— 2014. *La philosophie delphique de Plutarque*. Paris, Les Belles Lettres.

———— and Giavatto, A. (eds.) 2010. *Les dialogues platoniciens chez Plutarque. Stratégies et méthodes exégétiques*. Leuven, Leuven University Press.

Bucher-Isler, B. 1972. *Norm und Individualität in den Biographien Plutarchs*. Bern and Stuttgart, Haupt.

Buckler, J. 1992. 'Plutarch and Autopsy', *ANRW* 2.33.6: 4788–830.

Burkert, W. 1996. 'Plutarco: religiosità personale e teologia filosofica', in Gallo 1996: 11–28.

Buszard, B. 2008. 'Caesar's Ambition: A Combined Reading of Plutarch's *Alexander–Caesar* and *Pyrrhus–Marius*', *TAPhA* 138: 185–215.

Caiazza, A. 1995. 'A proposito della paternità plutarchea del *De unius*', *Prometheus* 21: 131–40.

Carrière, J.-C. 1977. 'A propos de la *politique* de Plutarque', *DHA* 3: 237–51.

———— and Cuvigny, M. (eds. and trans.) 1984. *Plutarque. Œuvres morales*, vol. 11, part 2: *Préceptes politiques; Sur la monarchie, la démocratie et l'oligarchie*. Collection des universités de France. Paris, Les Belles Lettres.

Carter, J. W. 2018. 'Plutarch's Epicurean Justification of Religious Belief', *JHPh* 56: 385–412.

Casanova, A. 2012. 'Plutarch as Apollo's Priest at Delphi', in Roig Lanzillotta and Muñoz Gallarte 2012: 151–7.

Casevitz M. and Babut, D. (eds. and trans.) 2002. *Plutarque. Œuvres morales*, vol. 15, part 2: *Traité 72. Sur les notions communes, contre les Stoïciens*. Collection des universités de France. Paris, Les Belles Lettres.

———— (eds. and trans.) 2004. *Plutarque. Œuvres morales*, vol. 15, part 1: *Traité 70. Sur les contradictions stoïciennes; Traité 71, Synopsis du traité 'Que les Stoïciens tiennent des propos plus paradoxaux que les poètes'*. Collection des universités de France. Paris, Les Belles Lettres.

Castelnérac, B. 2007. 'Plutarch's Psychology of Moral Virtue: "Pathos", "Logos", and the Unity of the Soul', *AncPhil* 27: 141–63.

Cherniss, H. 1976. *Plutarch. Moralia Vol. XIII, Part I*. Loeb Classical Library. Cambridge, MA, and London, Harvard University Press.

Chlup, R. 2000. 'Plutarch's Dualism and the Delphic Cult', *Phronesis* 45: 138–58.

Chrysanthou, C. S. 2018. 'Plutarch's Rhetoric of *Periautologia*: *Demosthenes* 1–3', *CJ* 113: 281–301.

Claassen, J.-M. 2004. 'Plutarch's Little Girl', *AClass* 47: 27–50.

Corlu, A. (ed. and trans.) 1970. *Plutarque. Le démon de Socrate*. Paris, Klincksieck.

Cornford, F. M. (ed. and trans.) 1937. *Plato's Cosmology. The Timaeus of Plato*. London, Routledge and Kegan Paul.

Corti, A. 2014. *L'Adversus Colotem di Plutarco. Storia di una polemica filosofica*. Leuven, Leuven University Press.

Darbo-Peschanski, C. 1998. 'Pourquoi chercher des causes aux coutumes? (Les *Questions romaines* et les *Questions grecques* de Plutarque)', in Payen 1998: 21–30.

de Blois, L. *et al.* (eds.) 2004. *The Statesman in Plutarch's Works. Volume I. Plutarch's Statesman and His Aftermath. Political, Philosophical, and Literary Aspects.* Leiden and Boston, MA, Brill.

—— *et al.* (eds.) 2005. *The Statesman in Plutarch's Works. Volume II. The Statesman in Plutarch's Greek and Roman Lives.* Leiden and Boston, MA, Brill.

Defradas, J. (ed. and trans.) 1954. *Plutarque. Le banquet des sept sages.* Paris, Klincksieck.

——, Hani, J., and Klaerr, R. (eds. and trans.) 1985. *Plutarque. Œuvres morales,* vol. 2: *Consolation à Apollonios, Préceptes de santé, Préceptes de mariage, Le banquet des sept sages, De la superstition.* Collection des universités de France. Paris, Les Belles Lettres.

Delvaux, G. 1995. 'Plutarque: Chronologie relative des *Vies Parallèles*', *LEC* 63: 97–113.

de Michele, L. 2005. 'Fimbria e Sertorio: *Proditores reipublicae?*', *Athenaeum* 93: 277–89.

Demulder, B. 2017. 'The Old Man and the Soul: Plato's *Laws* 10 in Plutarch's *De animae procreatione*', in Sanz Morales *et al.* 2017: 141–51.

—— 2018. '*The Good Universe and the Universal Good: Plutarch's Cosmological Ethics*', PhD thesis, Leuven University.

den Boer, W. 1985. 'Plutarch's Philosophic Basis for Personal Involvement', in J. W. Eadie and J. Ober (eds.), *The Craft of the Ancient Historian. Essays in Honor of Chester G. Starr.* Lanham, MD, New York, and London, University Press of America: 373–85.

de Romilly, J. 1979. *La douceur dans la pensée grecque.* Paris, Les Belles Lettres.

De Rosalia, A. 1991. 'Il latino di Plutarco', in G. D'Ippolito and I. Gallo (eds.), *Strutture formali dei 'Moralia' di Plutarco. Atti del III Convegno plutarcheo. Palermo, 3–5 maggio 1989.* Naples, D'Auria: 445–59.

Desideri, P. 1986. 'La vita politica cittadina nell'impero: Lettura dei *Praecepta gerendae rei publicae* e dell'*An seni res publica gerenda sit*', *Athenaeum* n.s. 64: 371–81.

—— 1992a. 'I documenti di Plutarco', *ANRW* 2.33.6: 4536–67.

—— 1992b. 'La formazione delle coppie nelle *Vite* plutarchee', *ANRW* 2.33.6: 4470–86.

Deuse, W. 2010. 'Plutarch's Eschatological Myths', in Nesselrath 2010: 169–97.

Dillon, J. 1977. *The Middle Platonists. A Study of Platonism 80 B.C. to A.D. 220.* London, Duckworth.

—— 1988. 'Plutarch and Platonist Orthodoxy', *ICS* 13: 357–64.

—— 1989. 'Tampering with the *Timaeus*: Ideological Emendations in Plato, with Special Reference to the *Timaeus*', *AJPh* 110: 50–72.

—— 1997. 'Plutarch and the End of History', in Mossman 1997a: 233–40.

—— 1999. 'Plutarch's Debt to Xenocrates', in Pérez Jiménez *et al.* 1999: 305–11.

—— 2002. 'Plutarch and God: Theodicy and Cosmogony in the Thought of Plutarch', in D. Frede and A. Laks (eds.), *Traditions of Theology. Studies in Hellenistic Theology, Its Background and Aftermath.* Leiden, Boston, MA, and Cologne, Brill: 223–37.

—— 2014. 'Plutarch and Platonism', in Beck 2014a: 61–72.

Dodds, E. R. 1933. 'The Portrait of a Greek Gentleman', *G&R* 5: 97–107.

Dognini, C. 2007. 'Il *De Herodoti malignitate* e la fortuna di Erodoto', in Y. Perrin (ed.), *Neronia VII. Rome, l'Italie et la Grèce. Hellénisme et philhellénisme au premier siècle après J.-C.* Brussels, Latomus: 481–502.

Donini, P. 1974. *Tre studi sull'aristotelismo nel II secolo d. C.* Turin, Paravia.

—— 1992. 'Il *De facie* di Plutarco e la teologia medioplatonica', in S. Gersh and C. Kannengiesser (eds.), *Platonism in Late Antiquity.* Notre Dame, IL, University of Notre Dame Press: 103–13.

—— 2004. 'Plutarco e Aristotele', in Gallo 2004: 255–73.

—— 2011a. *Commentary and Tradition. Aristotelianism, Platonism, and Post-Hellenistic Philosophy.* Berlin and New York, De Gruyter.

—— (ed. and trans.) 2011b. *Plutarco. Il volto della luna.* Naples, D'Auria.

—— (ed. and trans.) 2017. *Plutarco. Il demone di Socrate.* Rome, Carocci.

Dorandi, T. 1991. 'Den Autoren über die Schulter geschaut: Arbeitsweise und Autographie bei den antiken Schriftstellern', *ZPE* 87: 11–33.

—— 2000. *Le stylet et la tablette. Dans le secret des auteurs antiques.* Paris, Les Belles Lettres.

Döring, K. 1984. 'Plutarch und das Daimonion des Sokrates (Plut., *de genio Socratis* Kap. 20–24)', *Mnemosyne* 37: 376–92.

Dörrie, H. 1969. 'Le platonisme de Plutarque', in *Actes du VIIIe Congrès de l'Association Guillaume Budé (Paris, 5–10 avril 1968).* Paris, Les Belles Lettres: 519–30.

—— 1971. 'Die Stellung Plutarchs im Platonismus seiner Zeit', in R. B. Palmer and R. Hamerton-Kelly (eds.), *Philomathes. Studies and Essays in the Humanities in Memory of Philip Merlan.* The Hague, Nijhoff: 36–56.

Duff, T. E. 1999a. 'Plutarch, Plato and "Great Natures"', in Pérez Jiménez *et al.* 1999: 313–32.

—— 1999b. *Plutarch's Lives. Exploring Virtue and Vice.* Oxford, Clarendon Press.

———— 2001. 'The Prologue to the *Lives of Perikles and Fabius* (*Per.* 1–2)',
in Pérez Jiménez and Casadesús Bordoy 2001: 351–63.

———— 2003. 'Plutarch on the Childhood of Alkibiades (*Alk.* 2–3)', *PCPhS*
49: 89–117.

———— 2004. 'Plato, Tragedy, the Ideal Reader and Plutarch's *Demetrios
and Antony*', *Hermes* 132: 271–91.

———— 2007–8. 'Plutarch's Readers and the Moralism of the *Lives*',
Ploutarchos 5: 3–18.

———— 2008a. 'Models of Education in Plutarch', *JHS* 128: 1–26.

———— 2008b. 'The Opening of Plutarch's *Life of Themistokles*', *GRBS* 48:
159–79.

———— 2009. '"Loving too much": The Text of Plutarch, *Themistokles* 2.3',
Philologus 153: 149–58.

———— 2010. 'Plutarch's *Themistocles and Camillus*', in Humble 2010:
45–86.

———— 2011a. 'Plutarch's *Lives* and the Critical Reader', in Roskam and
Van der Stockt 2011: 59–82.

———— 2011b. 'The Structure of the Plutarchan Book', *ClAnt* 30: 213–78.

———— 2015. 'Aspect and Subordination in Plutarchan Narrative', in Ash,
Mossman, and Titchener 2015: 129–48.

Dumortier, J. 1969. 'Le châtiment de Néron dans le mythe de Thespésios
(*De sera numinis vindicta*, 31, 267E–568A)', in *Actes du VIIIe Congrès
de l'Association Guillaume Budé (Paris, 5–10 avril 1968)*. Paris, Les
Belles Lettres: 552–60.

———— (ed. and trans.) 1975. *Plutarque. Œuvres Morales*, vol. 7, part 1:
Traités de morale 27–36. Collection des universités de France. Paris,
Les Belles Lettres.

Effe, B. 2002. 'Die Liebe der Ismenodora: Zur Funktion der
Rahmenhandlung in Plutarchs *Erotikos*', *WJA* 20: 99–111.

———— 2008. 'Πράξεις und λόγοι: Zur literarischen Technik in Plutarchs
Dialog *De genio Socratis*', *WJA* 32: 159–72.

Egelhaaf-Gaiser, U. 2013. 'Gelehrte Tischgespräche beim panhellenischen
Fest: Bildungs- und Deutungskonkurrenz in den Symposialdialogen
des Plutarch', in S. Föllinger and G. M. Müller (eds.), *Der Dialog
in der Antike. Formen und Funktionen einer literarischen Gattung zwischen
Philosophie, Wissensvermittlung und dramatischer Inszenierung*. Berlin
and Boston, MA, De Gruyter: 295–325.

Erbse, H. 1956. 'Die Bedeutung der Synkrisis in den Parallelbiographien
Plutarchs', *Hermes* 89: 398–424.

Erler, M. and Stadler, M. A. (eds.) 2017. *Platonismus und spätägyptische
Religion. Plutarch und die Ägyptenrezeption in der Römischen Kaiserzeit*.
Berlin and Boston, MA, De Gruyter.

Eshleman, K. 2013. '"Then our symposium becomes a grammar school"': Grammarians in Plutarch's *Table Talks*', *SyllClass* 24: 145–71.

Feldman, L. H. 1996. 'The Jews as Viewed by Plutarch', in *Studies in Hellenistic Judaism*. Leiden, New York, and Cologne, Brill: 529–52.

Fernández Delgado, J. A. and Pordomingo Pardo, F. (eds.) 1996. *Estudios sobre Plutarco. Aspectos formales. Actas del IV Simposio español sobre Plutarco. Salamanca, 26 a 28 de Mayo de 1994*. Salamanca, Ediciones clásicas.

Ferrari, F. 1995. *Dio, idee e materia. La struttura del cosmo in Plutarco di Cheronea*. Naples, D'Auria.

——— 1996. Dio: padre e artifice. La teologia di Plutarco in *Plat. quaest.* 2', in Gallo 1996: 395–409.

——— 1999a. 'Platone, *Tim.* 35a1–6 in Plutarco, *An. procr.* 1012B–C: Citazione ed esegesi', *RhM* 142: 326–39.

——— 1999b. 'Πρόνοια platonica e Νόησις νοήσεως aristotelica: Plutarco e l'impossibilità di una sintesi', in Pérez Jiménez *et al.* 1999: 63–77.

——— 2001a. 'La letteratura filosofica di carattere esegetico in Plutarco', *SicGymn* 54: 259–83.

——— 2001b. 'Struttura e funzione dell'esegesi testuale nel medioplatonismo: Il caso del *Timeo*', *Athenaeum* 89: 525–74.

——— 2004. 'Platone in Plutarco', in Gallo 2004: 225–35.

——— 2005a. 'Der Gott Plutarchs und der Gott Platons', in Hirsch-Luipold 2005b: 13–25.

——— 2005b. 'Plutarco e lo scetticismo ellenistico', in A. Casanova (ed.), *Plutarco e l'età ellenistica*. Florence, Università degli studi di Firenze: 369–84.

——— 2007–8. 'I fondamenti metafisici dell'etica di Plutarco', *Ploutarchos* 5: 19–31.

——— 2010. 'La costruzione del platonismo nel *De E apud Delphos* di Plutarco', *Athenaeum* 98: 71–87.

——— 2015. 'Le système des causes chez Plutarque', *RPhA* 33: 95–114.

——— and Baldi, L. (eds. and trans.) 2002. *Plutarco. La generazione dell'anima nell Timeo*. Naples, D'Auria.

Ferreira, J. R. (ed.) 2002. *Plutarco educador da Europa*. Porto: Fundaçao Eng. António de Almeida.

Flacelière, R. 1943. 'Plutarque et la Pythie', *REG* 56: 72–111.

——— 1959. 'Plutarque et l'épicurisme', in *Epicurea, in memoriam Hectoris Bignone. Miscellanea philologica*. Genoa, Istituto di filologia classica e medioevale: 197–215.

——— 1964. *Sagesse de Plutarque*. Paris, Presses universitaires de France.

——— 1974. 'La théologie selon Plutarque', in *Mélanges de philosophie, de littérature et d'histoire ancienne offerts à Pierre Boyancé*. Rome, École française de Rome: 273–80.

———— 1976. 'Trajan, Delphes et Plutarque', in *Recueil Plassart. Études sur l'antiquité grecque offertes à André Plassart par ses collègues de la Sorbonne.* Paris, Les Belles Lettres: 97–103.

———— and Chambry, É. (eds. and trans.) 1973. *Plutarque. Vies. Tome VIII. Sertorius–Eumène; Agésilas–Pompée.* Collection des universités de France. Paris, Les Belles Lettres.

———— and Irigoin, J. 1987. 'Introduction générale', in *Plutarque. Œuvres morales,* vol. 1, part 1: *De l'éducation des enfants et Comment lire les poètes.* Collection des universités de France. Paris, Les Belles Lettres: vii–cccx.

———— and Juneaux, M. (eds. and trans.) 1961. *Plutarque. Vies. Tome II. Solon–Publicola; Thémistocle–Camille.* Collection des universités de France. Paris, Les Belles Lettres.

Frazer, R. M. 1971. 'Nero the Singing Animal', *Arethusa* 4: 215–8.

Frazier, F. 1987. 'A propos de la composition des couples dans les *Vies parallèles* de Plutarque', *RPh* 61: 65–75.

———— 1988. 'A propos de la *philotimia* dans les *Vies*: Quelques jalons dans l'histoire d'une notion', *RPh* ser. 3, 62: 109–27.

———— 1992. 'Contribution à l'étude de la composition des *Vies* de Plutarque: L'élaboration des grandes scènes', *ANRW* 2.33.6: 4487–535.

———— 1995. 'Principes et décisions dans le domaine politique d'après les *Vies* de Plutarque', in Gallo and Scardigli 1995: 147–71.

———— 2011. 'Autour du miroir: Les miroitements d'une image dans l'œuvre de Plutarque', in Roskam and Van der Stockt 2011: 297–326.

———— 2014. 'The Perils of Ambition', in Beck 2014a: 488–502.

———— 2016. *Histoire et morale dans les Vies parallèles de Plutarque.* Paris, Les Belles Lettres.

———— 2019. *Quelques aspects du platonisme de Plutarque. Philosopher en commun, tourner sa pensée vers Dieu.* Leiden and Boston, MA, Brill.

———— and Leão, D. 2010. *Tychè et Pronoia. La marche du monde selon Plutarque.* Coimbra, Centro de Estudos Clássicos e Humanísticos da Universidade de Coimbra.

Froidefond, C. 1987. 'Plutarque et le platonisme', *ANRW* 2.36.1: 184–233.

Frost, F. J. 1980. *Plutarch's Themistocles. A Historical Commentary.* Princeton, NJ, Princeton University Press.

Fuhrmann, F. 1964. *Les images de Plutarque,* inaugural diss., University of Paris.

Gallo, I. (ed.) 1996. *Plutarco e la religione. Atti del VI Convegno plutarcheo (Ravello, 29–31 maggio 1995).* Naples, D'Auria.

———— (ed.) 1998. *L'eredità culturale di Plutarco dall'antichità al Rinascimento.* Naples, D'Auria.

—— (ed.) 2004. *La biblioteca di Plutarco. Atti del IX Convegno plutarcheo. Pavia, 13–15 giugno 2002*. Naples, D'Auria.

—— and Moreschini, C. (eds.) 2000. *I generi letterari in Plutarco. Atti del VIII Convegno plutarcheo. Pisa, 2–4 giugno 1999*. Naples, D'Auria.

—— and Scardigli, B. (eds.) 1995. *Teoria e prassi politica nelle opere di Plutarco*. Naples, D'Auria.

García Moreno, L. A. 1992. 'Paradoxography and Political Ideals in Plutarch's *Life of Sertorius*', in Stadter 1992: 132–58.

García Valdés, M. (ed.) 1994. *Estudios sobre Plutarco. Ideas Religiosas. Actas del III Simposio Internacional sobre Plutarco. Oviedo 30 de abril a 2 de mayo de 1992*. Madrid, Ediciones clásicas.

Geiger, J. 1981. 'Plutarch's Parallel Lives: The Choice of Heroes', *Hermes* 109: 85–104.

—— 1995. 'Plutarch on Hellenistic Politics: The Case of Eumenes of Cardia', in Gallo and Scardigli 1995: 173–85.

—— 2002. '*Felicitas temporum* and Plutarch's Choice of Heroes', in Stadter and Van der Stockt 2002: 93–102.

—— 2005. 'Plutarch's Choice of Roman Heroes: Further Considerations', in Pérez Jiménez and Titchener 2005: 231–42.

—— 2010. 'Plutarch, Dionysus, and the God of the Jews Revisited (An Exercise in *Quellenforschung*)', in Van der Stockt *et al.* 2010: 211–19.

—— 2014. 'The Project of the *Parallel Lives*: Plutarch's Conception of Biography', in Beck 2014a: 292–303.

Georgiadou, A. 1988. 'The *Lives of the Caesars* and Plutarch's Other *Lives*', *ICS* 13: 349–56.

—— 1995. 'Vita activa and vita contemplativa: Plutarch's *De genio Socratis* and Euripides' *Antiope*', in Gallo and Scardigli 1995: 187–200.

—— 2014. 'The *Lives of the Caesars*', in Beck 2014a: 251–66.

—— and Oikonomopoulou, K. (eds.) 2017. *Space, Time, and Language in Plutarch*. Berlin and Boston, MA, De Gruyter.

Gianakaris, C. J. 1970. *Plutarch*. New York, Twayne.

Giangrande, G. 1992. 'La lingua dei *Moralia* di Plutarco: Normativismo e questioni di metodo', in I. Gallo and R. Laurenti (eds.), *I Moralia di Plutarco tra filologia e filosofia*. Naples, D'Auria: 29–46.

Giavatto, A. 2010a. 'Le dialogue des sources dans les *Questions Platoniciennes* de Plutarque', in Brouillette and Giavatto 2010: 117–29.

—— 2010b. 'Répertoire des citations de Platon dans les *Moralia*', in Brouillette and Giavatto 2010: 131–41.

Gill, C. 1983. 'The Question of Character-Development: Plutarch and Tacitus', *CQ* n.s. 33: 469–87.

—— 1994. 'Peace of Mind and Being Yourself: Panaetius to Plutarch', *ANRW* 2.36.7: 4599–640.

Gioè, A. 1996. 'Aspetti dell'esegesi medioplatonica: La manipolazione e l'adattamento della citazioni', in *RAL*, ser. 9, 7: 287–309.

Glucker, J. 1978. *Antiochus and the Late Academy*. Göttingen, Vandenhoeck und Ruprecht.

Goessler, L. 1962. *Plutarchs Gedanken über die Ehe*. Zurich, Berichthaus.

Goldhill, S. 1995. *Foucault's Virginity. Ancient Erotic Fiction and the History of Sexuality*. Cambridge, Cambridge University Press.

——— (ed.) 2001. *Being Greek under Rome. Cultural Identity, the Second Sophistic and the Development of Empire*. Cambridge, Cambridge University Press.

Gómez, P. and Mestre, F. 1997. 'Historia en Plutarco: Los Griegos y los Romanos', in Schrader *et al.* 1997: 209–22.

Görgemanns, H. 1970. *Untersuchungen zu Plutarchs Dialog De facie in orbe lunae*. Heidelberg, Winter.

——— 2005. 'Eros als Gott in Plutarchs "Amatorius"', in Hirsch-Luipold 2005b: 169–95.

Graf, F. 1996. 'Plutarco e la religione romana', in Gallo 1996: 269–83.

Graninger, D. 2010. 'Plutarch on the Evacuation of Athens (*Themistocles* 10.8–9)', *Hermes* 138: 308–17.

Gréard, O. 1885. *De la morale de Plutarque*. Paris, Hachette.

Griffiths, J. G. (ed. and trans.) 1970. *Plutarch's De Iside et Osiride*. Cardiff, University of Wales Press.

Grube, G. M. A. 1932. 'The Composition of the World-Soul in *Timaeus* 35 A–B', *CPh* 27: 80–2.

Guerrier, O. (ed.) 2005. *La tradition des Œuvres morales de Plutarque de l'Antiquité au début de la Renaissance, Pallas* 67: 71–210.

Hadley, R. A. 2001. 'A Possible Lost Source for the Career of Eumenes of Kardia', *Historia* 50: 3–33.

Halliday, W. R. (ed. and trans.) 1928. *The Greek Questions of Plutarch*. Oxford, Clarendon Press.

Hamilton, J. R. 1969. *Plutarch Alexander. A Commentary*. Oxford, Clarendon Press.

Hani, J. 1976. *La religion égyptienne dans la pensée de Plutarque*. Paris, Les Belles Lettres.

Hardie, P. R. 1992. 'Plutarch and the Interpretation of Myth', *ANRW* 2.33.6: 4743–87.

Harrison, G. W. M. 1987. 'Rhetoric, Writing and Plutarch', *AncSoc* 18: 271–9.

——— 1995. 'The Demise of the Periclean Ideal (Plutarch, *ad Principem ineruditum*)', in Gallo and Scardigli 1995: 201–7.

——— 2000. 'Problems with the Genre of *Problems*: Plutarch's Literary Innovations', *CPh* 95: 193–9.

—— and Francis, J. 2008. 'Plutarch in Crete', in Nikolaidis 2008: 791–803.

Heftner, H. 1995. *Plutarch und der Aufstieg des Pompeius. Ein historischer Kommentar zu Plutarchs Pompeiusvita. Teil I: Kap. 1–45.* Frankfurt, Lang.

Helmbold, W. C. and O'Neil, E. N. 1959. *Plutarch's Quotations.* Baltimore, MD, American Philological Association.

Helmig, C. 2005. 'A Jumble of Disordered Remarks? Structure and Argument of Plutarch's *De sera numinis uindicta*', in Jufresa *et al.* 2005: 323–32.

Herbert, K. 1957. 'The Identity of Plutarch's Lost *Scipio*', *AJPh* 78: 83–8.

Herchenroeder, L. 2008. 'Τί γὰρ τοῦτο πρὸς τὸν λόγον: Plutarch's *Gryllus* and the So-Called *Grylloi*', *AJPh* 129: 347–79.

Hershbell, J. P. 1987. 'Plutarch's *De animae procreatione in Timaeo*: An Analysis of Structure and Content', *ANRW* 2.36.1: 234–47.

—— 1992a. 'Plutarch and Epicureanism', *ANRW* 2.36.5: 3353–83.

—— 1992b. 'Plutarch and Stoicism', *ANRW* 2.36.5: 3336–52.

—— 1993. 'Plutarch and Herodotus: The Beetle in the Rose', *RhM* 136: 143–63.

—— 1997. 'Plutarch's Concept of History: Philosophy from Examples', *AncSoc* 28: 225–43.

Hillyard, B. P. (ed.) 1988. *Plutarch. De audiendo.* Salem, MA, Ayer Company.

Hirsch-Luipold, R. 2002. *Plutarchs Denken in Bildern. Studien zur literarischen, philosophischen und religiösen Funktion des Bildhaften.* Tübingen, Mohr Siebeck.

—— 2005a. 'Der eine Gott bei Philon von Alexandrien und Plutarch', in Hirsch-Luipold 2005b: 141–68.

—— (ed.) 2005b. *Gott und die Götter bei Plutarch. Götterbilder – Gottesbilder – Weltbilder.* Berlin and New York, De Gruyter.

—— 2014. 'Religion and Myth', in Beck 2014a: 163–76.

—— 2016. 'The Dividing Line: Theological/Religious Arguments in Plutarch's Anti-Stoic Polemics', in Opsomer *et al.* 2016: 17–36.

—— and Roig Lanzillotta, L. (eds.) 2021. *Plutarch's Religious Landscapes.* Leiden and Boston, MA, Brill.

Hirzel, R. 1895. *Der Dialog. Ein literarhistorischer Versuch.* 2 vols. Leipzig, Hirzel.

—— 1912. *Plutarch.* Leipzig, Dieterich.

Holzhausen, J. 1993. 'Zur Inspirationslehre Plutarchs in *De Pythiae oraculis*', *Philologus* 137: 72–91.

Hopfner, T. (ed. and trans.) 1941. *Plutarch. Über Isis und Osiris. II. Teil: Die Deutungen der Sage.* Prague, Orientalni Ustav.

Horky, P. S. 2017. 'The Spectrum of Animal Rationality in Plutarch', *Apeiron* 50: 103–33.

Humble, N. (ed.) 2010. *Plutarch's Lives. Parallelism and Purpose.* Swansea, Classical Press of Wales.

Hunter, R. and Russell, D. (eds.) 2011. *Plutarch. How to Study Poetry (De audiendis poetis).* Cambridge, Cambridge University Press.

Hutchinson, G. O. 2018. *Plutarch's Rhythmic Prose.* Oxford, Oxford University Press.

Indelli, G. (ed. and trans.) 1995. *Plutarco. Le bestie sono esseri razionali.* Naples, D'Auria.

Ingenkamp, H. G. 1971. *Plutarchs Schriften über die Heilung der Seele.* Göttingen: Vandenhoeck und Ruprecht.

———— 1984. 'Plutarch as Pragmatist', *CB* 60: 79–82.

———— 1985. 'Luciano e Plutarco: Due incontri con il divino', *AFLS* 6: 29–45.

———— 1999. '*De virtute morali*: Plutarchs Scheingefecht gegen die Stoische Lehre von der Seele', in Pérez Jiménez *et al.* 1999: 79–93.

———— 2000. 'Rhetorische und philosophische Mittel der Seelenheilung: Ein Vergleich zwischen Ciceros Tusculaner Disputationen und Plutarchs Seelenheilungsschriften', in Van der Stockt 2000b: 251–66.

———— 2001. 'Juridical and Non-Juridical Eschatologies – and Mysteries', in Pérez Jiménez and Casadesús Bordoy 2001: 131–41.

———— 2016. 'De Plutarchi malignitate', in Opsomer *et al.* 2016: 229–42.

Jacobs, S. G. 2018. *Plutarch's Pragmatic Biographies. Lessons for Statesmen and Generals in the Parallel Lives.* Leiden and Boston, MA, Brill.

Jaillard, D. 2007. 'Plutarque et la divination: La piété d'un prêtre philosophe', *RHR* 224: 149–69.

Jazdzewska, K. 2009–10. 'Not an "Innocent Spectacle": Hunting and *venationes* in Plutarch's *De sollertia animalium*', *Ploutarchos* 7: 35–45.

———— 2013. 'A Skeleton at a Banquet: Death in Plutarch's *Convivium septem sapientium*', *Phoenix* 67: 301–19.

———— 2016. 'Laughter in Plutarch's *Convivium septem sapientium*', *CPh* 111: 74–88.

———— 2018. 'Plutarch's *Greek Questions*: Between Glossography and *Problemata*-Literature', *Hermes* 146: 41–53.

Jeuckens, R. 1907. *Plutarch von Chaeronea und die Rhetorik.* Strassburg: Trübner.

Jones, C. P. 1966. 'Towards a Chronology of Plutarch's Works', *JRS* 56: 61–74.

———— 1967. 'The Teacher of Plutarch', *HSCPh* 71: 205–13.

———— 1971. *Plutarch and Rome.* Oxford, Clarendon Press.

Jones, R. M. 1916. *The Platonism of Plutarch.* Menasha, Collegiate Press (reprinted New York, Garland, 1980).

Jufresa, M., Mestre, F., Gómez, P., and Gilabert, P. (eds.) 2005. *Plutarc a la seva època. Paideia i societat*. Barcelona, Sociedad Española de Plutarquistas.

Kaesser, C. 2004. 'Tweaking the Real: Art Theory and the Borderline between History and Morality in Plutarch's *Lives*', *GRBS* 44: 361–74.

Karamanolis, G. E. 2006. *Plato and Aristotle in Agreement? Platonists on Aristotle from Antiochus to Porphyry*. Oxford, Clarendon Press.

Katz, B. R. 1983. 'Notes on Sertorius', *RhM* 126: 44–68.

Kechagia, E. 2011a. 'Philosophy in Plutarch's *Table Talk*: In Jest or in Earnest?', in Klotz and Oikonomopoulou 2011: 77–104.

——— 2011b. *Plutarch Against Colotes. A Lesson in History of Philosophy*. Oxford, Oxford University Press.

——— 2014. 'Plutarch and Epicureanism', in Beck 2014a: 104–20.

Klaerr, R., Philippon, A., and Sirinelli, J. (eds. and trans.) 1989. *Plutarque. Œuvres morales*, vol. 1, part 2. Collection des universités de France. Paris, Les Belles Lettres.

Klotz, F. 2007. 'Portraits of the Philosopher: Plutarch's Self-Presentation in the *Quaestiones convivales*', *CQ* 57: 650–67.

——— 2014. 'The Sympotic Works', in Beck 2014a: 207–22.

——— and Oikonomopoulou, K. (eds.) 2011. *The Philosopher's Banquet. Plutarch's Table Talk in the Intellectual Culture of the Roman Empire*. Oxford, Oxford University Press.

König, I. 2000. 'Q. Sertorius: Ein Kapitel des frühen römischen Bürgerkriegs', *Klio* 82: 441–58.

König, J. 2011. 'Self-Promotion and Self-Effacement in Plutarch's *Table Talk*', in Klotz and Oikonomopoulou 2011: 179–203.

Konrad, C. F. 1987. 'Some Friends of Sertorius', *AJPh* 108: 519–27.

——— 1994. *Plutarch's Sertorius. A Historical Commentary*. Chapel Hill, NC, University of North Carolina Press.

Konstan, D. 2004. '"The Birth of the Reader": Plutarch as a Literary Critic', *Scholia* 13: 3–27.

——— 2010–11. 'A Pig Convicts Itself of Unreason: The Implicit Argument of Plutarch's *Gryllus*', *Hyperboreus* 16–17: 371–85.

Konstantinovic, I. 1989. *Montaigne et Plutarque*. Geneva, Droz.

Koster, A. J. (ed.) 1937. *Plutarchi Vitam Arati*. Leiden, Brill.

Krauss, F. 1912. *Die rhetorischen Schriften Plutarchs und ihre Stellung im Plutarchischen Schriftenkorpus*. Nuremberg, Stich.

La Matina, M. 2000. 'La conferenza in Plutarco', in Gallo and Moreschini 2000: 177–216.

Lamberton, R. 2001. *Plutarch*. New Haven, CT, and London: Yale University Press.

Larmour, D. H. J. 1992. 'Making Parallels: *Synkrisis* and Plutarch's *Themistocles and Camillus*', *ANRW* 2.33.6: 4154–200.

——— 2014. 'The *Synkrisis*', in Beck 2014a: 405–16.

Lather, A. 2017. 'Taking Pleasure Seriously: Plutarch on the Benefits of Poetry and Philosophy', *CW* 110: 323–49.

Latzarus, B. 1920. *Les idées religieuses de Plutarque*. Paris, Leroux.

Leão, D. F. 2003–4. 'Plutarch and the Dark Side of Solon's Political Activity', *Ploutarchos* 1: 51–62.

——— 2008. 'Plutarch and the Character of the *Sapiens*', in Nikolaidis 2008: 481–8.

——— 2009. 'The *Tyrannos* as a *Sophos* in the *Septem sapientium convivium*', in Ribeiro Ferreira *et al.* 2009: 511–21.

——— 2019a. 'Anacharsis: La sagesse atypique de l'étranger avisé', in Leão and Guerrier 2019: 57–67.

——— 2019b. 'A Statesman of Many Resources: Plutarch on Solon's Use of Myth and Theatricality for Political Purposes', in Leão and Roig Lanzillotta 2019: 41–58.

——— 2020. 'Barbarians, Greekness, and Wisdom: The Afterlife of Croesus' Debate with Solon', in T. Figueira and C. Soares (eds.), *Ethnicity and Identity in Herodotus*. London and New York, Routledge: 271–95.

——— and Guerrier, O. (eds.) 2019. *Figures de sages, figures de philosophes dans l'oeuvre de Plutarque*. Coimbra, Coimbra University Press.

——— and Roig Lanzillotta, L. (eds.) 2019. *A Man of Many Interests. Plutarch on Religion, Myth, and Magic. Essays in Honor of Aurelio Pérez Jiménez*. Leiden and Boston, MA, Brill.

Lendle, O. 1967. 'Ciceros ὑπόμνημα περὶ τῆς ὑπατείας', *Hermes* 95: 90–109.

Liddel, P. 2008. 'Scholarship and Morality: Plutarch's Use of Inscriptions', in Nikolaidis 2008: 125–37.

Liebert, H. 2016. *Plutarch's Politics. Between City and Empire*. Cambridge, Cambridge University Press.

Lo Cascio, F. (ed. and trans.) 1997. *Plutarco. Il convito dei sette sapienti*. Naples, D'Auria.

Long, A. 2006. 'How does Socrates' Divine Sign Communicate with Him?', in S. Ahbel-Rappe and R. Kamtekar (eds.), *A Companion to Socrates*. Oxford, Blackwell: 63–74.

Longo, O. 1992. 'La teoria plutarchea del *primum frigidum*', in I. Gallo (ed.), *Plutarco e le scienze*. Genoa, Sagep: 225–30.

López Férez, J. A. 2007. 'Zeus en Plutarco: El dios y sus mitos', in Nieto Ibáñez and López López 2007: 801–22.

Marincola, J. M. 1994. 'Plutarch's Refutation of Herodotus', *AncW* 25: 191–203.

Marr, J. L. (ed. and trans.) 1998. *Plutarch. Life of Themistocles*. Warminster, Aris & Phillips.

Martin, H. 1960. 'The Concept of *Praotes* in Plutarch's *Lives*', *GRBS* 3: 65–73.

———— 1961. 'The Character of Plutarch's Themistocles', *TAPhA* 92: 326–39.

Martin, J. 1931. *Symposion. Die Geschichte einer literarischen Form*. Paderborn, Schöningh.

Massaro, D. 1996. 'Τὸ θεῖον e ὁ θεός in Plutarco', in Gallo 1996: 337–55.

McAlhany, J. 2016. 'Sertorius between Myth and History: The Isles of the Blessed Episode in Sallust, Plutarch & Horace', *CJ* 112: 57–76.

Meeusen, M. 2012. 'Matching in Mind the Sea Beast's Complexion: On the Pragmatics of Plutarch's Hypomnemata and Scientific Innovation: the Case of *Q.N.* 19 (916BF)', *Philologus* 156: 234–59.

———— 2013. 'How to Treat a Bee Sting? On the Higher Cause in Plutarch's *Causes of Natural Phenomena*: The Case of *Q.N.* 35–36', *QUCC* 105: 131–57.

———— 2014. 'Plutarch and the Wonder of Nature: Preliminaries to Plutarch's Science of Physical Problems', *Apeiron* 47: 310–41.

———— 2016. *Plutarch's Science of Natural Problems. A Study with Commentary of Quaestiones Naturales*. Leuven, Leuven University Press.

———— 2017. 'Egyptian Knowledge at Plutarch's Table: Out of the Question?', in Georgiadou and Oikonomopoulou 2017: 215–26.

———— and Van der Stockt, L. (eds.) 2015. *Natural Spectaculars. Aspects of Plutarch's Philosophy of Nature*. Leuven, Leuven University Press.

Melandri, E. 2003. 'I cosiddetti frammenti dell'opera *An virtus docenda sit* di Plutarco', *Humanitas* 55: 111–27.

Minon, S. 2015. 'Plutarque (*Thém.* 24) transpose Thucydide (I 136): De l'harmonie austère au péan delphique. Pragmatique et rythmique de deux modes de composition stylistique', *REG* 128: 29–99.

Moellering, H. A. 1963. *Plutarch on Superstition. Plutarch's De superstitione, Its Place in the Changing Meaning of Deisidaimonia and in the Context of His Theological Writings*. Boston, MA, Christopher.

Moles, J. L. (ed. and trans.) 1988. *Plutarch. The Life of Cicero*. Warminster, Aris & Phillips.

———— (ed.) 2017. *A Commentary on Plutarch's Brutus*. Newcastle, Histos.

Montes Cala, J. G., Sánchez Ortiz de Landaluce, M., and Gallé Cejudo, R. J. (eds.) 1999. *Plutarco, Dioniso y el vino. Actas del VI Simposio Español sobre Plutarco. Cádiz, 14–16 de mayo de 1998*. Madrid, Ediciones clásicas.

Mora, F. 2007. 'Nuclei d'interesse e strategie interpretative nelle *Quaestiones Romanae* di Plutarco', *Gerión* 25: 329–70.

Morel, P.-M. (ed.) 2013. *Lecture du 'Contre Colotès' de Plutarque, Aitia* 3, https://doi.org/10.4000/aitia.591.

Moreschini, C. 1996. 'Religione e filosofia in Plutarco', in Gallo 1996: 29–48.

——— (ed. and trans.) 1997. *Plutarco. L'E di Delfi*. Naples, D'Auria.

Morgan, T. 2011. 'The Miscellany and Plutarch', in Klotz and Oikonomopoulou 2011: 49–71.

Mossman, J. M. (ed.) 1992. 'Plutarch, Pyrrhus, and Alexander', in Stadter 1992: 90–108.

——— (ed.) 1997a. *Plutarch and His Intellectual World. Essays on Plutarch*. London, Duckworth.

——— 1997b. 'Plutarch's *Dinner of the Seven Wise Men* and Its Place in *Symposion* Literature', in Mossman 1997a: 119–40.

——— 1999. 'Is the Pen Mightier than the Sword? The Failure of Rhetoric in Plutarch's Demosthenes', *Histos* 3: 77–101.

——— 2010. 'A Life Unparallelled: *Artaxerxes*', in Humble 2010: 145–68.

——— 2019. 'Plutarch's Ghosts', in Leão and Roig Lanzillotta 2019: 59–75.

Moya del Baño, F. and Carrasco Reija, L. 1991. 'Plutarco, traductor del Latín al Griego', in J. García López and E. Calderón Dorda (eds.), *Estudios sobre Plutarco. Paisaje y Naturaleza. Actas del II Simposio Español sobre Plutarco. Murcia 1990*. Madrid, Ediciones clásicas: 287–96.

Muccioli, F. 2012. *La storia attraverso gli esempi. Protagonisti e interpretazioni del mondo greco in Plutarco*. Milan and Udine, Mimesis.

Mueller, H.-F. 1995. 'Images of Excellence: Visual Rhetoric and Political Behaviour', in Gallo and Scardigli 1995: 287–300.

Müller, A. 2012. 'Dialogic Structures and Forms of Knowledge in Plutarch's *The E at Delphi*', *SHPS* 43: 245–9.

Muñoz Gallarte, I. 2008. 'El judaísmo en las *Vitae* y *Moralia* de Plutarco', in Nikolaidis 2008: 815–30.

——— 2010–11. 'Hérodote et Plutarque: À propos de la rencontre entre Solon et Crésus', *Ploutarchos* 8: 117–31.

——— 2019. 'A Road to Wisdom: The Case of Revenants in Plutarch', in Leão and Guerrier 2019: 183–95.

Nesselrath, H.-G. (ed.) 2010. *Plutarch. On the Daimonion of Socrates. Human Liberation, Divine Guidance and Philosophy*. Tübingen, Mohr Siebeck.

Newmyer, S. T. 2006. *Animals, Rights and Reason in Plutarch and Modern Ethics*. New York and London, Routledge.

——— 2014. 'Animals in Plutarch', in Beck 2014a: 223–34.

Nieto Ibáñez, J. M. and López López, R. (eds.) 2007. *El amor en Plutarco*. León, Universidad de León.

Nikolaidis, A. G. 1982–4. ʻΟ σκοπός τῶν Βίων τοῦ Πλουτάρχου καὶ οἱ διάφορες συναφεῖς θεωρίες', *Archaiognosia* 3: 93–114.

───── 1986. ʻΕλληνικός – βαρβαρικός: Plutarch on Greek and Barbarian Characteristics', *WS* 20: 229–44.

───── 1991. ʻPlutarch's Contradictions', *C&M* 42: 153–86.

───── 1995. ʻPlutarch's Heroes in Action: Does the End Justify the Means?', in Gallo and Scardigli 1995: 301–12.

───── 1997a. ʻPlutarch on Women and Marriage', *WS* 110: 27–88.

───── 1997b. ʻPlutarch's Criteria for Judging His Historical Sources', in Schrader *et al.* 1997: 329–41.

───── 1999. ʻPlutarch on the Old, Middle and New Academies and the Academy in Plutarch's Day', in Pérez Jiménez *et al.* 1999: 397–415.

───── 2005. ʻPlutarch's Methods: His Cross-References and the Sequence of the *Parallel Lives*', in Pérez Jiménez and Titchener 2005: 283–323.

───── (ed.) 2008. *The Unity of Plutarch's Work. ʻMoralia' Themes in the ʻLives', Features of the ʻLives' in the ʻMoralia'*. Berlin and New York, De Gruyter.

───── 2009. ʻWhat did Apollo Mean to Plutarch?', in L. Athanassaki, R. P. Martin, and J. F. Miller (eds.), *Apolline Politics and Poetics. International Symposium*. Athens, European Cultural Centre of Delphi: 569–86.

───── 2014. ʻMorality, Characterization, and Individuality', in Beck 2014a: 350–72.

───── 2017. ʻPast and Present in Plutarch's *Table Talk*', in Georgiadou amd Oikonomopoulou 2017: 257–70.

Obbink, D. 1992. ʻWhat All Men Believe – Must be True: Common Conceptions and *Consensio omnium* in Aristotle and Hellenistic Philosophy', *OSAPh* 10: 193–231.

Obsieger, H. (ed.) 2013. *Plutarch. De E apud Delphos. Über das Epsilon am Apolltempel in Delphi*. Stuttgart, Steiner.

Oikonomopoulou, K. 2011. ʻPeripatetic Knowledge in Plutarch's *Table Talk*', in Klotz and Oikonomopoulou 2011: 105–30.

───── 2013. ʻPlutarch's Corpus of *Quaestiones* in the Tradition of Imperial Greek Encyclopaedism', in J. König and G. Woolf (eds.), *Encyclopaedism from Antiquity to the Renaissance*. Cambridge, Cambridge University Press: 129–53.

───── 2017. ʻSpace, Delphi and the Construction of the Greek Past in Plutarch's *Greek Questions*', in Georgiadou and Oikonomopoulou 2017: 107–16.

Opsomer, J. 1994. ʻL'âme du monde et l'âme de l'homme chez Plutarque', in García Valdés 1994: 33–49.

———— 1996. 'Ζητήματα: Structure et argumentation dans les *Quaestiones Platonicae*', in Fernández Delgado and Pordomingo Pardo 1996: 71–83.

———— 1997. 'Quelques réflexions sur la notion de providence chez Plutarque', in Schrader *et al.* 1997: 343–56.

———— 1998. *In Search of the Truth. Academic Tendencies in Middle Platonism*. Brussels, Koninklijke Academie voor Wetenschappen, Letteren en Schone Kunsten van België.

———— 2002. 'Is a Planet Happier than a Star? Cosmopolitanism in Plutarch's *On Exile*', in Stadter and Van der Stockt 2002: 281–95.

———— 2004. 'Plutarch's *De animae procreatione in Timaeo*: Manipulation or Search for Consistency', in P. Adamson, H. Baltussen and M. W. F. Stone (eds.), *Philosophy, Science and Exegesis in Greek, Arabic and Latin Commentaries. Vol. 1*. London, Institute of Classical Studies: 137–62.

———— 2005. 'Plutarch's Platonism Revisited', in M. Bonazzi and V. Celluprica (eds.), *L'eredità platonica. Studi sul platonismo da Arcesilao a Proclo*. Naples, Bibliopolis: 163–200.

———— 2006. 'Éléments stoïciens dans le *De E apud Delphos* de Plutarque', in Boulogne *et al.* 2006: 147–70.

———— 2007a. 'The Place of Plutarch in the History of Platonism', in Volpe Cacciatore and Ferrari 2007: 281–309.

———— 2007b. 'Plutarch on the One and the Dyad', in R. W. Sharples and R. Sorabji (eds.), *Greek and Roman Philosophy 100 BC–200 AD*. London, Institute of Classical Studies: 379–95.

———— 2009a. 'M. Annius Ammonius, a Philosophical Profile', in M. Bonazzi and J. Opsomer (eds.), *The Origins of the Platonic System. Platonisms of the Early Empire and Their Philosophical Contexts*. Leuven, Peeters: 123–86.

———— 2009b. 'Eine platonische Abhandlung über die freimütige Rede: Plutarchs *De adulatore et amico*', in E. Düsing, K. Düsing, and H.-D. Klein (eds.), *Geist und Sittlichkeit. Ethik-Modelle von Platon bis Levinas*. Würzburg, Königshausen und Neumann: 91–119.

———— 2010. 'Arguments non-linéaires et pensée en cercles: Forme et argumentation dans les *Questions Platoniciennes* de Plutarque', in Brouillette and Giavatto 2010: 93–116.

———— 2011. 'Virtue, Fortune, and Happiness in Theory and Practice', in Roskam and Van der Stockt 2011: 151–73.

———— 2014. 'Plutarch and the Stoics', in Beck 2014a: 88–103.

———— 2015. 'Plutarch on the Geometry of the Elements', in Meeusen and Van der Stockt 2015: 29–55.

———— 2016. 'The Cruel Consistency of *De sera numinis vindicta*', in Opsomer *et al.* 2016: 37–56.

————— 2017. 'Why Doesn't the Moon Crash into the Earth? Platonist and Stoic Teleologies in Plutarch's *Concerning the Face which Appears in the Orb of the Moon*', in J. Rocca (ed.), *Teleology in the Ancient World. Philosophical and Medical Approaches.* Cambridge, Cambridge University Press: 76–91.

————— 2020. 'The Platonic Soul, From the Early Academy to the First Century CE', in B. Inwood and J. Warren (eds.), *Body and Soul in Hellenistic Philosophy.* Cambridge, Cambridge University Press: 171–98.

—————, Roskam, G., and Titchener, F. B. (eds.) 2016. *A Versatile Gentleman. Consistency in Plutarch's Writing. Studies Offered to Luc Van der Stockt on the Occasion of His Retirement.* Leuven, Leuven University Press.

Oudot, E. 2016. '"La table fabrique les amis": Quelques remarques sur le savoir-vivre dans les *Propos de table* de Plutarque', *Camenae* 19: 1–18.

Pade, M. 2007. *The Reception of Plutarch's Lives in Fifteenth-Century Italy.* Copenhagen, Museum Tusculanum Press.

Panagopoulos, C. 1977. 'Vocabulaire et mentalité dans les *Moralia* de Plutarque', *DHA* 3: 197–235.

Patterson, C. 1999. 'Plutarch's *Advice to the Bride and Groom*: Traditional Wisdom through a Philosophic Lens', in Pomeroy 1999: 128–37.

Payen, P. (ed.) 1998. *Plutarque. Grecs et Romains en Questions.* Saint-Bertrant-de-Comminges, Musée archéologique departemental de Saint-Bertrant-de-Comminges.

————— 2002. 'Sertorius et l'Occident dans les *Vies parallèles* de Plutarque: Acculturation et contraintes narratives', *Pallas* 60: 93–115.

————— 2014. 'Plutarch the Antiquarian', in Beck 2014a: 235–48.

Pelling, C. B. R. (ed.) 1988. *Plutarch. Life of Antony.* Cambridge, Cambridge University Press.

————— 1989. 'Plutarch: Roman Heroes and Greek Culture', in M. Griffin and J. Barnes (eds.), *Philosophia Togata. Essays on Philosophy and Roman Society.* Oxford, Clarendon Press: 199–232.

————— 2002. *Plutarch and History. Eighteen Studies.* London, Duckworth.

————— 2005. '*Synkrisis* Revisited', in Pérez Jiménez and Titchener 2005: 325–40.

————— 2007. 'De malignitate Plutarchi: Plutarch, Herodotus, and the Persian Wars', in E. Bridges, E. Hall, and P. J. Rhodes (eds.), *Cultural Responses to the Persian Wars. Antiquity to the Third Millennium.* Oxford, Oxford University Press: 145–64.

————— 2010. 'Plutarch's "Tale of Two Cities": Do the *Parallel Lives* Combine as Global Histories?', in Humble 2010: 217–35.

———— (ed. and trans.) 2011a. *Plutarch. Caesar*. Oxford, Oxford University Press.

———— 2011b. 'What is Popular about Plutarch's "Popular Philosophy"?', in Roskam and Van der Stockt 2011: 41–58.

———— 2014. 'Political Philosophy', in Beck 2014a: 149–62.

———— 2019. 'Plutarch on the Great Battles of Greece', in Leão and Roig Lanzillotta 2019: 92–113.

Pérez Jiménez, A. 1995. '*Proairesis*: Las formas de acceso a la vida pública y el pensamiento político de Plutarco', in Gallo and Scardigli 1995: 363–81.

———— 2004. 'Los héroes de Plutarco y su elección entre la justicia y la utilidad', in de Blois *et al.* 2004: 127–36.

———— 2005. 'Δικαιοσύνη als Wesenszug des Göttlichen', in Hirsch-Luipold 2005b: 101–9.

———— (ed.) 2010. *Plutarco renovado. Importancia de las traducciones modernas de Vidas y Moralia*. Málaga, Grupo Editorial 33.

———— and Casadesús Bordoy, F. (eds.) 2001. *Estudios sobre Plutarco. Misticismo y religiones mistéricas en la obra de Plutarco*. Madrid and Málaga, Ediciones clásicas.

———— and Titchener, F. (eds.) 2005. *Historical and Biographical Values of Plutarch's Works. Studies devoted to Professor Philip A. Stadter by the International Plutarch Society*. Málaga and Logan, International Plutarch Society.

———— García López, J., and Aguilar, R. M. (eds.) 1999. *Plutarco, Platón y Aristóteles. Actas del V Congreso Internacional de la I.P.S. (Madrid–Cuenca, 4–7 de mayo de 1999)*. Madrid, Ediciones clásicas.

Peter, H. 1865. *Die Quellen Plutarchs in den Biographieen der Römer*. Halle, Buchhandlung des Waisenhauses (reprinted Amsterdam, Hakkert, 1965).

Petrucci, F. M. 2016a. 'Argumentative Strategies in the 'Platonic Section' of Plutarch's *De Iside et Osiride* (chapters 45–64)', *Mnemosyne* 69: 226–48.

———— 2016b. 'Plutarch's Theory of Cosmological Powers in the *De Iside et Osiride*', *Apeiron* 49: 329–67.

———— 2018a. 'Wave-Like Commentaries: The Structure and Philosophical Orientation of Middle Platonist Commentaries', *JHS* 138: 209–26.

———— 2018b. 'What Is an "Ideological Emendation" (Really)? Taurus T27 and Middle Platonist *Philologia Philosophica*', *Méthexis* 30: 128–53.

Plácido, D. 1995. 'La demokratía de Plutarco', in Gallo and Scardigli 1995: 383–9.

Pomeroy, S. B. (ed.) 1999. *Plutarch's Advice to the Bride and Groom and A Consolation to His Wife. English Translations, Commentary, Interpretive Essays, and Bibliography.* New York and Oxford, Oxford University Press.

Pordomingo Pardo, F. 1999. 'El banquete de Plutarco: ¿Ficción literaria o realidad histórica?', in Montes Cala *et al.* 1999: 379–92.

Porter, W. H. (ed.) 1937. *Plutarch's Life of Aratus.* Dublin and Cork, Cork University Press.

Postiglione, A. (ed. and trans.) 1991. *Plutarco. L'amore fraterno. L'amore per i figli.* Naples, D'Auria.

Preston, R. 2001. 'Roman Questions, Greek Answers: Plutarch and the Construction of Identity', in Goldhill 2001: 86–119.

Puech, B. 1992. 'Prosopographie des amis de Plutarque', *ANRW* 2.33.6: 4831–93.

Ragogna, G. 2002. 'Alcune considerazioni sul *De Herodoti malignitate* di Plutarco', *Patavium* 19: 23–41.

Rémy, B. 1976. 'Ornati et ornamenta quaestoria, praetoria et consularia sous le haut empire romain', *REA* 78–9: 160–98.

Renoirte, T. 1951. *Les 'Conseils politiques' de Plutarque. Une lettre ouverte aux Grecs à l'époque de Trajan.* Louvain, Publications universitaires de Louvain.

Rescigno, A. (ed. and trans.) 1995. *Plutarco. L'eclissi degli oracoli.* Naples, D'Auria.

Ribeiro Ferreira, J. *et al.* (eds.) 2009. *Symposion and Philanthropia in Plutarch.* Coimbra, Centro de Estudos Clássicos e Humanísticos da Universidade de Coimbra.

Richter, D. S. 2001. 'Plutarch on Isis and Osiris: Text, Cult, and Cultural Appropriation', *TAPhA* 131: 191–216.

Riley, M. 1977. 'The Purpose and Unity of Plutarch's *De genio Socratis*', *GRBS* 18: 257–73.

Rist, J. M. 2001. 'Plutarch's *Amatorius*: A Commentary on Plato's Theories of Love?', *CQ* 51: 557–75.

Roig Lanzillotta, L. 2011. 'Plutarch of Chaeronea and the Gnostic Worldview: Middle Platonism and the Nag Hammadi Library', in J. M. Candau Morón, F. J. González Ponce, and A. L. Chávez Reino (eds.), *Plutarco Transmisor. Actas del X Simposio internacional de la Sociedad Española de Plutarquistas. Sevilla, 12–14 de noviembre de 2009.* Seville, Secretariado de publicaciones de la Universidad de Sevilla: 401–17.

——— 2012. 'Plutarch's Idea of God in the Religious and Philosophical Context of Late Antiquity', in Roig Lanzillotta and Muñoz Gallarte 2012: 137–50.

―――― 2015. 'Plutarch's Anthropology and Its Influence on His Cosmological Framework', in Meeusen and Van der Stockt 2015: 179–95.

―――― and Muñoz Gallarte, I. (eds.) 2012. *Plutarch in the Religious and Philosophical Discourse of Late Antiquity*. Leiden and Boston, MA, Brill.

Roisman, J. 2011. 'The Silver Shields, Eumenes, and Their Historian', in A. Erskine and L. Llewellyn-Jones (eds.), *Creating a Hellenistic World*. Swansea, Classical Press of Wales: 61–81.

Rose, H. J. (ed. and trans.) 1924. *The Roman Questions of Plutarch*. Oxford, Clarendon Press.

Roskam, G. 1999a. 'Dionysus Sublimated: Plutarch's Thinking and Rethinking of the Traditional Dionysiac', in Montes Cala *et al.* 1999: 433–45.

―――― 1999b. 'Le pari de Plutarque: Computing Pros and Cons in the Face of Death', in Pérez Jiménez *et al.* 1999: 463–74.

―――― 2004a. 'From Stick to Reasoning: Plutarch on the Communication between Teacher and Pupil', *WS* 117: 93–114.

―――― 2004b. 'Plutarch on Self and Others', *AncSoc* 34: 245–73.

―――― 2004–5. 'Τὸ καλὸν αὐτό [...] ἔχοντας τέλος (*Praec. ger. reip.* 799A): Plutarch on the Foundation of the Politician's Career', *Ploutarchos* 2: 89–103.

―――― 2005a. 'A Great and Sacred Thing? Plutarch's Attempt to Revaluate the Political Office', in Pérez Jiménez and Titchener 2005: 399–410.

―――― 2005b. *On the Path to Virtue. The Stoic Doctrine of Moral Progress and Its Reception in (Middle-)Platonism*. Leuven, Leuven University Press.

―――― 2006. 'Apollon est-il vraiment le dieu du Soleil? La théorie Plutarquéenne des symboles, appliquée à un cas concret', in Boulogne *et al.* 2006: 171–210.

―――― 2007a. *A Commentary on Plutarch's De latenter vivendo*. Leuven, Leuven University Press.

―――― 2007b. *Live Unnoticed (Λάθε βιώσας). On the Vicissitudes of an Epicurean Doctrine*. Leiden and Boston, MA, Brill.

―――― 2009a. 'Educating the Young ... over Wine? Plutarch, Calvenus Taurus, and Favorinus as Convivial Teachers', in Ribeiro Ferreira *et al.* 2009: 369–83.

―――― 2009b. *Plutarch's Maxime cum principibus philosopho esse disserendum. An Interpretation with Commentary*. Leuven, Leuven University Press.

―――― 2010. 'Plutarch's "Socratic Symposia": The *Symposia* of Plato and Xenophon as Literary Models in the *Quaestiones convivales*', *Athenaeum* 98: 45–70.

―――― 2011a. 'Ambition and Love of Fame in Plutarch's Lives of Agis, Cleomenes and the Gracchi', *CPh* 106: 208–25.

—— 2011b. 'Aristotle in Middle Platonism: The Case of Plutarch of Chaeronea', in T. Bénatouïl, E. Maffi, and F. Trabattoni (eds.), *Plato, Aristotle, or Both? Dialogues between Platonism and Aristotelianism in Antiquity*. Hildesheim, Zurich, and New York, Olms: 35–61.

—— 2011c. 'Plutarch against Epicurus on Affection for Offspring: A Reading of *De amore prolis*', in Roskam and Van der Stockt 2011: 175–201.

—— 2012. 'Plutarch in a Limit Situation: Literature and Tradition in the *Consolatio ad uxorem*', *Eranos* 106: 111–23.

—— 2013. 'Theocritus' View of Socrates' Divine Sign in *De genio Socratis* 580CF', in A. Casanova (ed.), *Figure d'Atene nelle opere di Plutarco*. Florence, Firenze University Press: 233–48.

—— 2014a. 'Ἀποθεωρεῖν / ἀποθεώρησις: A Semasiological Study', *Glotta* 90: 180–91.

—— 2014b. 'Plutarch's Yearning after Divinity: The Introduction to *On Isis and Osiris*', *CJ* 110: 213–39.

—— 2015a. 'An Exegetical Note on Plutarch, *Isis and Osiris* 351E', *Emerita* 83: 157–64.

—— 2015b. 'Plutarch's Reception of Plato's *Phaedo*', in S. Delcomminette, P. d'Hoine, and M.-A. Gavray (eds.), *Ancient Readings of Plato's Phaedo*. Leiden and Boston, MA, Brill: 107–33.

—— 2017a. 'Considering Tit for Tat: The Programmatic Introduction to *Non posse suaviter vivi secundum Epicurum*', in Sanz Morales *et al.* 2017: 345–56.

—— 2017b. 'Discussing the Past: Moral Virtue, Truth, and Benevolence in Plutarch's *On the Malice of Herodotus*', in Georgiadou and Oikonomopoulou 2017: 161–73.

—— 2017c. 'On the Multi-Coloured Robes of Philosophy: Plutarch's Approach in *On Isis and Osiris*', in Erler and Stadler 2017: 199–218.

—— and Van der Stockt, L. (eds.) 2011. *Virtues for the People. Aspects of Plutarchan Ethics*. Leuven, Leuven University Press.

—— De Pourcq, M., and Van der Stockt, L. (eds.) 2012. *The Lash of Ambition. Plutarch, Imperial Greek Literature and the Dynamics of Philotimia*. Louvain, Peeters.

Russell, D. A. 1963. 'Plutarch's Life of Coriolanus', *JRS* 53: 21–8.

—— 1966. 'On Reading Plutarch's *Lives*', *G&R* 13: 139–54.

—— 1968. 'On Reading Plutarch's *Moralia*', *G&R* 15: 130–46.

—— 1972. *Plutarch*. London, Duckworth.

—— 1993a (trans.). *Plutarch. Selected Essays and Dialogues*. Oxford, Oxford University Press.

—— 1993b. 'Self-Disclosure in Plutarch and in Horace', in G. W. Most, H. Petersmann, and A. M. Ritter (eds.), *Philanthropia kai Eusebeia*.

Festschrift für Albrecht Dihle zum 70. Geburtstag. Göttingen, Vandenhoeck und Ruprecht: 426–37.

Russo, F. 2002. 'I *Commentarii* sillani come fonte della *Vita* plutarchea di Silla', *SCO* 48: 281–305.

Saïd, S. 2005a. 'Plutarch and the People in the *Parallel Live*s', in de Blois *et al.* 2005: 7–25.

———— 2005b. 'Poésie et éducation chez Plutarque ou comment convertir la poésie en introduction à la philosophie', in Jufresa *et al.* 2005: 147–76.

Salcedo Parrondo, M. 2005. 'Retórica visual y carácter político, *Alc.* 10: Un modelo negativo de *enargeia*', in de Blois *et al.* 2005: 179–86.

Sandbach, F. H. 1982. 'Plutarch and Aristotle', *ICS* 7: 207–32.

Sanz Morales, M., González Delgado, R., Librán Moreno, M., and Ureña Bracero, J. (eds.) 2017. *La (inter)textualidad en Plutarco.* Cáceres and Coimbra, Universidad de Extremadura.

Scannapieco, R. 2012. 'Μυστηριώδης θεολογία: Plutarch's fr. 157 Sandbach between Cultual Traditions and Philosophical Models', in Roig Lanzillotta and Muñoz Gallarte 2012: 193–214.

Scardigli, B. 1979. *Die Römerbiographien Plutarchs.* Munich, Beck.

Scheid, J. 2012. *À Rome sur les pas de Plutarque.* Paris, Vuibert.

Schenkeveld, D. M. 1996. 'Plutarch's First Table Talk (612E–615C)', in Van der Stockt 1996: 257–64.

Schepens, G. 2000. 'Plutarch's View of Ancient Rome: Some Remarks on the *Life of Pyrrhus*', in L. Mooren (ed.), *Politics, Administration and Society in the Hellenistic and Roman World. Proceedings of the International Colloquium, Bertinoro 19–24 July 1997.* Leuven, Peeters: 349–64.

Scherr, J. 2015. 'Die Jünglinge von Osca: Bemerkungen zu Plutarch, Sertorius 14,1–4', in R. Lafer and K. Strobel (eds.), *Antike Lebenswelten. Althistorische und papyrologische Studien.* Berlin and Boston, MA, De Gruyter: 282–91.

Schettino, M. T. 2014. 'The Use of Historical Sources', in Beck 2014a: 417–36.

Schmidt, T. S. 1999. *Plutarque et les barbares. La rhétorique d'une image.* Louvain and Namur, Peeters.

———— 2008. 'Les *Questions barbares* de Plutarque: Un essai de reconstitution', in M. Chassignet (ed.), *L'étiologie dans la pensée antique.* Turnhout, Brepols: 165–83.

————, Vamvouri, M., and Hirsch-Luipold, R. (eds.) 2020. *The Dynamics of Intertextuality in Plutarch.* Leiden and Boston, MA, Brill.

Schmitt Pantel, P. 2008. 'Anecdotes et histoire chez Plutarque: État de la question et interrogations', in B. Mezzadri (ed.), *Historiens de l'Antiquité.* Paris, Europe: 236–51.

Schmitz, T. A. 2012. 'Sophistic *Philotimia* in Plutarch', in Roskam *et al.* 2012: 69–84.

Schneeweiss, G. 1979. 'History and Philosophy in Plutarch: Observations on Plutarch's Lycurgus', in G. W. Bowersock, W. Burkert, and M. C. J. Putnam (eds.), *Arktouros. Hellenic Studies Presented to Bernard M. W. Knox on the Occasion of His 65th Birthday.* Berlin and New York, De Gruyter: 376–82.

Schoppe, C. 1994. *Plutarchs Interpretation der Ideenlehre Platons.* Münster, LIT.

Schrader, C., Ramón, V., and Vela, J. (eds.) 1997. *Plutarco y la historia. Actas del V Simposio Español sobre Plutarco. Zaragoza, 20–22 de junio de 1996.* Zaragoza, Universidad de Zaragoza.

Schröder, S. (ed.) 1990. *Plutarchs Schrift De Pythiae oraculis.* Stuttgart, Teubner.

——— 1994–5. 'Platon oder Chrysipp: Zur Inspirationstheorie in Plutarchs Schrift *De Pythiae oraculis*', *WJA* 20: 233–56.

Schubert, C. and Weiss, A. 2015. 'Die Hypomnemata bei Plutarch und Clemens: Ein Textmining-gestützter Vergleich der Arbeitsweise zweier "Sophisten"', *Hermes* 143: 447–71.

Schütrumpf, E. 1987. 'The *Rhetra* of Epitadeus: A Platonist's Fiction', *GRBS* 28: 441–57.

Scott-Kilvert, I. (trans.) 1960. *Plutarch. The Rise and Fall of Athens. Nine Greek Lives.* Harmondsworth, Penguin Books.

Sedley, D. N. 1976. 'Epicurus and His Professional Rivals', in J. Bollack and A. Laks (eds.), *Études sur l'Épicurisme antique.* Lille, Presses universitaires du Septentrion: 119–59.

Setaioli, A. 2007. 'Plutarch's Assessment of Latin as a Means of Expression', *Prometheus* 33: 156–66.

Sfameni Gasparro, G. 1996. 'Plutarco e la religione delfica: Il dio "filosofo" e il suo esegeta', in Gallo 1996: 157–88.

Sheppard, A. R. R. 1984–6. '*Homonoia* in the Greek Cities of the Roman Empire', *AncSoc* 15–17: 229–52.

Shiffman, M. 2010. 'Erotic Wisdom and the Socratic Vocation in Plutarch's *Platonic Question* 1', *GRBS* 50: 243–71.

Shipley, D. R. 1997. *A Commentary on Plutarch's Life of Agesilaos. Response to Sources in the Presentation of Character.* Oxford, Clarendon Press.

Simonetti, E. G. 2017. *A Perfect Medium? Oracular Divination in the Thought of Plutarch.* Leuven, Leuven University Press.

Sirinelli, J. 2000. *Plutarque de Chéronée. Un philosophe dans le siècle.* Paris, Fayard.

Soares, C. 2007. 'Rules for a Good Description: Theory and Practice in the *Life of Artaxerxes* (§§1–19)', *Hermathena* 182: 85–100.

Soury, G. 1942. *La démonologie de Plutarque. Essai sur les idées religieuses et les mythes d'un platonicien éclectique.* Paris, Les Belles Lettres.

Stadter, P. A. 1984. 'Searching for Themistocles: A Review Article', *CJ* 79: 356–63.

―――― 1988. 'The Proems of Plutarch's *Lives*', *ICS* 13: 275–95.

―――― 1989. *A Commentary on Plutarch's Pericles.* Chapel Hill, NC, and London, University of North Carolina Press.

―――― (ed.) 1992. *Plutarch and the Historical Tradition.* London and New York, Routledge.

―――― 1996. 'Anecdotes and the Thematic Structure of Plutarchean Biography', in Fernández Delgado and Pordomingo Pardo 1996: 291–303.

―――― 1999. 'Drinking, Table Talk, and Plutarch's Contemporaries', in Montes Cala *et al.* 1999: 481–90.

―――― 2003–4. 'Mirroring Virtue in Plutarch's *Lives*', *Ploutarchos* n.s. 1: 89–95.

―――― 2008. 'Notes and Anecdotes: Observations on Cross-Genre *Apophthegmata*', in Nikolaidis 2008: 53–66.

―――― 2011. 'Competition and Its Costs: φιλονικία in Plutarch's Society and Heroes', in Roskam and Van der Stockt 2011: 237–55.

―――― 2014. 'Plutarch's Compositional Technique: The Anecdote Collections and the *Parallel Lives*', *GRBS* 54: 665–86.

―――― 2015a. '"The Love of Noble Deeds": Plutarch's Portrait of Aratus of Sicyon', in Ash, Mossman, and Titchener 2015: 161–75.

―――― 2015b. *Plutarch and His Roman Readers.* Oxford, Oxford University Press.

―――― 2016. 'Sulla's Three-Thousand-νοῦμμοι Apartment: Plutarch's Problematic Code-Switching', in Opsomer *et al.* 2016: 197–209.

―――― and Van der Stockt, L. (eds.) 2002. *Sage and Emperor. Plutarch, Greek Intellectuals, and Roman Power in the Time of Trajan (98–117 A.D.).* Leuven, Leuven University Press.

Stamatopoulou, Z. 2014. 'Hesiodic Poetry and Wisdom in Plutarch's *Symposium of the Seven Sages*', *AJPh* 135: 533–58.

Strisino, J. 2002. 'Sulla and Scipio "Not to be Trusted"? The Reasons why Sertorius Captured Suessa Aurunca', *Latomus* 61: 33–40.

Strobach, A. 1997. *Plutarch und die Sprachen. Ein Beitrag zur Fremdsprachenproblematik in der Antike.* Stuttgart, Steiner.

Swain, S. C. R. 1989a. 'Character Change in Plutarch', *Phoenix* 43: 62–8.

―――― 1989b. 'Plutarch: Chance, Providence, and History', *AJPh* 110: 272–302.

―――― 1990. 'Hellenic Culture and the Roman Heroes of Plutarch', *JHS* 110: 126–45.

―――― 1992. 'Plutarchan Synkrisis', *Eranos* 90: 101–11.

———— 1996. *Hellenism and Empire. Language, Classicism, and Power in the Greek World AD 50–250.* Oxford, Clarendon Press.

———— 1997. 'Plutarch, Plato, Athens, and Rome', in J. Barnes and M. Griffin (eds.), *Philosophia Togata 2.* Oxford, Clarendon Press: 165–87.

Tatum, W. J. 2010. 'Why *Parallel* Lives?', in Humble 2010: 1–22.

———— 2014. 'Antiquarianism and Its Uses: Plutarch's *Roman Questions* and His *Lives* of Early Romans', *Athenaeum* 102: 104–19.

Teixeira, E. 1995. 'Démocratie et monarchie chez Plutarque', *DHA* 21: 139–46.

Teodorsson, S.-T. 1989. *A Commentary on Plutarch's Table Talks, Vol. I (Books 1–3).* Göteborg, Acta Universitatis Gothoburgensis.

———— 1990. *A Commentary on Plutarch's Table Talks, Vol. II (Books 4–6).* Göteborg, Acta Universitatis Gothoburgensis.

———— 1996. *A Commentary on Plutarch's Table Talks, Vol. III (Books 7–9).* Göteborg, Acta Universitatis Gothoburgensis.

———— 1997. 'Ethical Historiography: Plutarch's Attitude to Historical Criticism', in Schrader *et al.* 1997: 439–47.

———— 2000. 'Plutarch's Use of Synonyms: A Typical Feature of His Style', in Van der Stockt 2000b: 511–8.

———— 2005–6. 'Plutarch's Thoughts about Happiness', *Ploutarchos* 3: 127–40.

———— 2009. 'The Place of Plutarch in the Literary Genre of *Symposium*', in Ribeiro Ferreira *et al.* 2009: 3–16.

Theander, C. 1951. *Plutarch und die Geschichte.* Lund, Gleerup.

Thévenaz, P. 1938. *L'âme du monde, le devenir et la matière chez Plutarque, avec une traduction du traité 'De la genèse de l'ame dans le Timée' (1re partie).* Paris, Les Belles Lettres.

Thum, T. 2013. *Plutarchs Dialog De E apud Delphos. Eine Studie.* Tübingen, Mohr Siebeck.

Timotin, A. 2012. *La démonologie platonicienne. Histoire de la notion de daimōn de Platon aux derniers néoplatoniciens.* Leiden and Boston, MA, Brill.

Tirelli, A. (ed. and trans.) 2005. *Plutarco. Ad un governante incolto.* Naples, D'Auria.

Titchener, F. B. 2002. 'Plutarch and Roman(ized) Athens', in E. N. Ostenfeld (ed.), *Greek Romans and Roman Greeks. Studies in Cultural Interaction.* Aarhus, Aarhus University Press: 136–41.

———— 2009. 'The Role of Reality in Plutarch's *Quaestiones convivales*', in Ribeiro Ferreira *et al.* 2009: 395–401.

———— 2011. 'Plutarch's *Table Talk*: Sampling a Rich Blend. A Survey of Scholarly Appraisal', in Klotz and Oikonomopoulou 2011: 35–48.

———— 2014. 'Fate and Fortune', in Beck 2014a: 479–87.

Torraca, L. 1998. 'Problemi di lingua e stile nei *Moralia* di Plutarco', *ANRW* 2.34.4: 3487–510.

Trapp, M. B. 2004. 'Statesmanship in a Minor Key?', in de Blois *et al.* 2004: 189–200.

Tritle, L. 1987. 'Leosthenes and Plutarch's View of the Athenian *Strategia*', *AHB* 1: 6–9.

Tsouvala, G. 2014. 'Love and Marriage', in Beck 2014a: 191–206.

Tuci, P. A. 2006. 'Temistocle e la manipolazione della volontà popolare: Gli oracoli delfici e la scomparsa del serpente sacro', *Aevum* 80: 37–61.

Valgiglio, E. (ed. and trans.) 1973. *Plutarco. De audiendis poetis*. Turin, Loescher.

———— 1988. *Divinità e religione in Plutarco*. Genoa, Compagnia dei librai.

———— 1992a. 'Dagli *Ethicà* ai *Bioi* in Plutarco', *ANRW* 2.33.6: 3963–4051.

———— (ed. and trans.) 1992b. *Plutarco. Gli oracoli della Pizia*. Naples, D'Auria.

Vamvouri Ruffy, M. 2011. 'Symposium, Physical and Social Health in Plutarch's *Table Talk*', in Klotz and Oikonomopoulou 2011: 131–57.

———— 2012. *Les vertus thérapeutiques du banquet. Médecine et idéologie dans les Propos de table de Plutarque*. Paris, Les Belles Lettres.

———— 2017. 'The Construction of a Cosmopolitan Space in Plutarch's *On Exile*', in Georgiadou and Oikonomopoulou 2017: 237–46.

Van der Stockt, L. 1992. *Twinkling and Twilight. Plutarch's Reflections on Literature*. Brussels, Koninklijke Academie voor Wetenschappen, Letteren en Schone Kunsten van België.

———— (ed.) 1996. *Plutarchea lovaniensia. A Miscellany of Essays on Plutarch*. Leuven.

———— 1999a. 'A Plutarchan Hypomnema on Self-Love', *AJPh* 120: 575–99.

———— 1999b. 'Three Aristotle's Equal but One Plato: On a Cluster of Quotations in Plutarch', in Pérez Jiménez *et al.* 1999: 127–40.

———— 2000a. 'Aspects of the Ethics and Poetics of the Dialogue in the *Corpus Plutarcheum*', in Gallo and Moreschini 2000: 93–116.

———— (ed.) 2000b. *Rhetorical Theory and Praxis in Plutarch*. Louvain and Namur, Peeters.

———— 2002. 'Καρπὸς ἐκ φιλίας ἡγεμονικῆς (*Mor.* 814C): Plutarch's Observations on the "Old-Boy Network"', in Stadter and Van der Stockt 2002: 115–40.

———— 2004a. 'Plutarch in Plutarch: The Problem of the Hypomnemata', in Gallo 2004: 331–40.

————— 2004b. "'With Followeth Justice Always" (Plato, *Laws* 716A): Plutarch on the "Divinity" of Rulers and Laws', in L. de Blois *et al.* 2004: 137–49.

————— 2005. 'No Cause for Alarm: Chthonic Deities in Plutarch', in Hirsch-Luipold 2005b: 229–49.

————— 2011. '*Semper duo, numquam tres*? Plutarch's *Popularphilosophie* on Friendship and Virtue in *On Having Many Friends*', in Roskam and Van der Stockt 2011: 19–39.

————— 2019. 'Plutarch on Philology and Philologists', in Leão and Roig Lanzillotta 2019: 295–306.

————— *et al.* (eds.) 2010. *Gods, Daimones, Rituals, Myths, and History of Religions in Plutarch's Works. Studies Devoted to Professor Frederick E. Brenk.* Málaga and Logan, International Plutarch Society.

Van Hoof, L. 2005–6. 'The Reader Makes the Text: Model Readers on the Move', *Ploutarchos* 3: 141–53.

————— 2010. *Plutarch's Practical Ethics. The Social Dynamics of Philosophy.* Oxford, Oxford University Press.

————— 2014. 'Practical Ethics', in Beck 2014a: 135–48.

Van Meirvenne, B. 1999. 'Puzzling over Plutarch: Traces of a Plutarchean Plato-Study Concerning *Lg.* 729 A–C in *Adul.* 32 (*Mor.* 71 B), *Coniug. Praec.* 46–47 (*Mor.* 144 F) and *Aet. Rom.* 33 (*Mor.* 272 C)', in Montes Cala *et al.* 1999: 527–40.

————— 2001. '"Earth and Ambrosia" (*De facie* §§ 24–25): Plutarch on the Habitability of the Moon', in Pérez Jiménez and Casadesús Bordoy 2001: 283–96.

Van Nuffelen, P. 2011. *Rethinking the Gods. Philosophical Readings of Religion in the Post-Hellenistic Period.* Cambridge, Cambridge University Press.

Verdegem, S. 2004–5. 'Plotting Alcibiades' Downfall: Plutarch's Use of His Historical Sources in *Alc.* 35.1–36.5', *Ploutarchos* n.s. 2: 141–50.

————— 2005. 'Envy at Work: Φθόνος in Plutarch's *Lives* of Fifth-Century Athenian Statesmen', in Jufresa *et al.* 2005: 673–8.

————— 2010a. 'Parallels and Contrasts: Plutarch's *Comparison of Coriolanus and Alcibiades*', in Humble 2010: 23–44.

————— 2010b. *Plutarch's Life of Alcibiades. Story, Text and Moralism.* Leuven, Leuven University Press.

Vernière, Y. 1977. *Symboles et mythes dans la pensée de Plutarque. Essai d'interprétation philosophique et religieuse des Moralia.* Paris, Les Belles Lettres.

————— 1989. 'Nature et fonction des démons chez Plutarque', in J. Ries (ed.), *Anges et démons. Actes du colloque de Liège et de Louvain-la-neuve, 25–26 novembre 1987.* Louvain-la-neuve, UCL Centre d'histoire des religions: 241–51.

Vesperini, P. 2012. '*Philosophia* et *polumathia*: À propos d'une correction fautive dans un passage des *Moralia* citant Aristote', *RPh* 86: 115–21.

Veyne, P. 1999. 'Prodiges, divination et peur des dieux chez Plutarque', *RHR* 216: 387–442.

Vicente Sánchez, A. 2008. 'Plutarco compositor de *Vitae* y *Moralia*: Análisis intratextual', in Nikolaidis 2008: 209–17.

Volkmann, R. 1869. *Leben, Schriften und Philosophie des Plutarch von Chaeronea.* 2 vols. Berlin, Calvary.

Volpe Cacciatore, P. (ed.) 2009. *Plutarco nelle traduzioni latine di età umanistica.* Naples, D'Auria.

——— and Ferrari, F. (eds.) 2007. *Plutarco e la cultura della sua età. Atti del X Convegno plutarcheo. Fisciano–Paestum, 27–29 ottobre 2005.* Naples, D'Auria.

Wardman, A. E. 1955. 'Plutarch and Alexander', *CQ* 5: 96–107.

——— 1971. 'Plutarch's Methods in the *Lives*', *CQ* 21: 254–61.

——— 1974. *Plutarch's Lives.* London, Elek.

Warren, J. 2011. 'Pleasure, Plutarch's *Non posse* and Plato's *Republic*', *CQ* 61: 278–93.

Waterfield, R. and Kidd, I. (eds. and trans.) 1992. *Plutarch. Essays.* Harmondsworth, Penguin Books.

Weber, H. 1959. *Die Staats- und Rechtslehre Plutarchs von Chaironeia.* Bonn, Bouvier.

Weissenberger, B. 1895. *Die Sprache Plutarchs von Chaeronea und die pseudoplutarchischen Schriften.* Straubing, Attenkofer.

Weisser, S. 2016. 'The Art of Quotation: Plutarch and Galen against Chrysippus', in S. Weisser and N. Thaler (eds.), *Strategies of Polemics in Greek and Roman Philosophy.* Leiden and Boston, MA, Brill: 205–29.

Westman, R. 1955. *Plutarch gegen Kolotes. Seine Schrift 'Adversus Colotem' als philosophiegeschichtliche Quelle.* Helsingfors, Societas philosophica.

——— 1987. 'Unbeachteter epikureischer Bericht bei Plutarch (Qu.conviv. 5,1)', *Arctos* 21: 195–201.

Whitmarsh, T. 2001. *Greek Literature and the Roman Empire. The Politics of Imitation.* Oxford, Oxford University Press.

——— 2006. 'The Sincerest Form of Imitation: Plutarch on Flattery', in D. Konstan and S. Saïd (eds.), *Greeks on Greekness. Viewing the Greek Past under the Roman Empire.* Cambridge, Cambridge Philological Society: 93–111.

Whittaker, J. 1989. 'The Value of Indirect Tradition in the Establishment of Greek Philosophical Texts or the Art of Misquotation', in J. N. Grant (ed.), *Editing Greek and Latin Texts.* New York, AMS: 63–95.

Wolman, H. B. 1972. 'The Philosophical Intentions of Plutarch's Roman Lives', in *Studi classici in onore di Quintino Cataudella*. 3 vols, Catania, Università di Catania, Facoltà di Lettere e Filosofia: ii.645–78.

Worthington, I. 1985. 'Plutarch *Demosthenes* 25 and Demosthenes' Cup', *CPh* 80: 229–33.

Xenophontos, S. 2012. 'Plutarch's Compositional Technique in the *An seni respublica gerenda sit*: Clusters vs. Patterns', *AJPh* 133: 61–91.

——— 2016. *Ethical Education in Plutarch. Moralising Agents and Contexts.* Berlin and Boston, MA, De Gruyter.

——— and Oikonomopoulou, K. (eds.) 2019. *Brill's Companion to the Reception of Plutarch.* Leiden and Boston, MA, Brill.

Yaginuma, S. 1992. 'Plutarch's Language and Style', *ANRW* 2.33.6: 4726–42.

Zacher, K.-D. 1982. *Plutarchs Kritik an der Lustlehre Epikurs. Ein Kommentar zu Non posse suaviter vivi secundum Epicurum, Kap. 1–8.* Königstein, Hain.

Zadorojnyi, A. V. 1997. 'Nero's Transformation Again: Plutarch, *De sera numinis vindicta* 567F–568A', *Pegasus* 40: 28–9.

——— 2002. 'Safe Drugs for the Good Boys: Platonism and Pedagogy in Plutarch's *De audiendis poetis*', in Stadter and Van der Stockt 2002: 297–314.

——— 2005. 'Plutarch and the Forbidden City: *Demosthenes* 1–2', in Pérez Jiménez and Titchener 2005: 493–512.

——— 2006. 'Plutarch's Themistocles and the Poets', *AJPh* 127: 261–92.

——— 2007. 'Cato's Suicide in Plutarch', *CQ* 57: 216–30.

——— 2010. '῞Ωσπερ ἐν ἐσόπτρῳ: The Rhetoric and Philosophy of Plutarch's Mirrors', in Humble 2010: 169–95.

——— 2011. 'The Ethico-Politics of Writing in Plutarch's *Life of Dion*', *JHS* 131: 147–63.

——— 2014. '*Kratein onomatôn*: Language and Value in Plutarch', in Beck 2014a: 304–20.

——— 2018. 'Plutarch's Heroes and the "Biographical Synecdoche"', in F. Cairns and T. Luke (eds.), *Ancient Biography. Identity through Lives*. Prenton, Francis Cairns: 213–28.

Ziegler, K. 1951. 'Plutarchos von Chaironeia', in *RE* 21.1, Stuttgart: 636–962.

Index of passages

Locations in ancient texts are given in bold, page numbers in this volume in italics.